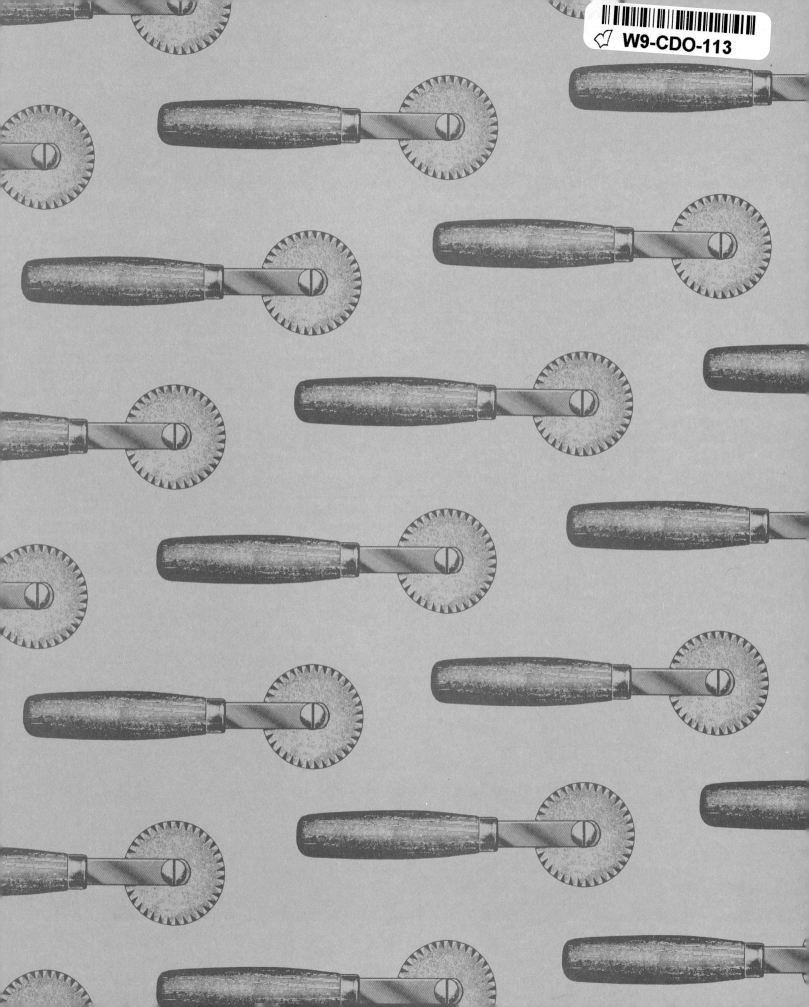

*This volume is one of a series that explains and demonstrates
how to prepare various types of food, and that offers in each
book an international anthology of great recipes.*

Pasta

BY
THE EDITORS OF TIME-LIFE BOOKS

TIME-LIFE BOOKS/ALEXANDRIA, VIRGINIA

Cover: Fresh young vegetables grace a mound of satiny, homemade egg noodles to make *pasta primavera*—Italy's springtime pasta. To keep them crisp, the sweet peppers, zucchini, asparagus, broccoli, snow peas and green beans were given the briefest possible precooking *(page 33),* then lightly turned in hot olive oil before being stirred immediately into the just-boiled pasta.

Time-Life Books Inc.
is a wholly owned subsidiary of
TIME INCORPORATED

Founder: Henry R. Luce 1898-1967
Editor-in-Chief: Henry Anatole Grunwald
President: J. Richard Munro
Chairman of the Board: Ralph P. Davidson
Corporate Editor: Jason McManus
Group Vice President, Books: Reginald K. Brack Jr.
Vice President, Books: George Artandi

TIME-LIFE BOOKS INC.

Editor: George Constable; *Executive Editor:* George Daniels; *Editorial General Manager:* Neal Goff; *Director of Design:* Louis Klein; *Editorial Board:* Dale M. Brown, Roberta Conlan, Gerry Schremp, Gerald Simons, Rosalind Stubenberg, Kit van Tulleken, Henry Woodhead; *Director of Research:* Phyllis K. Wise; *Director of Photography:* John Conrad Weiser; *Copy Room:* Diane Ullius; *Production:* Celia Beattie; *Quality Control:* James J. Cox (director), Sally Collins; *Library:* Louise D. Forstall

President: William J. Henry; *Senior Vice President:* Christopher T. Linen; *Vice Presidents:* Stephen L. Bair, Robert A. Ellis, John M. Fahey Jr., Juanita T. James, James L. Mercer, Joanne A. Pello, Paul R. Stewart, Christian Strasser

THE GOOD COOK

The original version of this book was created in London for Time-Life Books B.V.
European Editor: Kit van Tulleken; *Photography Director:* Pamela Marke; *Chief of Research:* Vanessa Kramer; *Special Projects Editor:* Windsor Chorlton; *Chief Sub-Editor:* Ilse Gray; *Production Editor:* Ellen Brush; *Quality Control:* Douglas Whitworth

Staff for *Pasta: Series Editor:* Alan Lothian; *Series Coordinator:* Liz Timothy; *Head Designer:* Rick Bowring; *Text Editor:* Gillian Boucher; *Anthology Editors:* Josephine Bacon, Liz Clasen; *Staff Writer:* Thom Henvey; *Researchers:* Krystyna Davidson, Deborah Litton, Margaret Hall; *Sub-Editors:* Katie Lloyd, Sally Rowland; *Design Assistants:* Cherry Doyle, Adrian Saunders; *Editorial Department:* Pat Boag, Kate Cann, Debra Dick, Beverly Doe, Philip Garner, Molly Sutherland, Julia West, Helen Whitehorn

U.S. Staff for *Pasta: Editor:* Gerry Schremp; *Assistant Editor:* Ellen Phillips; *Designer:* Ellen Robling; *Chief Researcher:* Juanita Wilson; *Picture Editor:* Adrian Allen; *Staff Writer:* Carol Dana; *Researchers:* Barbara Fleming (techniques), Patricia Kim (anthology), Karin Kinney; *Assistant Designer:* Peg Schreiber; *Copy Coordinators:* Nancy Berman, Allan Fallow, Tonna Gibert; *Art Assistant:* Robert Herndon; *Picture Coordinator:* Alvin Ferrell; *Editorial Assistants:* Brenda Harwell, Rosalie Yates

CHIEF SERIES CONSULTANT

Richard Olney, an American, has lived and worked for some three decades in France, where he is highly regarded as an authority on food and wine. A regular contributor to such influential journals as *La Revue du Vin de France* and *Cuisine et Vins de France,* he also has written numerous articles for other gastronomic magazines in the United States and France. He is, too, the author of *The French Menu Cookbook* and the award-winning *Simple French Food,* has directed cooking courses in France and in the United States, and is a member of several distinguished gastronomic societies, including L'Académie Internationale du Vin, La Confrérie des Chevaliers du Tastevin and La Commanderie du Bontemps de Médoc et des Graves. Working in London with the series editorial staff, he has been basically responsible for the planning of this volume, and has supervised the final selection of recipes submitted by other consultants. The United States edition of The Good Cook has been revised by the Editors of Time-Life Books to bring it into complete accord with American customs and usage.

CHIEF AMERICAN CONSULTANT

Carol Cutler is the author of three cookbooks, including the award-winning *The Six-Minute Soufflé and Other Culinary Delights.* During the 12 years she lived in France, she studied at the Cordon Bleu and the École des Trois Gourmandes, and with private chefs. She is a member of the Cercle des Gourmettes, a long-established French food society limited to just 50 members, and is also a charter member of Les Dames d'Escoffier, Washington Chapter.

SPECIAL CONSULTANT

Jeremiah Tower is an eminent American restaurateur who lived for many years in Europe, and is a member of La Commanderie du Bontemps de Médoc et des Graves and La Jurade de Saint-Emilion. He has been largely responsible for the step-by-step photographic sequences in this volume.

PHOTOGRAPHER

Aldo Tutino, a native of Italy, has worked in Milan, New York City and Washington, D.C. He has won a number of awards for his photographs from the New York Advertising Club.

INTERNATIONAL CONSULTANTS
GREAT BRITAIN: *Jane Grigson* has written a number of books about food and has been a cookery correspondent for the London *Observer* since 1968. *Alan*

Davidson, a former member of the British Diplomatic Service, is the author of three cookbooks. J Reynolds, who prepared many of the dishes for photographs in this volume, is from San Francis She trained as a cook in the kitchens of severa France's great restaurants. FRANCE: *Michel Lem nier,* the cofounder and vice president of Les A itiés Gastronomiques Internationales, is a frequ lecturer on wine and vineyards. GERMANY: *Joc Kuchenbecker* trained as a chef, but worked fo years as a food photographer in several Euro an countries before opening his own restaurar Hamburg. *Anne Brakemeier* is the co-autho three cookbooks. ITALY: *Massimo Alberini* is a w known food writer and journalist, with a partic interest in culinary history. His many books inclu *Storia del Pranzo all'Italiana, 4000 Anni a Tavc* and *100 Ricette Storiche.* THE NETHERLANDS: *Hugh J* has published cookbooks and his recipes app in several Dutch magazines. THE UNITED STATES: *J Dannenbaum,* the director of a cooking schoo Philadelphia, Pennsylvania, also conducts cook classes at the Gritti Palace in Venice, Italy, anc the Greenbrier in White Sulphur Springs, West ginia. She is the author of two cookbooks and merous magazine articles. *Judith Olney,* autho *Comforting Food* and *Summer Food,* received culinary training in England and France. In addi to conducting cooking classes, she regularly c tributes articles to gastronomic magazines. *Rol Shoffner,* wine and food editor of *The Washing ian* magazine for five years, has written many c cles on food and wine.

Correspondents: Elisabeth Kraemer-Singh (Bonn); Marg Hapgood, Dorothy Bacon (London); Miriam Hsia, Susa Jonas, Lucy T. Voulgaris (New York); Maria Vincenza Aloisi, Josephine du Brusle (Paris); Ann Natanson (Rom Valuable assistance was also provided by: Lesley Coleman, Karin B. Pearce (London); Bona Schmid, Mar Teresa Marenco (Milan); Carolyn T. Chubet, Christina Lieberman (New York); Michèle le Baube (Paris); Mimi Murphy (Rome).

CONTENTS

An Esteemed Staple

odles and couscous, dumplings and won tons, macaroni, riga-ni, spaghetti, tubetti, vermicelli, fettucini—this agreeable t catalogues only a few of the many varieties of pasta, the ost diverse food made from grain. All pasta preparations begin th a dough, or paste—*pasta* means paste in Italian—made by ixing ground grain or flour and liquid; but the ingredients, eir proportions and the methods of mixing and shaping the ugh all are variables. Most Western pasta, for instance, is ade from finely ground wheat or wheat flour; many Oriental stas are based on rice flour or starches derived from potatoes, ans or even acorns. The dough may be colored, flavored and rmed in many ways; once shaped, the pasta can be used fresh, t it can also be dried and stored indefinitely.

However they are prepared, all well-cooked pastas share rtain characteristics: flavor that is subtle, texture that is ten-rly firm. Pastas are perfect vehicles to be used in combination th almost any other food and they appear in an astonishing ofusion of presentations. Some pastas give body to soups, me are coated with sauces and some are mixed with meat, afood, vegetables, cheese or even with fruit.

This book will serve as a guide through the delightful maze pasta cookery. On the pages immediately following appear scriptions of many of the dried pastas available in markets, as ll as demonstrations of how to make basic sauces. From the cceeding chapter you will learn how you can make fresh pas-, either by hand or with a machine, how to flavor it, and how to t it into ribbons or fold it around fillings to make such pack-es as ravioli. Later chapters demonstrate the art of cooking d presenting pasta. The chapter on boiling shows the proper chniques for cooking pasta shapes both large and small, plain d filled, Western and Oriental, and includes examples of ickly made sauces. Following this section are chapters devot- to elaborations on boiled pasta—assemblies that are baked fried. Finally, the demonstrations that complete the first half this book serve as a primer on dumplings in all of their differ-t guises. To complement the techniques demonstrations, the cond half of the volume presents an anthology of pasta recipes awn from cuisines around the world.

brief history

e pasta of today is the result of a long process of accident and olution that began well before recorded history. In the Middle st, 100 centuries ago, wheat grew wild in great abundance. 9000 B.C., villages had been established near the fields by rmerly nomadic peoples who first gathered the wild grain,

then learned to cultivate it themselves. Early Neolithic man found that the wheat grains, once harvested and freed from the chaff that covered them, had to be cooked. He probably toasted the grains on hot stones, then mixed them with water to make them palatable. This grain paste was a staple of most prehistoric civilizations, and remained so well into Classical times.

From grain paste it was but a short step to dumplings: The paste needed only to be shaped into balls and dropped into boiling water. Once somebody decided to flatten the dumplings for quicker cooking, a new pasta had been invented; indeed, some pastas still are shaped by flattening the dough with the thumbs *(page 22)*. Other common pasta shapes—strips or squares, for instance—could also be easily cut from the flattened dough.

By the 4th and 3rd Centuries B.C., many cultures had some form of pasta. It is referred to in the records of the Han Dynasty in China. In Italy, the Etruscans made fresh pasta much as we do now, as evidenced by a bas-relief carved on a 4th Century B.C. tomb about 30 miles north of Rome. The bas-relief shows all the tools of pasta making: a rolling-out table, a receptacle for flour and a pastry wheel for cutting the dough into strips.

As civilizations developed, pasta entered the language. By the early Middle Ages, every country had a word for this string-like food. In India, it was called *sevika,* or thread. Germans referred to their pasta as *Nudeln,* the French called it *nouilles,* and the English knew it as noodles—the European words were probably derived from the Latin *nodellus* (knot), in acknowledgment of the way skeins of pasta inevitably tangle on a plate.

Italy, melting pot of the ancient and medieval worlds, has always abounded in names for pasta. In medieval Sicily, long under Arab influence, the term for pasta derived from the Arabic; in the 12th Century, the geographer Al-Idrisi published a book called *Entertainment for Travellers,* in which he observed that Sicilians near Palermo made a food from flour in the form of threads, which they called *itriyah,* or string. (That name evolved into *trii,* still used for Sicilian pasta.) A hundred years later, in Genoa, a soldier named Ponzio Bastone made a will that included a bequest of a *bariscella piena de macaroni*—a small basket full of macaroni. The word Bastone used probably descends from the Sicilian *macco,* meaning a flour-and-water paste; a more charming possibility is that it derives from the Greek *makac,* translated as "food of the blessed."

Bastone's bequest, written in 1279, gives an idea of how much pasta was valued at the time. The will also is the ultimate evidence disproving the popular view that Marco Polo introduced pasta to Italy after discovering it in China, for the great

Venetian traveler did not arrive home until 1295. However, Marco Polo did mention in his ambitiously titled *Description of the World* that he ate Chinese pasta at the court of Kubla Khan, and lasagne in Sumatra; the latter, he remarked with interest, was prepared from breadfruit-tree flour.

The making of pasta

For centuries now, most pasta has been prepared in one of two ways. The basic method—still in use *(pages 16-17)*—is simply to mix wheat flour with eggs, roll the resultant dough thin and cut it into whatever shape is desired. This dough has a delectably tender texture and a pale golden color, lent it by the eggs.

Pasta also can be formed by kneading a flour-and-water dough until it is firm and cohesive, then forcing the mass by means of a screw mechanism through a perforated mold so that it emerges as long strings, tubes or whatever shape the holes in the mold determine; this is how spaghetti is made. The best molded pastas were—and are—based on semolina: coarsely ground, hard durum wheat, which produces a strong, resilient dough that is, however, difficult to knead and rarely used for homemade pasta. For molded pastas, the kneading once was done in a large wooden trough, called a *madia*, by men who trampled the dough with their bare feet. Eventually, a wheel that rotated in the trough replaced the feet, while mechanized presses speeded the molding process.

Southern Italy, warm and breezy, had the perfect climate for drying the mass-produced pasta outdoors, and a medieval pasta industry, complete with a powerful guild, flourished there, eventually centering in Naples. Until the early decades of this century, when manufacturing was modernized and enclosed in factories, visitors to Naples were greeted by curtains of drying pasta that festooned the city's streets, alleys and courtyards. Almost every street corner was manned by a *maccheronaro*—a macaroni seller, who not only sold dried pasta to passersby, but also cooked and sauced it for them right on the street.

The ubiquitous pasta of Naples was itself a tourist attraction. It fascinated Thomas Jefferson, for one. When the ever-curious statesman visited the city in the late 18th Century, he took meticulous notes—still extant—on the pasta-making procedure, ordered four crates of "maccarony" to be shipped home and also instructed a friend to buy him a pasta machine.

Despite Jefferson's enthusiasm, Americans were not dedicated pasta eaters until relatively recently, although they were familiar with German and English dishes featuring dumplings and noodles. A pasta factory was established in Brooklyn in 1848, but it was not until the great Italian immigrations between 1880 and 1920 that pasta began to appear with regularity on American tables. The immigrants, mostly from Southern Italy, first imported and then began to manufacture their own colorfully named dried pastas—among them rigatoni (from *rigati,* meaning grooved), spaghetti (from *spago,* or string), vermicelli (literally, little worms) and tubetti (little tubes).

Cooking pasta

Of the pasta varieties now available to the American cook, the best Western types are tender, egg-rich, fresh pastas made at home or bought from a specialty shop. Also excellent are t firm, nutty-tasting, dried pastas made from durum wheat a water. Among the latter, imported Italian pastas are a go choice; by law, they are made only with durum wheat. Mc commercial American pastas also are made from this prefer wheat and the fact is announced on their package labels. Dri pastas made with egg also are available, but they suffer in co parison with fresh egg pasta. Besides Western-style pasta there are Oriental varieties, which require slightly differe cooking treatments *(pages 38 and 39)*.

Whatever the pasta, its preliminary, and sometimes on cooking takes place in a liquid that is usually water and usua boiling *(pages 30-31)*. During the cooking, the pasta absor some water, and thereby softens and becomes properly moi Simple though this cooking method is, it requires attentic Pasta's unassertive flavor makes its texture overridingly i portant to the success of a dish. The texture should always be, the Italian phrase, *al dente*—tender but still quite firm to t bite. To put it another way, soft pasta is overcooked pasta.

Sauces and assemblies

If you plan to sauce and serve your pasta after boiling it, t sauce should be ready to use the instant the pasta is draine Pasta cools rapidly, and as it cools it begins to stick togethe Hot sauce and warmed plates help prevent cooling. But speed of the essence: The pasta should be drained, sauced, served a eaten within moments of the time it leaves the pot.

For boiled pasta that is to receive further cooking—baki or frying, for instance—the initial process can be accomplish

with less haste. Since the boiled pasta will soften further in t frying pan or in the oven, it should be cooked only until it flexible—not until it is *al dente*. Because it will be handl during various stuffing, saucing and layering operations, t boiled pasta should be cooled as described on pages 54-55.

Possible sauces and fillings for pasta are legion and no str rules govern their use, except that the pasta should not be ove whelmed by its accompaniments: Pasta aswim in a sea of sau is badly served. Many American cooks associate pasta primari with tomato sauce or tomato-flavored meat sauce, and inde both raw and cooked tomatoes make excellent sauces *(pages and 33)*. The association is not surprising, since pasta was pop larized here by immigrants from Italy's South, where the tom to is used much more than in Northern Italy. However, t tomato was not introduced to Italy until the 16th Century, a t used in cooking until the 18th Century; many of the most ‸nous pasta dishes include no tomato at all.

A dish of boiled pasta may, for instance, be unadorned ex‸pt for a light coating of olive oil and sautéed garlic *(page 34).* ‸, as is frequently the case, oil- or cream-and-butter-coated ‸sta may be flavored simply with grated cheese. Other famous ‸uces for boiled pasta include the pungent, basil-and-garlic-‸sed blend known as *pesto (page 35),* and the parboiled, sau-‸d combinations of fresh vegetables used for *pasta prima-*‸*a*—springtime pasta *(page 33).* From the Orient come sauces ‸ing chopped, sautéed meat, seafood or vegetables, soy sauce, ‸nger and other spicy ingredients. The choice of sauces, in ‸ort, is practically limitless; improvisation is always in order.

The same holds true for baked and fried pasta dishes. The ‸any manifestations of lasagne are cases in point. In the United ‸ates, lasagne is most often served in the style of Bologna: It ‸nsists of large flat noodles interlayered with white sauce, ‸eat sauce and cheese *(pages 52-53).* In Italy, however, the ‸riations of lasagne are countless. Calabrian lasagne includes ‸ its filling hard-boiled eggs, soft cheese and meat croquettes; a ‸ssic Sicilian lasagne incorporates eggplant, yellow peppers, ‸chovies, olives, capers, tomato pulp, garlic and parsley.

‸e dexterous diner

‸any pastas offer little challenge to the diner. Small filled ‸apes such as ravioli or neatly segmented casseroles such as ‸sagne are easily handled with a fork and knife. Long strands ‸ pasta—spaghetti or linguini, for instance—are harder to eat: ‸nveying the slippery strands to the mouth with dignity needs ‸xterity and has received a certain amount of attention, espe-‸ally from Italians, who have had reason over the centuries to ‸ both entertained and concerned by the problem.

Their light-hearted approach is perhaps best exemplified by ‸e tradition of Pulcinella. Pulcinella was a stock character ‸atured by traveling troupes of Italian comedians known col-‸ctively as the Commedia dell' Arte, who began touring the ‸untryside in the 15th Century. Pulcinella, a zany servant, ‸emplar of coarse behavior, was easy to identify: He had a ‸rge hooked nose and he ate continuously from a steaming bowl ‸ pasta—using his hands. In later centuries, as the Pulcinella ‸aracter evolved into the English puppet Punch, his pasta bowl ‸sappeared. His manners, however, were exploited in the ‸reets of Naples well into the 18th Century. Prints of the period ‸ow the Neapolitan *maccheronaro* on his street corner, accom-‸nied by a crowd-attracting assistant—a barefoot man who ‸ised long strands of pasta over his head with one hand, and ‸opped them from on high into his mouth.

This amusing if somewhat untidy technique stands in con-‸ast to another Italian tradition: that of elegant—not to say, ‸fected—manners for everything from public conversation to ‸ivate dining. An example of the latter is the Italian use of the ‸rk. This simple tool came late to Northern Europe. Until the ‸th Century most people ate their food with the aid of a knife, a ‸ece of bread for sopping up sauce and sometimes a spoon. Italy, ‸wever, accepted the dainty Byzantine habit of eating with a ‸rk as early as the 16th Century, a fact much commented on by

respectful travelers. As a French silk merchant remarked in 1518, "These gentlemen, when they want to eat, take up the meat with a silver fork."

And with a fork—nothing else—the eating of long strings of pasta is simplicity itself. The fork, held vertically, should be pushed directly into the mass of pasta, quickly twirled to catch the strands in a neat bundle and immediately put in the mouth.

Serving pasta and wine

Pastas, in their infinite variety, can appear at any point in a meal. Small Chinese won tons *(pages 72-73),* for instance, make delectable snacks or hors d'oeuvre. In Italy, small portions of pasta often become a first course, to be followed by meat and dessert. Only heavier, meaty pasta assemblies such as the rich,

filled roll demonstrated on pages 36-37, would be main dishes. Dumplings *(pages 76-86)* most often appear as side dishes, as do small pasta shapes such as croquettes *(pages 74-75).* And sweet pastas or dumplings can be served as desserts.

The drinks that accompany a pasta dish depend on its sauces and garnishes, which means the choice of drinks is broad in-deed. A general rule to keep in mind is that aggressively sea-soned ingredients—frequently found with pasta—will kill the taste of a fine, delicate wine. Chinese pasta assemblies, for ex-ample, with their complex interplays of tastes, are usually best accompanied by beer. Beer also is a good drink for many dump-ling dishes, which usually are earthy stews too hearty for a fine wine. Or serve dumplings with a fresh young wine—a simple California Chardonnay for poultry stews; a light, fruity Zinfan-del for beef or veal.

The same guidelines obtain for Italian pasta dishes. In addi-tion, it is pleasant, where possible, to serve the wine of the region that produced the dish. *Fettucini all' Alfredo,* for in-stance, that rich combination of butter, cream and cheese *(rec-ipe, page 89),* is most often associated with Rome; a delicious partner would be the favorite table wine of Rome, sturdy white Frascati. Sicilian fish-and-pasta dishes are well served by Sic-ily's dry white Corvo. Filled pastas heavy with meat and cheese deserve a hearty wine such as Tuscany's Chianti Classico. And seafood dishes from the Adriatic, such as pasta with clam sauce, marry happily with dry, white Verdicchio.

These recommendations are no more than that: There is as much scope for experiment with wines as there is with pasta. Making your own discoveries is a large part of the enjoyment.

A Primer of Shapes

Pasta shapes such as those displayed here have been made commercially in Italy since about 1400, and in the United States since 1848. By extruding pasta dough through dies, or molds, manufacturers have created hundreds of forms—a sampling of 26 is arrayed on these pages—ranging from plain spaghetti to whimsical cartwheels and butterflies.

All of the pasta shapes are formed from wheat-and-water paste, sometimes tinted with the juices of a vegetable such as spinach. The quality of a pasta and its cooking properties depend on the type of wheat and how it was milled. You can identify the flour used by the labels on the pasta packages.

The best commercial pasta is made with durum wheat that has been ground either into the fine granules called semolina or into durum flour. A particularly hard type of wheat, durum is high in the gluten that makes dough firm and elastic—easy to shape by machine and sturdy enough to hold up well in boiling.

Whole-wheat flour includes particles of bran and wheat germ. It yields a somewhat softer, brownish pasta with a pronounced nutty flavor. Soy flour produces a still softer product, with a bland taste and grayish color but high in protein.

Whatever the basic ingredient, most shapes can be used interchangeably to vary the appearance of pasta dishes. As a rule, twisted and curved shapes such as the wheels and shells included at right are used with meaty sauces, as they trap more chunky particles than strands and ribbons do. The wide bands of lasagne are best reserved for layered casseroles, the broad tubes of manicotti for filling.

Commercial pasta can be stored almost indefinitely if it is kept in a tightly sealed package or a snugly covered container in a cool, dry place.

Identifying shapes. Each of the pastas at right is labeled with its most commonly used name — or, in the case of mostaccioli/penne, two equally familiar names. Where the Italian name may not be generally understood, the English translation is also given.

Margherite
Daisies

Ruote
Cartwheels

Fusilli
Twists

Mostaccioli/Penne
Small mustaches/Per

Spinach fettucini

Ditali
Thimbles

Whole-wheat and vegetable elbow macaroni

Manicotti rigati
Grooved muffs

Fettucini

Ziti tagliati
Cut bridegrooms

Cut grooved macaroni

Ziti
Bridegrooms

Mafalde
Ripple-edged noodles

Rotelle
Wheels

**Elbow
macaroni**

Farfalle
Butterflies

Conchigliette
Small shells

**Whole-wheat
shells**

**Ripple-edged
spinach lasagne**

Conchiglie
Shells

Soy-rice shells

Artichoke spaghetti

Capelli d'angelo
Angel's hair

Lasagne

Linguini

Spaghetti

International Variations

Pastas from countries as far apart as China and Morocco can expand a cook's repertoire by providing new options in flavor, texture, size and uses. All of the varieties shown at right are now imported to, or made in, the United States. Indeed, egg flakes and Pennsylvania Dutch potpie *(right)* are American innovations.

The most exotic imports originate in the Orient, where pasta is made with a wide range of flours, or vegetable or nut starches. Mung-bean starch, for example, is used in China for transparent cellophane noodles; potato starch is turned into similarly transparent noodles in Japan as well as China; acorn starch yields the peanut-flavored Korean noodles.

Rice flour is the basic ingredient of the sweet noodle sticks—thin or thick—of China and the Philippines; buckwheat flour yields sweet-sour Japanese noodles; white-wheat flour is used in Japan for noodles similar to Italian spaghetti and in China for fragile egg noodles.

White-wheat flour, often from soft varieties of the grain, and whole-wheat flour are the bases for the bland, firm egg noodles of Germany and Central Europe. But hard-wheat semolina is essential to the tiny Italian pastas known as *pastina* and the granular couscous of North Africa, which would lose their shapes when cooked if made with soft flour.

Couscous—pellets made of semolina-and-water dough—is so fine that it must be cooked by steam *(pages 44-47)*, and bean, potato or rice noodles must be gently poached *(pages 38-39)* because they are too gelatinous for boiling. All of the other pastas on these pages can be boiled in salted water, then served with sauce, baked or fried. Or they can be boiled in soup or stew. The miniature pastas can be cooked in soup, or boiled and used as a stuffing for vegetables *(pages 56-57)*.

A worldwide sampler. Arrayed at right are noodles from China, Japan, Korea and the Philippines; North African couscous and Pennsylvania Dutch potpie *(center, top)*; Italian *pastina* and American egg flakes *(center, bottom)*; and German-style egg noodles. The Oriental and Italian pastas are labeled with their original names as well as with English translations of those names.

Mi fen
Rice-stick noodles

Fen ssu
Bean-thread noodles/
Cellophane noodles

Mo mil kook so
Acorn-starch noodles

Udon
Thick wheat-flour
noodles

Somen
Thin wheat-flour noodles

Tan mien
Egg noodles

Harusame/Sai fun
Potato-starch noodles

Lug-lug
Thick rice-stick noodles

Potpie

Broad egg noodles

Couscous

Narrow egg noodles

Soba
Buckwheat noodles

Orzo
Barley

Acini di pepe
Peppercorns

Stelline
Little stars

Egg flakes

Spinach egg noodles

**Whole-wheat
egg noodles**

Three Basic Sauces

Sauces for pasta can range from simple glosses of melted butter or warm olive oil to rich concoctions of eggs and cream; any of them can be improvised at will *(pages 32-35)*. Every cook's repertoire should, however, include the three basic sauces shown on these pages: a white sauce, a tomato sauce and a meat sauce *(recipes, pages 166-167)*. All can be varied according to the contents of your larder.

A white sauce *(right)*, for instance, always begins with a roux—a paste made by heating butter and flour, adding milk, and simmering the mixture for about 40 minutes, until it has lost its floury taste. The result can be used as is, or it can be enriched with cream or flavored with cheese or herbs. White sauces usually appear in such baked dishes as lasagne *(pages 52-53)*, but a similar mixture is the basis of many soufflés *(pages 60-61)*.

A basic cooked tomato sauce *(opposite, top)* is made by simmering quartered, unpeeled tomatoes in their own juice until they disintegrate, straining out the skins and seeds, and cooking the sauce until it is the thickness you want. If fresh tomatoes are not in season, use canned ones.

Alternatively, fresh tomatoes may be peeled and seeded before cooking. To do this, immerse the tomatoes briefly in boiling water to make them easier to peel. Pull off their skins, halve the tomatoes crosswise and scoop out their seeds. Sauté them rapidly to obtain a rough-textured, fresh-flavored sauce. Both of the sauces can be varied by adding aromatic vegetables and herbs; both can be enriched with cream, and both are served with boiled and baked dishes.

A meat sauce *(bottom right)* is simply a thick stew for which all of the ingredients have been chopped fine. Meat and vegetables are sautéed, then simmered in liquid for an hour or two until they are tender. You can use raw meat or any leftover cooked meat. Aromatic vegetables such as onions, leeks, celery and carrots flavor the sauce; tomatoes are important for color as well as flavor. In this demonstration, dried cepes—wild mushrooms available at specialty markets—give the sauce a special smoky taste, but other dried mushrooms could be used instead. Like tomato sauce, a meat sauce can enhance both boiled and baked pasta.

Butter, Flour and Milk for Smoothness

1 **Adding milk.** Melt butter in a saucepan over low heat. Add an equal quantity of flour. With a whisk, stir the flour and butter together until the mixture is smooth. Cook this roux gently for two or three minutes, then pour in cold milk, whisking briskly at the same time *(above)*.

2 **Cooking the sauce.** Continue to whisk the sauce until it comes to a boil. Reduce the heat so that the sauce barely simmers. Let it cook, uncovered, for about 40 minutes, stirring from time to time, until the sauce is thick and smooth *(above)*. Season to taste.

Hearty Flavorings from Mixed Meats

1 **Sautéing.** Chop carrots and onions fine and cook them gently in oil until soft—about 10 minutes. Raise the heat and add chopped or ground beef. Stir the beef until all traces of pink disappear, then add cooked meats — chopped ham and pork are shown.

2 **Pouring in wine.** Cook the meat and vegetables for about 10 minutes, until the meat is well browned. Add red or white wine and scrape the pan with a wooden spoon to dissolve any savory brown deposits. Add stock *(recipe, page 167)* or water.

A Fragrant Tomato Purée

1 **Seasoning tomatoes.** Quarter tomatoes and place them in a pan with herbs — here, bay leaf and a thyme sprig — salt and, if you like, a sliced onion or crushed garlic clove. Bring the tomatoes to a boil, crushing them and stirring frequently.

2 **Puréeing the tomatoes.** Reduce the heat and cook for about 10 minutes. When the tomatoes are pulpy, remove the herbs. Use a pestle or wooden spoon to push the tomatoes through a strainer into a bowl. Discard the seeds and skins in the strainer.

3 **Reducing the sauce.** Return the purée to the pan. Cook the tomato purée over low heat until it has reduced to about half its original volume. Taste the sauce, season it with salt and pepper, then add chopped fresh herbs — in this case, basil and parsley.

Adding flavorings. Soften dried mushrooms — cepes are used here — in warm water for about 30 minutes. Drain the mushrooms and add them to the sauce (above) together with chopped garlic and parsley, and a strip of fresh lemon peel.

4 **Adding tomatoes.** Core tomatoes and immerse them for 20 seconds in boiling water, then drain and skin them. Halve the tomatoes crosswise, seed them and chop them into chunks. Add the tomatoes to the sauce and stir to mix the ingredients.

5 **Testing the consistency.** Simmer the sauce gently until it is almost thick enough to hold its shape in a spoon — about one and a half hours. Leave the lid of the pan ajar so that you can monitor the simmer, allowing liquids to reduce without letting solids burn.

1
Making Fresh Pasta
A Simple Art
with Rich Rewards

Making pasta is one of the most straightforward of culinary techniques: Flour is simply moistened with egg and a little oil, kneaded to develop its natural elasticity, rolled out and cut to whatever shape you desire. As with most foods, variations in ingredients abound. The very firm pasta popular in Southern Italy, for instance, is prepared from nothing more than flour and water *(recipe, page 88)*. An especially rich and luxurious pasta contains flour and egg yolks alone, instead of whole eggs *(recipe, page 138)*. And a basic pasta may be colored and flavored with such ingredients as chopped fresh herbs, powdered saffron or puréed vegetables including tomatoes and spinach *(page 21)*.

The process of making any of these pastas is akin to pastry making. Pasta dough must be rolled out thinner than most pastry, but achieving that involves care and patience rather than special skill. Once the pasta has been rolled out, it can be formed into a spectrum of shapes—strips, squares, butterflies and figure 8s, to name a few examples—using a knife, a pastry wheel or your thumbs *(pages 22-23)*. And many of the finished shapes may be stuffed, as ravioli is, with homemade fillings based on meat, fish, vegetables or cheese *(recipes, pages 112-118)*. All these homemade pastas will have a distinctive texture—firm and springy, yet deliciously tender.

When you use a pasta machine *(opposite and page 22)*, pasta making becomes even simpler. The machine both kneads and rolls the pasta. The two processes are achieved by passing the dough between a single set of rollers, which are kept a set distance apart for the kneading and are then brought progressively closer together to squeeze and stretch out the dough. Finally, individual cutting rollers convert the thin sheets of dough into noodles.

Dedicated pasta eaters claim that handmade pasta has more flavor than machine-made pasta because it is treated less roughly. The difference can be minimized by not overdoing the machine kneading; the fewer times the dough is passed through the machine, the more it resembles handmade pasta. The machine's drawbacks are in any case outweighed by its usefulness. For most cooks, a machine ensures that homemade pasta will make a regular appearance on the dinner table, instead of being just an occasional treat.

strip of floured dough, flattened into
thin sheet by being passed repeatedly
etween the rollers of the pasta
achine, is cranked through a set of
tting rollers that slice it into fine
odles. The machine has a second set
rollers for broader noodles.

First Steps: Mixing, Kneading and Rolling

To make pasta by hand, you need only moisten flour to produce dough, then knead the dough, roll it out *(opposite, below),* and cut it into the desired shape *(pages 22-23).* The process is simplicity itself, once you understand the properties of wheat flour.

The substance that turns flour into dough is gluten, a complex of proteins that, when moistened and kneaded, fuses discrete flour particles into a network of microscopic strands. The more gluten a flour has, the stronger this network will be and the firmer the dough.

Most commercial pasta is made from gluten-rich semolina, milled from hard durum wheat; it is available at specialty markets but yields a dough so firm that it is difficult to manipulate. A better choice is bread flour, made from hard wheats with a slightly lower gluten content. All-purpose flour is made from softer wheat

than bread flour and so has less gluten, but the unbleached variety still produces a properly firm, tender pasta. Bleached all-purpose flour, however, makes pasta too soft for most tastes: Bleaching diminishes flour's gluten.

Although the flour can be made into a dough with water as the moistener, egg confers a richer flavor. If you are making pasta for rolling out, use one egg for about ¾ cup [175 ml.] of flour; the exact proportion will depend on the size of the eggs and the absorbency of the flour, which can vary with the brand and with the humidity of the kitchen. Adding a little oil or melted butter softens the dough, making it easier to handle *(recipe, page 164).* However, do not use oil or butter when you are making Hungarian-style pasta shreds *(right);* this pasta, used in soups and soufflés *(pages 60-61),* is made from stiff dough that can be grated.

It is easiest to adjust the proportions ingredients by adding flour gradually once dough gets stiff, eggs or other liquids cannot be incorporated to soften Mix a large quantity of dough on a fl work surface, a small quantity in a bowl. On a flat surface, heap up more flour than you will need, place the liquid in the center, and gradually mix in flour from the perimeter, stopping when the dough forms a cohesive mass. When using bowl, start with less flour than you think you will need.

Once the dough is mixed, it should kneaded for a minimum of five minut to develop the gluten network. Kneading should leave the dough smooth and silky at which point the gluten is so elastic that the dough springs back on itself you try to roll it. After it rests for an hour however, the gluten relaxes so that the dough can be rolled out thin.

A Standard Dough for Every Purpose

1 **Adding egg to flour.** Form a mound of flour on a smooth surface. Make a well in the center of the mound. Break whole eggs into the well, or lightly beat them and pour in the beaten egg *(above).* Add salt and, if you like, pour a little olive oil into the well to soften the dough and make it easier to manipulate.

2 **Mixing the dough.** With one hand, gradually push the flour from around the edge of the well into the egg mixture. Stir with your fingers to form a batter inside the well. To prevent the batter from flowing out, support the perimeter of the flour with your free han *(above).* Continue to incorporate flour into the egg mixture until the batter becomes a firm paste. Gather it into a ball.

Breaking eggs into flour. On a work surface, form a mound of flour. Make a deep well in the mound. Break eggs into the well *(above)*. Add salt; with your finger tips, stir the flour into the eggs gradually, working outward, to make a stiff paste.

2 **Incorporating extra flour.** Lightly flour the work surface. Knead the dough by repeatedly folding it and pressing it flat *(above)*. During the kneading process, constantly add more flour; the dough should become stiff but not crumbly. Continue kneading until the dough is smooth and firm.

3 **Grating.** Shape the dough into a ball and enclose it in plastic wrap. Freeze the ball for about 30 minutes. Using the large holes of a box grater, grate the dough onto a sheet of parchment or wax paper. If you do not use the pasta shreds immediately, flour them to prevent sticking, and refrigerate them.

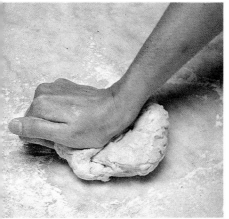

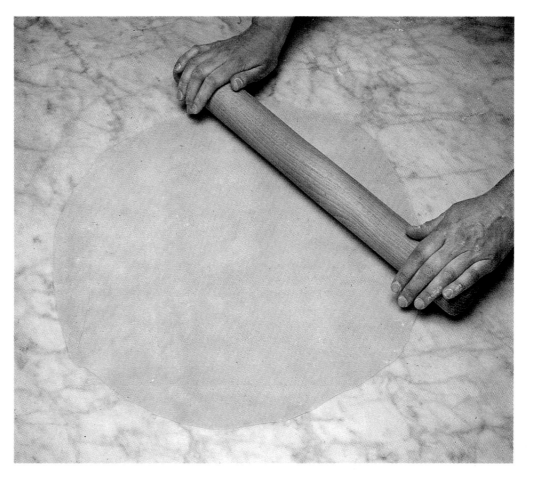

Kneading. With the heel of your hand, press the dough flat on a lightly floured surface. Fold the dough, then press again. Repeat for five to 10 minutes, until the dough is silky. Cover the dough and let it rest for one hour.

Rolling the dough. Divide the dough into portions about the size of your fist. Roll out each one on a lightly floured surface. Turn the dough sheet halfway around at regular intervals to maintain an even thickness. When the dough is almost translucent, it is thin enough to cut into shapes.

The Laborsaving Pasta Machine

With mechanical help, every phase of the pasta-making process can be simplified and accelerated. The preliminary steps of blending the dough ingredients can be accomplished with an electric mixer or a food processor. And, as demonstrated here, kneading can be done with a pasta machine, which performs the additional task of rolling out the dough—and cutting it up, if you wish.

Pasta machines come in both electric-powered and hand-cranked versions, but they all operate in similar ways. A typical one, used here, consists of three pairs of rollers set in a sturdy frame. One pair is smooth, with an adjustable knob at the side of the machine to vary the width of the gap between the pair. These rollers first knead and then roll out the dough. The other pairs of rollers are fitted with cutters that slice the rolled dough into noodles of different widths. The handle that turns the rollers is moved from pair to pair as needed.

The dough itself is mixed from the same ingredients used in handmade pasta: usually flour, eggs and salt, often with a little olive oil, manually kneaded just enough to bind them together. For the machine kneading, the dough is floured to keep it from sticking and then passed through the smooth rollers five or six times. Because the dough must be thick enough to be pressed firmly by the rollers—the essence of kneading—rather than slipping easily between them, it must be folded over between passages. If you are making a large quantity of pasta, divide the dough mixture into portions the size of your fist, so as to produce sheets of manageable proportions.

The kneading is complete and the pasta is ready to be rolled out when the dough is very smooth and has reached the width of the rollers. A resting period before rolling is unnecessary; the powerful machine will easily roll out the stiff dough. During the rolling-out stage, the gap between the rollers is decreased after each passage of the sheet through them. Careful handling is needed to keep the sheet from tearing as it becomes progressively thinner and longer. When it has attained the desired thickness, the dough can be cut into shapes by hand or with the machine's cutters (pages 22-23).

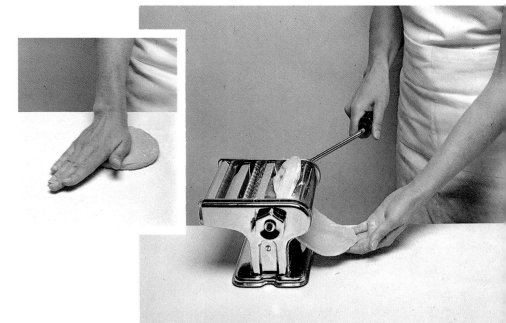

1 **Preparing the dough.** Mix pasta dough (pages 16-17) and lightly knead it. Divide the dough into fist-sized portions. Flatten one portion with your hand (inset) and set the others aside, covered with plastic wrap. Set the rollers of the machine fully open. Flour the dough and pass it between the rollers.

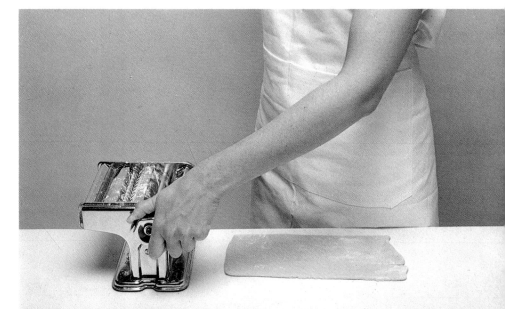

4 **Rolling out the dough.** Decrease the gap between the rollers by turning the knob at the side of the machine one notch (above). Flour the dough and, without folding it, pass it between the rollers. Flour the dough lightly once more.

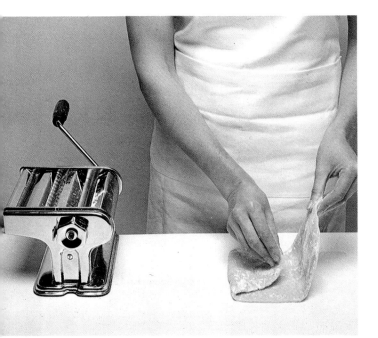

2 **Folding the rolled dough.** Lightly flour a work surface. Lay the rolled dough out on it. Fold one end of the dough toward the middle and fold the other end on top of it to make three layers *(above)* that are approximately as long and as wide as the original portion. Sprinkle on a little more flour.

3 **Kneading the dough by machine.** Turn the dough 90 degrees to help produce a neat rectangular shape, and pass it between the smooth rollers again. Repeat the flouring, folding, rolling and turning four or five times until the dough is very smooth and shaped to the width of the machine.

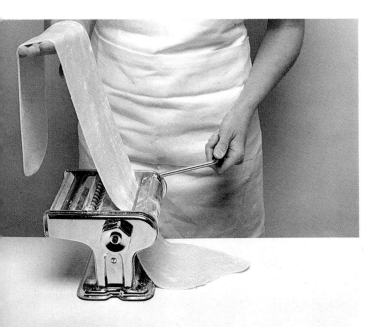

5 **Rolling the dough thinner.** Decrease the gap between the rollers by another notch. Pass the dough through the machine again. Because the pasta sheet will now be quite long, support it with one hand as you feed it into the machine *(above)*. As it emerges, stop cranking from time to time and slide the rolled sheet along the work surface rather than letting it fall in folds.

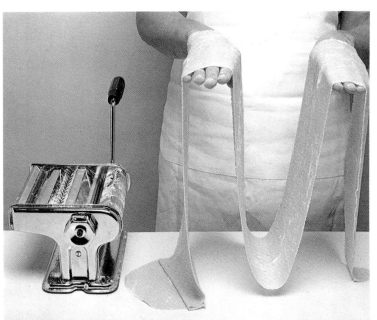

6 **Drying the rolled dough.** Flour the dough and roll it as thin as you require; the machine's next-to-finest setting produces a thickness suitable for most purposes. Unless you intend to make filled pasta shapes, hang the dough up to dry: You can suspend it over a broomstick balanced across the backs of two chairs. Repeat Steps 2 to 5 with the rest of the dough. When all of the dough feels dry — not sticky — cut it into the lengths desired.

Diverse Colors and Flavors

Colored pasta requires little more effort to make than plain pasta does, yet the results, especially if you use different-colored pastas in a single dish *(page 59)*, are spectacular. The coloring elements—herbs for speckled green pasta, beets for red, tomatoes for orange, spinach or chard for solid green, and saffron for yellow—also flavor the pasta subtly.

So that they will be evenly assimilated into the dough, all the colorings except saffron require preparation before they are mixed with the other pasta ingredients. The herbs are simply chopped.

Spinach is parboiled, squeezed dry and puréed if the pasta is to be hand-rolled; if you use a machine, however, it is enough to chop the dried parboiled spinach into fine bits: The machine's rollers spread the color uniformly. For a tomato coloring, use a well-reduced sauce. Beets are so dense that they must be boiled and puréed, no matter how you make the pasta; they can be pounded to a purée with a mortar and pestle, but an electric food processor makes the work easier.

The vegetable purées and the herbs can be combined with the other pasta ingredients in a single mixing step. But saffron, available ground or as easily

crushed dry threads, should be combin with the flour before the moist ingre ents are added.

Once the colorings have been inc porated into the dough, you can kne and roll the pasta by hand *(page 1* or by machine *(pages 18-19)*. To comp sate for the moistness of most of the col ings, add extra flour to the dough duri kneading. Some colorings, such as spi ach and herbs, release their moistu progressively; to counter stickiness, y will have to dust the pasta with mc flour than usual when you roll it out.

Sheets of fresh pasta in rainbow tones hang to dry over a broomstick. From left to right are herb-, beet-, tomato-, spinach- and saffron-colored pas

A Muted Green from Spinach

1 **Preparing spinach.** Cook stemmed spinach in boiling salted water for two minutes. Drain and rinse it. Squeeze the spinach dry and chop it fine; then add it to flour, egg, salt and oil.

2 **Kneading in spinach.** Mix all of the ingredients for the green pasta thoroughly with a fork. Knead the dough briefly by hand *(above)*, then use a pasta machine to knead and roll it out.

A Speckling of Fresh Herbs

1 **Chopping herbs.** Chop a selection of fresh herbs — parsley, sorrel, thyme, sage, tarragon and lovage are shown — to a fine consistency. Basil, marjoram, hyssop and fennel are other options.

2 **Stirring in herbs.** Using a fork, stir the chopped herbs into the other pasta ingredients — flour, olive oil, salt and eggs. Knead the pasta and roll it out.

A Lively Pink from Beets

1 **Puréeing beets.** Boil unpeeled beets in salted water until tender — 40 minutes to two hours, depending on their size. Peel and chop the beets and purée them in a food processor *(above)*.

2 **Stirring in beets.** Stir the beet purée with the other pasta ingredients in a mixing bowl or on a flat surface. Knead the pasta and roll it out.

An Orange Glow from Tomato

Blending in tomato. To make orange-colored pasta, stir puréed tomato *(recipe, page 167)* into the other ingredients before kneading and rolling out the dough.

A Warm Gold from Saffron

1 **Mixing in saffron.** Add a knife tip of pulverized or ground saffron to the dry ingredients — flour and salt — and stir it in well to distribute the color evenly.

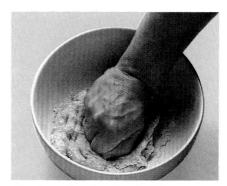

2 **Kneading the dough.** When the saffron is evenly spread throughout the flour, mix in the liquid — in this instance, eggs and oil. Knead and roll out the dough.

Cutting and Shaping the Dough

Homemade pasta can be fashioned into noodles with a pasta machine *(right)*, but with the aid of a knife or pastry wheel and a little practice in folding and pinching, you can make not only noodles but also such exotic shapes as butterflies and mushroom caps by hand.

Folding expedites the production of pasta shapes based on rolled-out sheets of dough. To make long noodles quickly by hand, for instance, you can fold a pasta sheet so that each slice of the knife cuts through several dough layers at once *(opposite, top)*. Similarly, pasta squares can be cut in quantity if you begin with a stack of pasta strips *(opposite, bottom right)*. A dexterous pinch can transform a flat pasta rectangle into a butterfly *(opposite, bottom left)*; pressing and twisting are the methods used to mold shapes based on cylinders or balls of dough rather than on sheets *(right, below)*.

The cylinders that are used for three-dimensional pasta shapes should be very malleable: Shape the dough as soon as you have kneaded it. Pasta sheets, on the other hand, should be left to dry for about 10 minutes to make them easier to cut and to prevent the sliced-up shapes from sticking together. For insurance against sticking, sprinkle both sheets and cylinders with flour, cornmeal or semolina— available at specialty stores—before and after shaping.

Once the pasta has been molded or cut, it should be left uncovered for about five minutes to dry and firm up slightly before it is cooked. If you do not plan to use it within an hour, cover it with plastic wrap to prevent excessive drying; as long as the pasta remains flexible, it will be as good as it was when freshly made. If you wish to store pasta overnight or longer, leave it uncovered at room temperature for three or four hours to dry it out and prevent sticking, then enclose it in tightly sealed plastic bags. Homemade pasta may be stored in the refrigerator for a week or in the freezer for a month.

Rapid Cutting with a Machine

Making noodles. Pasta machines *(pages 18-19)* have two or more cutting rollers with blades spaced at different intervals. For medium-sized noodles, insert the handle beside the wide-cutting roller and crank rolled dough through the machine. Support the emerging noodles with your hand.

Cutting fine noodles. Insert the handle of the machine beside the narrow-cutting roller, and pass the sheet of pasta through the machine. Once the roller has gripped the pasta, leave the uncut sheet draped over the machine and use your free hand to catch the emerging noodles.

Pressing Out Figure Eights

Pressing with your thumbs. Tear off small, walnut-sized pieces of dough that has been kneaded but not rolled, and form them into small egg shapes with your fingers. On a floured surface, flatten the pieces into ovals. Using your thumbs, press down firmly at both ends of each oval, leaving an imprint on either side of a central ridge of dough to form the shape of a figure 8.

Creating Mushrooms

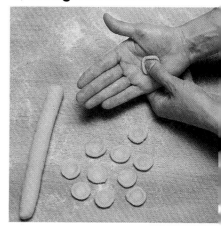

Molding in your palm. On a floured surface, form a piece of dough into a cylinder approximately ¾ inch [2 cm.] in diameter. Slice the cylinder into rounds ⅛ inch [3 mm.] thick. Place a round in the palm of your hand. With the thumb of the other hand, make a dent and, at the same time, twist the round slightly to make it broader and thinner so that it resembles a mushroom cap.

Slicing by Hand

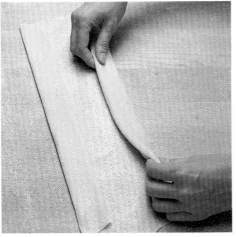

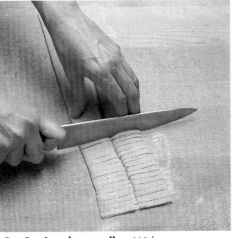

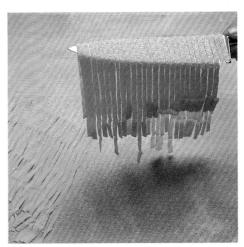

1 **Folding the dough.** Roll a piece of pasta dough into a roughly circular shape. Sprinkle the sheet with cornmeal to prevent it from sticking. Repeatedly fold the pasta very loosely over onto itself, working from both sides toward the center until the two folds meet. Do not press the folded pasta, or it may stick together.

2 **Cutting the noodles.** With a sharp knife or, for decorative edges, a fluted pastry wheel, cut across the folded dough to make even strips *(above)*. The noodles may be cut as wide or as narrow as you like them.

3 **Unrolling the noodles.** Slide the blade of a large knife under the folded sheet at the center line — the point where the two folds meet. Raise the knife, blunt edge uppermost: The rolled-up noodles will unroll, dropping down on either side of the blade *(above)*.

Fashioning Butterflies

Pinching neat rectangles. Using a fluted pastry wheel, cut along each edge of a rectangular sheet of dough to serrate it. With the cutter, divide the sheet into rectangles about 2 inches [5 cm.] long and 1 inch [2½ cm.] wide. Pinch the center of each rectangle to form butterflies *(farfalle in Italian).*

Mass-producing Small Squares

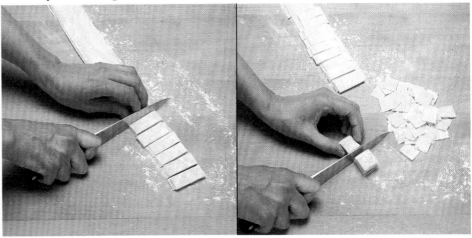

Stacking layers for speedy cutting. Roll out sheets of dough and cut them into long strips, each about 2 inches [5 cm.] wide to form lazanki, but 4 inches [10 cm.] wide for potpie. Flour the strips and stack them on top of each other. Cut this stack across at 1-inch [2½-cm.] intervals for lazanki *(left)*, at 2-inch intervals for potpie. Cut the pieces in half to make squares *(right)*.

Filling Pasta Packages

Among the most appealing of fresh-pasta dishes are those based on small pasta shapes sealed around a filling. As demonstrated here and on pages 26-27, both fillings and package shapes lend themselves to almost inexhaustible variation.

Fillings may include meats, fish, vegetables or cheese, either alone or in such combinations as the meat-and-spinach and cheese-and-spinach mixtures shown at bottom (recipes, pages 163 and 113). Meat, fish and vegetable bases for fillings are normally precooked, because these ingredients (unless they are used in extremely small quantities) will not cook through in the brief time it takes to boil fresh pasta. Any filling must be puréed or chopped fine to fit tidily into its small wrapper; it must also be fairly dry so that it does not make the pasta soggy and fragile. Boiled vegetables should be drained and squeezed to eliminate excess fluid; braising liquids used in making

fillings should be strained off if they do not evaporate during the cooking.

The pasta dough that is used to enclose these fillings should be rolled out a little thicker than dough that is used for unstuffed pasta—about ⅛ inch [3 mm.] is the right thickness—because the packages must be sturdy. And the dough must be moist and flexible: Cut and shape it as soon as you have rolled it out.

You can shape packages assembly-line fashion, as demonstrated with the ravioli at right. To make it, pasta dough is trimmed to a rectangle and dotted at regular intervals with small heaps of filling. Then the pasta between the mounds is moistened so that it will stick to a second pasta sheet laid over the first. By running a knife or pastry wheel carefully between the mounds of filling, you can quickly shape the pasta dough into individual ravioli.

For the more complex shapes shown on pages 26-27, the dough is first cut into squares or circles, then folded in various

ways over the filling. Pasta circles, f example, may be folded over to form si ple half-moons. For a more elaborate fect, the half-moons can be curled make the packages known as tortelli Or a pasta circle can be folded envelop fashion to produce a neat rectangle. P ta squares whose opposite corners a pinched together become star shapes.

Each of these packages should provi a margin of at least ¼ inch [6 mm.] sealed pasta around its filling to enclo it securely. Make sure no stray filling li between the edges: It will prevent t pasta from sealing.

Because of the dough's moistness, t pasta tends to be sticky. If you stack pa ta circles or squares before filling a folding them, dust them with flour cornmeal to keep them apart. So that t filled shapes do not stick and tear, pla them, well separated, on a floured clo until you are ready to boil them.

A Tangy Blend of Vegetables and Meats

1 **Cooking meats.** Chop onions and meat—in this case, veal, beef and ham. Sauté the onions in oil until soft. Stir in the meat, turning it until brown. Add thyme, bay leaf and a glass each of wine and stock. Partly cover and simmer for one to one and a half hours, until the meat is tender and the liquid reduced.

2 **Mashing the stuffing.** Parboil trimmed spinach for two to three minutes; drain, and squeeze it dry. Chop it fine. Remove the thyme and bay leaf from the cooked meat. Transfer the meat and onions to a large bowl, and mash them thoroughly with a fork.

3 **Mixing in the spinach.** Add the chopped spinach to the mashed meat and onions and stir in egg yolks to bind the mixture. Use a fork to blend the ingredients thoroughly. Taste the filling and, if necessary, season it with salt and freshly ground pepper.

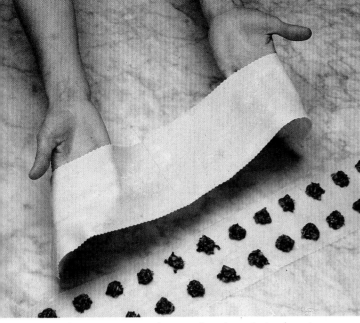

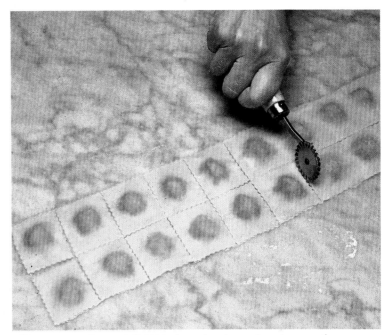

Filling. Roll out two strips of pasta dough and trim them to identical size. Leaving about a 1-inch [2½-cm.] margin around the edges, place 1-teaspoon [5-ml.] mounds of filling *(opposite)* on one of the strips at about 2-inch [5-cm.] intervals. Brush water between the mounds. Lay the second pasta strip over the first.

2 **Cutting the ravioli.** With the side of your hand, press the pasta around each mound of filling, so that the two moistened strips stick together firmly. Using a fluted pastry wheel, carefully cut along and across the pasta dough midway between the rows of filling to separate the individual ravioli.

A Creamy Mixture of Spinach and Cheese

A Pounded Meat Paste

1 **Mixing cheese and egg.** Trim the stems from spinach leaves and parboil the leaves for two or three minutes. Drain the spinach, rinse it under cold water, then squeeze it dry and chop it fine. Mix ricotta cheese with eggs and some freshly grated Parmesan *(above)*.

2 **Stirring in the spinach.** Add the chopped spinach to the other filling ingredients in the bowl. Stir to combine them *(above)*. Season to taste with salt, pepper and ground allspice.

Preparing the filling. Trim fat and connective tissue from a piece of lamb shoulder. Chop the meat into small pieces. In a mortar, pound the lamb with garlic, salt and pepper, and herbs — mint, oregano and parsley are used here — until the mixture is a fairly smooth paste. Or purée the meat and flavorings in a food processor.

Curling Tortellini

1 **Adding the filling.** With a biscuit cutter or the rim of a glass, stamp circles about 3 inches [8 cm.] in diameter from a sheet of pasta dough. In the middle of each circle, put a teaspoon [5 ml.] of stuffing — in this case, a spinach-and-ricotta-cheese mixture *(page 25)*. Using a pastry brush or your finger, moisten the edge of each of the pasta circles with water *(above)*.

2 **Making the first fold.** Fold the circle of dough in half over the stuffing. To seal in the stuffing, pinch the moistened edges of the dough together between your thumb and forefinger *(above)* to make a half-moon. You can cook the pasta in this form, if you like or go on to make tortellini *(Steps 3 and 4)*.

Folding Tidy Packets

Folding circles for a trim package. Stamp circles about 3 inches [8 cm.] in diameter from a sheet of pasta dough. Put a teaspoon [5 ml.] of stuffing — in this case, a meat-and-spinach mixture *(page 24)* — in the center of each circle. Brush the rim of the circle with a little water. Fold two opposite sides of the circle over the stuffing. Fold up the other two sides over the first two, and press gently to seal the envelope-like container.

Pinching squares for a starlike shape. With a fluted or plain pastry wheel, cut a sheet of pasta dough into 3-inch [8-cm.] squares. Place a teaspoon [5 ml.] of stuffing — here, a meat-and-spinach mixture — in the center of each square, and moisten the edge of the square with water. Pinch together two opposite corners over the stuffing, then fold the other two corners into the center. To enclose the stuffing securely, pinch the cut edges together.

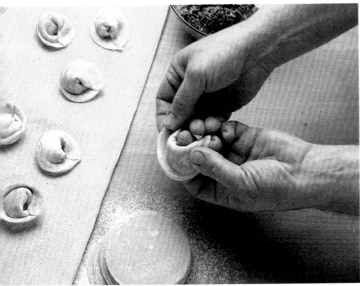

3 **Bending the half-moon into a ring.** Grasp each half-moon, its folded edge uppermost, between your thumb and index finger. Curve the half-moon around the index finger until the ends almost touch. At the same time, turn the sealed lower edge of the half-moon up toward the folded edge to form a cuff *(above)*.

4 **Fixing the shape.** Pinch the ends of the curled half-moon firmly together to secure the ring. Lay the completed tortellini on a floured towel, spacing them well apart so that they do not touch. Let the tortellini dry for a few minutes before you cook them.

nching corners. Cut a pasta sheet into /₄-inch [3-cm.] squares. On each, smear a *tle* stuffing — in this case, pounded meat, *ft* raw since the minuscule amount will cook as *e* pasta boils. Join the opposite corners of *ach* square *(above)* and pinch all four corners *gether (right)*. Do not seal all the edges: *e* stuffing will adhere during cooking.

2
Boiling, Poaching and Steaming
Tenderizing with Liquid

Whether pasta is to be dressed in sauce and served immediately, or combined with other ingredients and baked or fried, it is usually cooked in liquid—a process that moistens and tenderizes it. Western pastas are usually boiled in a roomy pot of rumbling water *(page 31)*. Most Oriental pastas are treated the same way; the exceptions are cellophane and rice-stick noodles, which are softened in hot or cold water—boiling water would make them gummy—before they are finally, and briefly, cooked *(pages 38-39)*. Instead of being immersed in liquid, couscous, a pellet-shaped North African pasta, is traditionally cooked in the steam that rises from a simmering stew, flavoring the tiny pellets while keeping them fluffy and separate *(pages 44-47)*.

Whereas boiling, poaching and steaming are among the simplest of cooking methods, all three must be carefully monitored to prevent the pasta from overcooking. An Italian saying, "Spaghetti loves company," reminds the cook to keep a watchful eye on a potful of boiling pasta. Cooking times will vary according to the thickness and freshness of the pasta and whether it is plain or stuffed. The best way to guard against overcooking is to test the pasta frequently by biting a piece or pinching it: The pasta will be done when it is flexible yet firm.

Boiled pasta may be glossed with butter, cream or olive oil, and sprinkled with herbs or grated cheese. Such a restrained treatment is especially appropriate for fresh pasta and for stuffed pasta shapes, whose savory fillings make extra flavoring redundant. Dried pasta can take a more assertive topping such as a robust meat-and-tomato sauce *(pages 12-13)* or the *carbonara* sauce shown opposite *(demonstration, page 35)*, a creamy blend emboldened with spicy Italian bacon. Between these extremes lie a plethora of seafood, meat and vegetable concoctions that can be made by formula *(recipes, pages 89-112)* or varied according to whim.

Instead of being presented in a sauce, pasta may be used to fortify stews—in which case, the pasta is boiled in the stew's own stock *(page 40)*. Boiled pasta also lends itself to more formal combinations with other foods. In the most spectacular of these preparations, long strands of boiled macaroni are coiled inside a round mold and cemented together with a mousseline to encase a pasta-based filling: When poached and unmolded, the dish has the appearance of a beehive *(pages 41-43)*.

uous strands of linguini enveloped
creamy *carbonara* sauce are
esented piping hot from a heated
wl. A rich combination of egg yolks,
avy cream and grated Parmesan
eese, enlivened with sage and the
ppery Italian bacon called
cetta, the sauce was cooked as it was
sed with the pasta in the skillet that
d been used to sauté the bacon.

A Straightforward Path to Perfection

Perfect boiled pasta, tender yet firm to the bite, is the result of a simple cooking method that works well with almost every size, shape and type of homemade and commercial wheat pasta.

The boiling process is governed by a few important rules. The first of these is that the pasta must be cooked in a large quantity of rapidly boiling water so that individual pieces can float freely; otherwise they will stick together in a gummy mass and cook unevenly. Allow 4 quarts [4 liters] of water for each pound [½ kg.] of pasta. But never try to boil more than 2 pounds [1 kg.] at a time; larger batches do not cook or drain satisfactorily.

To keep the water from boiling over as it absorbs starch from the pasta, add oil—using 1 tablespoonful [15 ml.] for every 4 quarts. To bring out the pasta's mild flavor, stir in about 1½ tablespoons [22 ml.] of salt.

The water must reach a vigorous, rolling boil before you add the pasta—in small amounts that will not cool the water too much and cause the pieces of pasta to clump. If the boil subsides despite your precautions, cover the pan briefly to bring the water back to a rolling boil as fast as possible.

How long a particular pasta is boiled varies with its moisture content as well as its size and shape. Fresh, homemade pasta rolled thin may be ready in as little as a minute; thicker pieces can take up to five minutes of cooking. Similarly, dried pasta can take anywhere from four to 15 minutes of boiling to reach doneness. The only way to tell when the pasta is ready is to lift a piece from the water, and pinch or bite it. The pasta should feel flexible b[ut] still firm inside.

Begin testing fresh pasta a minute [af]ter you put it in the pot; begin testi[ng] dried pasta when it starts to look opaqu[e]. The moment the pasta is done, stop t[he] cooking by pouring the contents of t[he] pot into a colander and shaking the c[ol]ander briefly to remove excess liquid.

Quickly transfer the pasta to a warm[ed] serving bowl. Pasta cools rapidly a[nd] starts to stick as it does so. To preve[nt] this, toss the pasta with olive oil or so[ft]ened butter, depending on the sauce y[ou] plan to use. The next step—which shou[ld] follow immediately—is to toss the pas[ta] with sauce. The sauce may be as simp[le] as garlic sautéed in oil or as complex a[s a] mélange of separately precooked veget[a]bles; a selection is shown on pages 32-3[.]

4 **Draining the pasta.** When the pasta is done, immediately pour the contents of the pot into a colander set in a sink *(left)*. Then, grasping the colander handles with potholders to protect your hands from heat and stea[m,] vigorously shake the colander to remove excess liquid *(above)*.

Adding the oil. Bring salted water to a boil in a large pot set over high heat: Allow 10 minutes or more for the water to reach a rolling boil. Add some oil to keep the water from foaming over. Olive oil is used here, but because the oil acts as a foam retardant, not a flavoring, corn or peanut oil may be used.

2 **Adding dried pasta.** Add about a fourth of the pasta at a time to the boiling water — spaghetti is shown. Using a long-handled fork, push down stiff strands as they soften. When all the pasta is added, stir it quickly to separate the pieces. If necessary, cover the pot to bring the water back to a boil.

3 **Testing for doneness.** Begin timing when the water returns to a boil. After about four minutes for thin pasta, or eight for thick, use a fork to lift out a sample. Let it cool briefly, then pinch a piece or bite it. The pasta should be flexible but slightly resistant. If not, keep boiling, testing every 30 seconds.

5 **Serving the spaghetti.** Pour the drained spaghetti onto a warmed platter that has been greased with olive oil (if the chosen sauce is oil based) or dotted with butter, as here (if the sauce contains butter). Briefly toss the pasta and oil or butter together, cover the pasta with sauce, toss again and serve at once.

The Care of Fresh Pasta

Adding the pasta. Bring salted water to a boil and add oil as in Step 1. Add all the fresh pasta — it will be flexible, as are the wide noodles shown above — and stir. Begin to test for doneness — as shown in Step 3 — about a minute or so later.

A Sampling of Quick Sauces

Just-boiled pasta, a savory sauce coating its curves and folds, makes a tempting dish—and, depending on the sauce, can be rich and delicate or robust and hearty. Besides the long-cooked varieties demonstrated on pages 12-13, there are countless sauces that require little or no cooking and lend themselves happily to variation and improvisation.

All these quick-cooked sauces begin with a moistening coat of butter or oil. The flavoring elements can be as spare as garlic or herbs alone, but may also incorporate vegetables, meats, seafoods or cheeses. Extra enrichment can be supplied by milk, cream, sour cream or eggs.

No rigid rules govern which sauce to use with which type of pasta, but a few common-sense precepts serve as guidelines for inventive cooks. Fresh, homemade pasta deserves the lightest, least assertive saucing; the pasta's fine flavor and exceptional texture might be masked by a heavy, highly seasoned mixture. The three sauces shown on these pages are examples of types appropriate for fresh pastas.

The richest is a blend of cream, egg yolks, butter and cheese *(below)*, which gives pasta a pale coating, light and satiny. For more color and texture, tomatoes and herbs marinated in olive oil—and left uncooked to retain the garden-fresh flavor—are a good choice *(opposite, top; recipe, page 98)*. But the sauce that invites the most variation is the type known as *primavera*, ideally made with the youngest of fresh spring produce, briefly precooked and heated together in olive oil *(opposite, bottom)*.

Dried pasta is sturdy enough to support the pungent sauces demonstrated on pages 34-35. The simplest of these is nothing more than olive oil flavored with as generous a lacing of garlic as the cook desires. For a more unctuous dish, the cream-and-egg-yolk mixture used to co fresh pasta can be made into the mo forceful sauce called *carbonara* by th addition of *pancetta*, a spicy Italian b con *(recipe, page 106)*. A classic summ sauce for dried pasta is pesto ("pounde in Italian), a highly aromatic paste ma from fresh basil leaves, pine nuts, chee and garlic *(recipe, page 93)*. Another f mous summer sauce capitalizes on fresh ly steamed clams accented with win garlic and onion.

Whatever the pasta-and-sauce comb nation may be, the same rules for cookir and serving apply. Because boiled past must be tossed with sauce and served th moment it reaches the proper textur the sauce must be prepared before th pasta goes into the pot. And sauce of ar kind should be used sparingly: It shoul coat the pasta pieces evenly and tho oughly, but should never be so abunda that the pasta drowns in a soupy sea.

A Satiny Coat of Cream and Cheese

1 **Mixing the sauce.** Separate the eggs and put the yolks in a mixing bowl. With a rotary or box grater *(above)*, grate fine a generous quantity of hard cheese — Parmesan is shown. Whisk the yolks smooth, then whisk in 1 or 2 tablespoons [15 or 30 ml.] of heavy cream for each yolk. Stir in salt, pepper and the grated cheese.

2 **Preparing the pasta.** In a skillet, melt enough butter to form a thin layer. Set the skillet aside. Boil fresh pasta *(page 31)* — medium-wide noodles are used here — drain it, put it into the skillet and turn it carefully in the butter. Add large chunks of cold butter and set the skillet over medium heat. Then pour in the cream mixture.

3 **Finishing the dish.** Turn the pasta gently in the sauce, or slide the pan ba and forth quickly over the heat, to coat the pieces evenly. After one or tw minutes, when the butter chunks are almost melted and the sauce is hot, th pasta is ready to serve.

sing Marinated Tomatoes

Preparing tomatoes. Core tomatoes and drop them into boiling water to loosen their skins. After about 20 seconds, transfer the tomatoes to a bowl of ice water to cool. Peel each tomato by grasping the skin between a knife blade and your thumb. Stem basil leaves and peel garlic cloves.

2 **Marinating.** Halve the tomatoes, squeeze out the seeds and chop the flesh into chunks. Chop the garlic and add it to the tomatoes; tear the basil leaves into pieces and add them, too. Toss with olive oil, salt and pepper; cover and marinate for at least two hours.

3 **Coating the pasta.** Boil fresh pasta and drain it; wide-cut noodles are used in this demonstration. Immediately transfer the pasta to a warmed serving dish and add the tomato mixture. Turn the pasta gently to coat it with the oil and to distribute the flavorings evenly. Serve at once.

Mélange of Fresh Vegetables

Preparing vegetables. Broil sweet red peppers, turning them frequently, for 10 minutes or until the skins are charred. Peel off and discard the loosened skins; seed, derib and slice the peppers. Top and tail green beans. Trim asparagus tips and broccoli florets *(above).* Slice unpeeled zucchini thin. String snow peas.

2 **Cooking the vegetables.** Blanch each raw vegetable separately in boiling water and drain it. Green beans, asparagus, broccoli and zucchini will take only about three minutes each, snow peas no more than 15 seconds. Heat olive oil in a skillet until a haze forms above it, then stir in the blanched vegetables and peppers.

3 **Coating the pasta.** Turn the vegetables in the oil until they are hot but still crisp — no more than three or four minutes. Season with salt and pepper, then add the vegetables to a warmed serving dish containing hot pasta, just boiled and drained. Turn the prepared vegetables and pasta together briefly. Serve immediately.

A Gloss of Garlic and Oil

1 **Flavoring the oil.** Crush two or three garlic cloves lightly with the flat of a knife blade to loosen their skins, then peel the cloves, slice them thin and drop them into a skillet. Pour in a generous layer of olive oil — in this case, oil in which whole, unpeeled garlic cloves have steeped for several days.

2 **Cooking the garlic.** Turn the heat to low and sauté the garlic slices until they are golden; do not let them burn, because this would give the oil a bitter flavor. Using a slotted spoon or skimmer, remove the garlic slices from the oil and discard them.

3 **Garnishing the pasta.** Toss the garlic-flavored oil with freshly cooked and drained pasta — dried linguini is shown here. Garnish, if you like, with Italian black olives that have been rinsed of brine, soaked in olive oil, then halved and pitted. Sprinkle the mixture with chopped fresh parsley.

A Bold Shellfish Sauce

1 **Cooking clams.** Pour a little white wine and water into a pot. Add parsley, chopped onion and garlic, and scrubbed, hard-shell clams. Cover, and cook over high heat. When the clams open — in about five minutes — transfer them to a plate; pick out and discard any unopened clams. Strain the clam cooking liquid and reserve it.

2 **Making sauce.** In a skillet set over low heat, gently cook a little olive oil, chopped onion and garlic until soft — about one minute. Add chopped parsley and freshly ground pepper. Pour in the strained clam cooking liquid, raise the heat to high and boil the sauce mixture for about five minutes, or until it has been reduced slightly.

3 **Serving.** Boil pasta — dried linguini, in this instance — drain it, and toss it in warmed serving bowl with a little olive oil. Strew the clams, still in their shells, over the pasta. Pour the reduced sauce mixture over all and serve at on

con for a Spicy Accent

1 **Cooking the bacon.** Cut *pancetta* — Italian bacon available at specialty markets — into thin strips and sauté it in a little olive oil for about 10 minutes, until it crisps. Add torn fresh sage leaves, if desired, near the end of cooking. Drain the bacon in a strainer and pour off most of the fat from the pan.

2 **Preparing sauce.** Whisk together egg yolks and a little heavy cream — about ½ tablespoonful [7 ml.] for each yolk — until smooth. Stir in enough freshly grated Parmesan cheese to make a thick but pourable sauce. Add pepper. Over medium heat, briefly warm the pan used for the *pancetta*.

3 **Finishing the dish.** Return the *pancetta* to the pan and cover it with freshly cooked, drained pasta; dried linguini is used above. Pour the egg-yolk-and-cream mixture over the pasta, mix all of the ingredients briefly together over the heat and serve at once. Do not salt the dish; *pancetta* is salty enough.

Garlicky Purée of Basil and Nuts

1 **Pounding the leaves.** Stem fresh basil leaves; then pound and grind them with peeled garlic cloves and salt in a mortar and pestle. Continue until the mixture is reduced to a pulpy paste.

2 **Adding flavorings.** Pound freshly grated cheese — Parmesan is used in this demonstration, but many cooks use pecorino Romano, or both — into the basil mixture, along with pine nuts. When the cheese is blended and the nuts crushed, pound in olive oil to dilute the pesto to a thick purée. If you like, add freshly ground pepper.

3 **Coating the pasta.** Boil pasta — dried linguini is shown — drain it, and toss it into a heated serving bowl with a little olive oil. Then add the pesto to the hot pasta and turn the ingredients about with two spoons to coat each piece of pasta with sauce.

Gentle Treatment for Filled Shapes

With slight adjustments to allow for the packages' size and thickness, boiling is as good a cooking method for filled pasta as it is for plain, whether the pasta is tiny ravioli or tortellini *(pages 25-27)*, or a giant cylinder *(below; recipe, page 114)*.

Small pastas, such as the ravioli shown opposite *(top)*, require relatively simple cooking methods. They cook almost as quickly as fresh, unfilled pasta and need similarly generous quantities of water. It is particularly important that these small packages not be crowded in the pan; if they are, they will cook unevenly, and some will overcook and become soggy. Cook the pasta in small batches and handle it very gently: The packages can easily fall apart. Use large skimmers or perforated spoons for lifting and draining: Small filled packages tossed in a colander will certainly break apart.

Large pasta rolls call for more demanding treatment. The rolls always are shaped from fresh dough because commercial pasta is not available in sheets that are big enough. The dough should be rolled out as described on pages 16-17 but, to minimize its fragility, the sheet should be slightly thicker than one that is used to make pasta ribbons: ¼ inch [6 mm.] is about right.

Many of the techniques used for shaping and cooking large rolls are designed to protect the rather unwieldy pasta. To prevent stretching and tearing, the pasta is manipulated as gently as possible. A large piece of muslin or cheesecloth is an invaluable tool: The cloth can be used to lift and roll the pasta around its filling *(Step 3, below)*, and then wrapped around the assembly and tied at both ends to contain the pasta during cooking.

For cooking the roll you will need a deep vessel fitted with a rack that sup-ports the pasta and allows you to mov without bending and possibly break it. Both the fish poacher shown here the roasting pan shown on page 86 effective; lacking these, make sma rolls that can be handled with spatul

Large pasta shapes are cooked in wa that boils very gently. In rapidly boil water, the outer pasta layers would come overcooked and soggy before the terior layers were cooked.

Cooked pasta packages are genera garnished with a sauce, and the rang sauces is as broad as the range of filli *(recipes, pages 112-118)*. Pasta and ing should complement each other. He for instance, cheese-filled ravioli are c ered with a rich meat sauce. The pa roll shown below, thick with cheese spinach, is topped with a light, chur fresh-tomato sauce.

Rolling and Poaching a Large Sheet of Dough

1 **Unrolling a pasta sheet.** Mix, knead and roll out a sheet of pasta to a thickness of about ¼ inch [6 mm.]. Lightly flour a large piece of muslin or double thickness of cheesecloth. Roll the pasta sheet loosely around a rolling pin, then carefully unroll it onto the cloth *(above).*

2 **Spreading the filling.** Prepare a filling—a mixture of spinach and ricotta *(page 25)* with chopped ham is shown. Spoon it onto the pasta sheet *(above)* and spread it to an even thickness of about ½ inch [1 cm.]. Leave a 1-inch [2½-cm.] margin uncovered around the edge of the sheet.

3 **Rolling the pasta.** Lift one side of the cloth off the work surface so that side of the pasta sheet rolls over. Gather up more cloth, nudging the pa along as you compact the roll with your hands. When the sheet is completely rolled, wrap the cloth around it and tie each end with string make a fabric cocoon for the pasta.

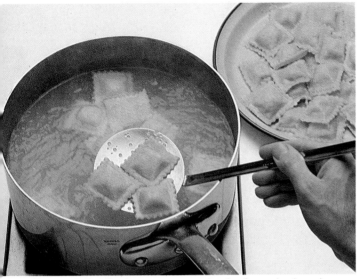

Boiling ravioli. Fill a large pan to a depth of two thirds with water; add salt and oil. Bring the water to a boil, then use a skimmer to lower fresh ravioli into the pan a few at a time. Cook ravioli in batches to avoid crowding the pan. After three minutes, remove a ravioli and bite or pinch it: It should feel tender yet firm. If not, let the batch boil for another minute and test again.

2 **Serving ravioli.** As soon as the ravioli are done, lift them with the skimmer and let excess water drain back into the pan. Transfer the drained pasta to a warmed serving dish and cover it with a hot sauce — in this case, meat sauce *(pages 12-13)* — to keep it warm while you cook the remaining batches.

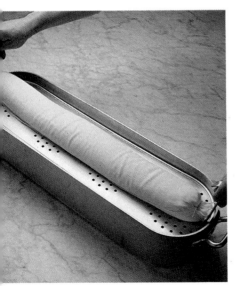

4 **Poaching.** Place the wrapped roll on the rack of a fish poacher and lower the rack into the poacher *(above)*. Pour in boiling water to immerse the roll. Cover the poacher and place it over two stove burners set at medium heat. Simmer the roll for about 40 minutes. Lift the rack out of the poacher and let the roll drain. As soon as the roll is cool enough to handle easily, cut off the strings and unwrap the cloth.

5 **Slicing and serving the roll.** Slide the roll from the cloth to a warmed serving dish and serve the roll as quickly as possible. Use a sharp knife to slice the roll, first dipping the knife into hot water so that the pasta does not stick to it. Serve the slices with a sauce — a chunky tomato sauce with basil leaves is used here.

Coping with Fragile Noodles

The primary cooking medium for Oriental pastas is water, just as it is for Western ones, and most Oriental pastas are boiled in exactly the same way as their Occidental counterparts. However, two types—rice-stick noodles and cellophane noodles—are manufactured differently from other pastas and, in consequence, must be handled in a different way.

To produce these noodles, rice, beans or potatoes are soaked, drained, ground, made into a paste, extruded into boiling water, cooled, frozen, defrosted and then dried, a time-consuming process yielding translucent strands that are mostly gelatin. Like any gelatin, the noodles would become rubbery if plunged directly into boiling water. Instead, they must be softened by soaking in hot or cold water, then briefly cooked in mixtures of frying or simmering ingredients.

Soaking times will vary with the temperature of the water, the thickness of the noodles and the use that will be made of them. When properly soaked—about 20 minutes in cold water, 10 minutes in hot—the noodles will be double in size and pliable but still chewy to the bite. At this stage they can be added to a simmering soup to give it body, briefly pan fried (*pages 66-67*) or quickly heated in a stew, as shown in this demonstration.

The stews of Oriental cookery are similar to the sauces for Western pasta in that they can incorporate almost any meat, fish or vegetable. Usually, they are pungently seasoned. Here, ground pork is marinated with scallions in sesame-seed oil and soy sauce, then browned in oil with garlic, ginger and hot-pepper paste—a fiery condiment available at Oriental markets. The addition of water turns the seasonings into a sauce for the stew; the softened cellophane noodles add textural interest, as do dried Chinese mushrooms—also available at Oriental markets—that have been soaked in water beforehand to rehydrate them. Other meats such as beef could replace the pork, and almost any vegetable—snow peas, for example—could be used instead of the mushrooms.

1 **Presoaking.** In a small bowl, soak dried Chinese mushrooms in warm water for 30 minutes. Using a large bowl, immerse bundles of cellophane noodles in very hot water; let them soak for 10 minutes or so, until soft and flexible.

2 **Marinating the meat.** While the noodles are soaking, mix ground po▸ with soy sauce and sesame-seed oil. Trim and slice scallions. Add half of t▸ scallions to the meat mixture; reserve▸ the rest. Cover the bowl and marinate▸ ingredients until ready to use.

5 **Cooking the noodles.** Add the cellophane noodles to the meat-and-vegetable mixture and stir them well. Let the noodles cook for about one minute while you cut their long strands in several places with the spatula or shovel.

3 **Stir frying the seasonings.** Drain the noodles and the mushrooms. Cut off the stiff stems of the mushrooms and slice the caps. In a large pan — a wok is used here — heat peanut oil until it begins to smoke. Add hot-pepper paste, and finely chopped ginger and garlic, stirring rapidly for about 30 seconds with a spatula or Chinese cooking shovel.

4 **Adding the meat.** Quickly stir the marinated meat into the seasonings, breaking up any chunks with the spatula or shovel. Cook the meat until all traces of pink disappear, about one minute. Pour in soy sauce, and stir and cook the combined ingredients for 30 seconds longer.

5 **Simmering and serving.** Add water to the pan, as well as the remaining scallions and the sliced mushroom caps. Season with salt to taste, cover the pan *(above),* and simmer for three or four minutes. For a piquant embellishment, grind fresh black pepper over the entire dish before serving it *(right).*

Potpie Squares Cooked in Broth

Boiled in a stew, pasta absorbs flavors as it becomes tender. Dried pasta will serve, but fresh pasta—it can be made while the stew cooks—will be done in a fraction of the time demanded by dried kinds.

To complement the heartiness of stew, the pasta should be a substantial variety such as penne, shells, butterflies or the potpie squares shown here. The only requirement for the stew itself is that it must have enough stock so the pieces of pasta can circulate freely as they boil.

In the demonstration below, chicken is poached whole to retain its succulence, then cut up and combined with potatoes, celery and potpie to produce the Pennsylvania Dutch stew that is also called potpie *(recipe, page 108)*. Large cuts of beef, pork or veal, or a whole rabbit, could replace the chicken; carrots, parsnips or leeks might substitute for or suppleme the vegetables shown.

Potpie stock gets its golden hue a faint pungency from saffron. The stock frequently served as a broth but it cou be turned into a gravy, after the solid i gredients are removed, by gradually st ring into it small bits of *beurre manié* butter and flour rubbed together to for a paste—as a thickener.

1 Poaching the chicken. Place a trussed roasting chicken in a large pot of cold water. Bring the water slowly to a boil, skimming any scum that rises. Add flavorings—celery, saffron, parsley, salt and pepper are used here. Reduce the heat until the liquid barely simmers. Cook for an hour, until tender.

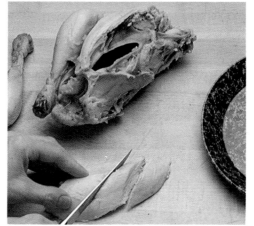

2 Preparing the meat. Transfer the chicken to a cutting board and carve it into sections. With a small, sharp knife, remove the skin and bones. Slice each section into serving portions and set these aside on a plate, covered with plastic wrap to keep them moist.

3 Straining the stock. Peel potatoes and cut them into 1-inch [2½-cm.] cube Cut celery into thick slices. Combine the vegetables in a medium-sized pot then set a strainer over the pot and lad the chicken stock through the strainer, adding about 2 quarts [2 liters] of stoc for each ½ pound [¼ kg.] of pasta.

4 Cooking the pasta. Bring the stock to a boil. Boil the vegetables for about 10 minutes, then add fresh potpie squares and boil for two to three minutes. Or add dried potpie with the vegetables as soon as the stock boils and cook for 12 to 15 minutes. Add the chicken, chopped parsley, pepper and salt to taste.

5 Serving the potpie. Let the stock simmer for a minute or so to heat the chicken through. Line a deep serving dish with the potpi and potatoes, and arrange the chicken pieces and celery on top. Sprinkle the surface with parsley and ladle stock over the ste to immerse it. Serve immediately in individual bowls.

Casing of Coiled Macaroni

hen boiled, long tubes of macaroni are
·xible enough to be coiled in a mold to
·m the walls of a timbale: a pasta or
·stry case containing a savory filling.
·ter the case is filled, the timbale is
·oked in a water bath, which gently
·ats and solidifies the filling without
·duly softening the macaroni. For serv-
·g, the timbale is unmolded.

Almost any plain round mold or bowl
·n be used to shape the timbale. A char-
·tte mold or soufflé dish will produce a
·umlike form. Here, the macaroni is
·iled in a hemispherical mold, which
·ves the finished timbale a beehive as-
·ct (page 43; recipe, page 119).

In addition to providing the case, pasta
·ves extra body to the filling. Macaroni
·ft over from lining the mold can be cut
·to short tubes, then mixed with differ-
·t sorts of precooked and chopped meat,
·afood and vegetables—sautéed chick-
·· livers and beef tongue, for example, or
·iled lobster and shrimp—and the com-
·nation can then be united with a sauce.

In this demonstration, the macaroni is
·ixed with veal sweetbreads—the soft-
·xtured, mild-flavored thymus glands.
·e sweetbreads require advance prepa-
·tion: First, they are soaked to draw off
·ood, then parboiled to firm the flesh
·d weighted to compact it, and finally
·aised with wine and aromatic vegeta-
·es. The braising liquid creates a stock
·at, thickened with a flour-and-butter
·ux, becomes the sauce.

To support the case and to prevent the
·acaroni from unraveling, the pasta is
·ated with a forcemeat mousseline be-
·re the case is filled. The mousseline,
·hich is forcemeat (very finely puréed
·eat) bound with egg white and enriched
·ith cream, firms as it cooks, cementing
·e macaroni strands together.

The chicken forcemeat shown on these
·ages will go well with any meat filling;
·ıbstitute a forcemeat made from whit-
·ıg, hake or pike if you choose a fish or
·ıellfish filling. The proportions among
·ıgredients for a mousseline may be var-
·d—within limits. More egg white will
·ake the mousseline firmer; more cream
·ill make it more delicate. A safe ratio
· use is the egg white of one large egg
·ıd 1 cup [¼ liter] of heavy cream to
· pound [¼ kg.] of forcemeat.

1 **Preparing sweetbreads.** Soak
veal sweetbreads in a bowl of cold water
for an hour. Transfer them to a
saucepan and cover them with fresh cold
water. Bring the water to a boil,
simmer the sweetbreads for two minutes,
then drain them. Plunge them into cold
water to stop the cooking. Remove gristle
and fat, and peel off the membrane.

2 **Flattening sweetbreads.** Place
the sweetbreads side by side on a towel.
Cover them with another towel. Place
a board on top of the sweetbreads and
use 1-pound [½-kg.] cans to weight
the board. Compress the sweetbreads
for about two hours to firm the flesh.

3 **Braising sweetbreads.** Sauté
finely chopped carrots, onion and herbs
in butter until soft—about 10 minutes.
Add the sweetbreads, in a single layer.
Pour in a splash of dry white wine and
boil to reduce the wine to half its original
volume. Add a bay leaf, cover the
sweetbreads with stock, set a lid on the
pan and simmer for 40 minutes.

4 **Straining the stock.** Remove the
sweetbreads from the pan and let them
cool. Tip the remaining contents of the
pan into a fine strainer set over a bowl.
Using a wooden spoon or pestle,
press the vegetables firmly, but without
grinding, to extract their juices.
Discard the vegetables and herbs. Slice
the sweetbreads and reserve them. ▶

5 **Preparing the case.** In a large pot, bring salted and oiled water to a boil. Add long macaroni and cook it until *al dente (pages 30-31)*. Drain the macaroni in a colander. Lay the strands side by side on a towel; make sure the strands do not touch or they may stick together. Thickly butter a hemispherical mold or a metal bowl. Starting at the center of the mold *(above)*, coil the macaroni end to end in a spiral, taking care to leave no gaps between the strands. Continue until the mold is completely lined *(inset)*. Set the remaining macaroni aside. Place the mold in the refrigerator so that the butter will harden, holding the macaroni firmly in place.

6 **Preparing the forcemeat.** Bone and skin a chicken breast. Chop the meat into pieces. In a food processor, grind the pieces fine, then combine them with an egg white. To make the purée very smooth, press it through a fine drum sieve *(above)*. Transfer the purée to a bowl and press a piece of plastic wrap against its surface. Refrigerate the purée for about an hour.

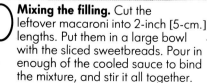

10 **Mixing the filling.** Cut the leftover macaroni into 2-inch [5-cm.] lengths. Put them in a large bowl with the sliced sweetbreads. Pour in enough of the cooled sauce to bind the mixture, and stir it all together.

11 **Filling the case.** Spoon the filling into the lined macaroni case. To eliminate any air pockets, gently press down on the filling. Level the top and, using a spatula, spread the remaining mousseline over the surface. Press a round of buttered wax or parchment paper over the mousseline.

12 **Cooking the timbale.** To protect the bottom of the timbale from direct heat, place a wire rack in a large pot half-filled with hot water. Set the mold on the rack. Cook the timbale on top of the stove over low heat, or in a preheated 350° F. [180° C.] oven for 45 minutes. Lift the mold out of the pot

7 Incorporating the cream. Set the bowl of chilled purée in a bowl of ice; slowly mix in heavy cream until the purée is soft enough to stir easily. Whip the rest of the cream until it is thick *(above)*, then blend it thoroughly into the purée. Leave the mousseline in ice so that it stays firm.

8 Lining the case. Remove the chilled mold from the refrigerator. Spoon three quarters of the mousseline into the mold and, using the back of the spoon, spread the mousseline evenly over the surface of the macaroni. Cover the mold and refrigerate it to firm the mousseline.

9 Making the sauce. In a small pan, heat butter and stir in a little flour. Whisk in the strained stock *(Step 4, page 41)*. Move the pan half off the heat and simmer the sauce for 40 minutes or so to reduce it by about half. Skim off the fatty skin that repeatedly forms over the cooler side of the surface.

13 Unmolding and serving. Peel off the paper round and let the timbale rest at room temperature for 10 minutes to firm and settle. Place a warmed serving plate on top of the mold. Turn over the plate and mold together. Lift off the mold. Cut the timbale into wedges *(left)*. Serve with tomato sauce *(page 13)* enriched with heavy cream *(inset)*.

Couscous: A Full Meal from One Pot

The tiny size of the dough pellets known as couscous dictates gentle handling. If cooked in boiling water, the pellets stick together. To keep them separate, tender and fluffy, couscous pellets are first moistened *(Steps 1-4),* then steamed in two stages as shown on pages 45-46. As a side dish, couscous can be cooked above boiling water. But in the North African countries where the pasta originated, it is cooked in the aromatic steam that rises from poaching fruit or from a meat-and-vegetable stew such as the one shown here *(recipes, pages 120-121 and 156).*

Imported couscous is available in fine, medium-sized and coarse pellets from specialty food shops. The sizes can be used interchangeably, although fine pellets are traditionally reserved for desserts. A precooked medium-sized variety, which cooks somewhat faster, can be found in some supermarkets.

The ideal steaming vessel is a *couscoussier*—a two-section pot with holes in both the base and the lid of the top section that allow steam to pass through the pellets and escape without condensing under the lid. The stew is simmered in the lower section while the couscous steams in the top one; to ensure that steam is driven upward, the sections are sealed with a cloth impregnated with flour-and-water paste *(Step 8).*

Couscoussiers can be purchased from kitchen-supply shops, but you can improvise by using a deep pot for the lower section and a cheesecloth-lined colander that fits snugly into the pot for the upper section. Seal the sections with a paste-coated cloth and use a piece of foil pierced with holes to cover the colander.

Because the stew demands more cooking time than the couscous, the meat and slow-cooking vegetables are simmered for about 30 minutes before the top section of the *couscoussier* is added. When partly cooked, the pellets will lump together; they must be removed from the pot and separated by hand. Before the top section is replaced, quick-cooking vegetables are added to the stew.

Once fully cooked, the pellets serve as a bed for the stew. Some broth is used to moisten individual servings. Hot *harissa* sauce *(box, page 47)* flavors the broth; more sauce is offered as extra seasoning.

1 **Dampening couscous.** Spread the couscous on a deep tray or baking pan. Sprinkle the pellets with just enough water to dampen them.

2 **Stirring the couscous.** Rake through the couscous with your finger until all of the pellets feel moistened. Let the pellets absorb the water and sw for about 15 minutes, then rake your fingers through them again.

5 **Preparing the ingredients for the stew.** Drain chickpeas that have been soaked in water overnight, and simmer them in fresh water for one to one and a half hours until they are tender. Drain them in a strainer set over a bowl. Cut up a chicken or a lamb shoulder — or both, as above — into large pieces. Chop an onion. Peel carrots and turnips and cut them into large chunks. Rinse a bunch of coriander leaves.

3 **Separating couscous.** Roll the pellets gently between your palms to break up any lumps. Sprinkle the couscous with a little more water and roll the pellets between your palms again. Continue adding water and rolling the pellets until all of them are saturated and have doubled in size.

4 **Sieving the couscous.** Put the damp couscous pellets into a coarse-meshed sieve and shake the sieve over the tray so that the couscous passes through. If some of the pellets have lumped together and will not pass through, sprinkle them with a little more water and roll them between your palms again, then sieve them.

5 **Assembling the stew.** Fill the bottom section of a *couscoussier* about halfway with cold water and drop in the prepared meat, vegetables and coriander leaves. Add a pinch each of ground saffron and cinnamon, and stir in a teaspoon or two of *harissa* sauce (box, page 47).

7 **Adding the top section.** Bring the water slowly to a boil; remove any scum from its surface and cook the stew at a bare simmer, uncovered, for about 30 minutes. Heap the couscous lightly in the top section of the *couscoussier*. Set the top section on the lower one and cover the *couscoussier* with its lid.

8 **Sealing the couscoussier.** Make a paste with three parts of flour to one part of water. Dip a long band of cheesecloth or muslin into this paste and squeeze the cloth to rid it of excess moisture. Wrap the cloth several times around the joint between the sections of the *couscoussier*. Tuck the end of the cloth under the last layer of wrapping. ▶

9 **Tipping out the couscous.** Raise the heat so that the liquid boils and produces steam to cook the couscous. After about 30 minutes, the pellets will lump together. To separate them, remove the cloth from the *couscoussier*; lift off the top section, leaving the stew in the bottom section to cook. Using a fork, push the couscous onto a tray.

10 **Fluffing up couscous.** Spread the couscous evenly on the tray. To help separate the pellets, sprinkle cold water over the couscous. Gently rake through the pellets with your fingers and break up any lumps. Leave the couscous pellets on the tray while you prepare the other ingredients for the stew *(Steps 11-13).*

11 **Preparing pumpkin.** Slice a small pumpkin — or half of a large one — into wedges; then scrape out the seeds and strings with a spoon. Using a small, sharp knife, peel the pumpkin wedges and cut them into large chunks.

12 **Cooking the pumpkin.** Pumpkin overcooks and turns mushy quickly; to keep the chunks intact, cook them separately so that you can easily check their progress. Put them in a small pan and cover them with liquid ladled from the *couscoussier*. Set the pan aside until you are ready to finish cooking the stew.

13 **Fixing other vegetables.** Broil peppers, turning them every few minutes, until the skins blister. Let the peppers cool, covered by a damp cloth, then peel and seed them. Immerse tomatoes in boiling water; peel, halve and seed them. Cut zucchini into large pieces. Add these vegetables to the stew.

14 **Completing the cooking.** Return the couscous to the top section of the *couscoussier*; replace the top section on the lower one and seal the joint *(Step 8, page 45)* with a new strip of cloth. Cook for 15 minutes, or until the peppers and zucchini are tender and the couscous is soft and fluffy. Meanwhile, simmer the pumpkin gently for 10 to 15 minutes until tender

A Fiery Sauce

Making harissa sauce. Soak a few dried hot chilies in cold water for an hour to soften them. Wearing rubber gloves, split the chilies and remove the stems and seeds. Pound the chilies in a mortar with 2 or 3 tablespoons [30 or 45 ml.] of caraway seeds, a garlic clove and some coarse salt until they form a paste. Mix in enough oil to make the paste fluid. Refrigerated, *harissa* sauce will keep for three months.

15 **Serving the couscous.** Place the pellets on a serving dish and ladle broth over them. Add butter and, using two forks, toss the couscous. Arrange the pumpkin around the edge of the dish, and ladle the meat and the other vegetables over the couscous. Serve the couscous with the rest of the broth and a bowl of *harissa* sauce *(above);* those who enjoy the sauce can dilute it in a spoonful of broth *(right)* and pour the mixture over their couscous.

Baking
Melding Flavors in the Oven

Pasta makes a fine foundation for baked assemblies: Satiny in texture and bland in flavor, it serves as a foil for rough-grained, assertive-tasting mixtures of meat, vegetables, seafood or cheese, and as a vehicle for rich, smooth sauces. Most baked dishes are of the kind known as *pasticci* in Italy; the pasta, the sauce that keeps it moist, and the ingredients used for extra flavor and texture are separately prepared, then combined and baked to unite the disparate elements into a harmonious entity.

Using this model, you can create a number of quite different effects, depending on the type of pasta you choose. Short varieties—elbow macaroni or shells, for instance—can be tossed with white sauce and shredded cheese and layered with sliced cheese; baking turns this simple assembly into an opulent kind of macaroni and cheese: a creamy mass with a crisp, golden veneer *(pages 50-51)*. Such pasta mixtures—enriched, if you like, with meats and chopped vegetables—make excellent fillings *(pages 56-57)*. Baked in a mold lined with a sliced vegetable such as eggplant, the pasta mixture provides a rich interior firm enough to support the assembly when it is unmolded. Very tiny pastas can be mixed with sauce and used to stuff whole, hollowed-out vegetables—tomatoes, zucchini or green peppers.

Longer pastas such as fettucini are too unwieldy to form a filling of this type. Such pasta can, however, be packed loosely into a pastry case and baked. By using several types of pasta this way, you can create a dish of kaleidoscopic color and subtly varied textures *(opposite)*.

Larger pastas may be used as casings for assemblies rather than as fillings. Outsize hollow pastas such as conchiglie come ready to be stuffed and bathed with sauce. Sheets of pasta, whole or cut into large squares, serve as a cover for layers of fillings and sauces. Or pasta may be cut into squares or long wide strips, wrapped around fillings, then topped by sauce and baked to produce tidy individual portions *(pages 54-55)*.

With slight alterations in proportions and preparation, the typical baked pasta assembly—pasta, filling and sauce—can be turned into the most unusual of baked pasta creations: soufflés. The addition of beaten egg whites to the other ingredients gives soufflés their distinction. During baking, the whites expand, yielding a dish that is airy and light, yet substantial because of the pasta concealed within *(pages 60-61)*.

pastas, both plain and flavored, d spinach-stuffed tortellini are served n a pie with a crust made from e-oil dough *(pages 58-59)*. The stness of the pie filling, enriched by n and cream, contrasts appetizingly the crisp texture of the golden wn pastry shell and lid.

Macaroni and Cheese: A Model Assembly

The principles for preparing baked pasta dishes are most readily displayed in that humble American classic, macaroni and cheese—a dish that, like its more complicated relatives, is essentially a mixture of pasta, sauce and flavorings (recipe, page 124).

The pasta for macaroni and cheese should be a short, contoured type that, unlike long pasta strands, will remain distributed evenly throughout the sauce during baking. Dried macaroni, rigatoni, ziti or penne are good choices, as are fresh pasta butterflies (page 23).

As with almost all baked pasta dishes, the pasta receives a preliminary, carefully gauged boiling. The pasta must be softened just enough so that it will bake to doneness with the other ingredients; if it were completely cooked beforehand, it would emerge from the oven an overcooked, characterless mush.

Fresh pasta may require no more than

20 seconds of boiling to soften it to the point where it is flexible but still firm to the bite. Dried pasta will reach this stage after as little as five minutes of boiling; begin testing it at this point. Drain any type of pasta thoroughly before adding it to other ingredients: Excess moisture could make the finished dish watery.

A plain white sauce (recipe, page 166) is the usual choice for macaroni and cheese: The sauce keeps the macaroni moist and serves as a bland, creamy binder for all the ingredients. Because the grated cheese used to flavor the dish will melt and thicken the sauce during baking, the sauce should be pourable when the dish is assembled. If it is too thick, dilute it with a little milk or cream.

As for the cheese, almost any type is suitable, and a combination of several types of cheeses adds interest to the dish. In this demonstration, Fontina—shredded to speed its melting time—is com-

bined with the macaroni before the sau is added, but either freshly grated P mesan or stronger-tasting pecorino mano would be equally good. To provid surprising contrast in flavor and text to these assertive hard cheeses, slices mild mozzarella are concealed in the sembled dish. They could be replaced young Gruyère or a mild Cheddar; a semisoft cheese prepared in this way w melt during baking to form a smoo molten sheet inside the pasta.

The assembly lends itself to a numl of simple but interesting variations. Y could, for example, augment the pas and-cheese mixture with cubed cool meats such as ham or turkey. Fresh ve tables such as sautéed mushrooms parboiled peas might also provide attr tive notes of color and flavor. And, fo particularly crisp finish, you can grat the cooked macaroni and cheese wit topping of bread crumbs, as shown he

4 **Preparing the baking dish.** Cut three thick slices of mozzarella cheese—preferably whole-milk mozzarella, which will melt more smoothly than the skim-milk kind. Set the slices aside. Generously coat the sides and bottom of an ovenproof casserole with butter.

5 **Adding the cheese.** Transfer half of the pasta mixture to the casserole and lay the mozzarella slices on top of it. Spread the remaining pasta mixture over the cheese. Cover the casserole with its lid or with aluminum foil, place it in an oven preheated to 350° F. [180° C.], and bake for 45 minutes.

6 **Buttering bread crumbs.** Melt butter in a skillet over low heat. Add fi fresh bread crumbs and sauté the crumbs in the warm butter, stirring constantly, until they are moist; be careful not to let them brown.

Shredding the cheese. Make a white sauce *(page 12)* and set it aside. Parboil elbow macaroni, drain it and place it in a deep bowl. Using a shredder with large holes, or the largest holes of a box grater, shred a generous amount of Fontina cheese onto the macaroni.

2 **Adding the sauce.** If necessary, add light cream or milk to the white sauce to thin it to pouring consistency. Then ladle enough warm sauce over the macaroni and Fontina to blanket the surface with a thick layer.

3 **Mixing the ingredients.** Stir with a large spoon until the sauce coats all of the macaroni pieces and the cheese is evenly distributed throughout. Stir in additional white sauce and Fontina until the pasta mixture is very moist but not soupy. Season with salt and pepper.

7 **Serving.** Remove the casserole from the oven, uncover it and distribute the buttered bread crumbs over the macaroni and cheese. Return the casserole to the oven and bake uncovered for 15 minutes, or until the pasta is bubbling and the crumbs are golden brown *(below)*. Serve the macaroni and cheese immediately *(right)*, spooning out some of the softened mozzarella with each portion.

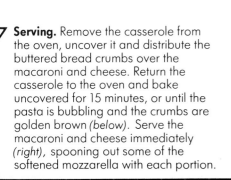

Layering Pastas and Sauces

The flat rectangles or broad strips of pasta known as lasagne make particularly distinctive baked assemblies: They are used to enclose other elements, either in individual packages *(pages 54-55)* or, more customarily, in layered arrangements such as the ones shown here.

In a layered dish, the size of the pasta pieces often determines the structure of the assembly. Large pasta squares, for instance, can be positioned so that they

enfold their sauces completely. In the demonstration below, for example, parboiled squares of spinach lasagne are formed into sheets that separate layers of meat sauce, white sauce *(page 12)* and grated cheese. For a decorative effect, the first layer of pasta is arranged so that it does not simply cover the base of the dish, but also lines the sides and overhangs the edges. When the subsequent layers are in place, the overhanging pasta is flipped

back toward the center of the dish to cr ate a tidy border.

Small pasta squares such as lazanki not lend themselves to such formal a rangements. If bound with sauce, howe er, they will cohere and form layers th can blanket other ingredients. In the a sembly at right, top, small squares a combined with egg yolks, sour crea melted butter and egg whites, then la ered with ham *(recipe, page 137).*

1 **Parboiling the lasagne.** Bring a pot of salted water to a boil. Add lasagne squares — in this case, spinach lasagne — a few at a time and boil them until they are just flexible: less than two minutes for fresh pasta and about five minutes for dried.

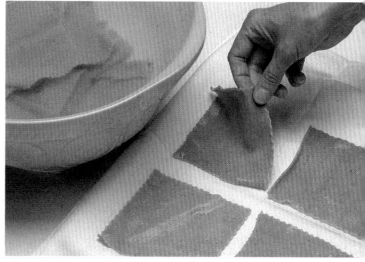

2 **Rinsing and drying.** Remove the lasagne squares from the pan with a wide spatula and briefly immerse them in cold water stop the cooking. Drain the lasagne squares side by side on a towel; do not allow them to touch one another.

3 **Layering the lasagne.** Butter a shallow ovenproof dish and cover the bottom with a layer of meat sauce *(pages 12-13)*. Cover with lasagne, arranging the squares so that they overlap by about ½ inch [1 cm.], and the edges overhang the rim of the dish.

4 **Adding the white sauce.** Shred mozzarella coarse, grate Parmesan fine, and blend the cheeses with your hands. Spoon layer of meat sauce over the lasagne; follow with a layer of white sauce. Sprinkle the cheese mixture over the white sauce.

Lazanki Squares with Diced Ham

1 **Adding egg whites.** Parboil small lazanki squares *(page 23)* in salted water. Drain them, cool briefly in cold water, and drain on paper towels. Separate eggs and whisk the yolks with melted butter and sour cream; add to the pasta. Whisk the egg whites to form stiff peaks and fold them into the mixture.

2 **Adding the ham.** Place a layer of the pasta mixture in the bottom of a buttered ovenproof dish. Sprinkle with diced cooked ham *(above)*. Continue to build up the dish with alternate layers of the pasta mixture and the ham, finishing with the pasta mixture.

3 **Baking the pasta.** Put the assembly in a preheated 350° F. [180° C.] oven. Bake it for about an hour. The top of the dish should be a light golden color. Let the pasta settle for a few minutes before serving it *(above)*.

5 **Building up the layers.** Place another layer of lasagne on top of the cheese, but arrange the squares inside the dish instead of overhanging the rim. Add more layers of meat sauce, white sauce and cheese, ending with cheese. Flip the overhanging lasagne back over the cheese so that it borders the dish.

6 **Baking.** Brush the border with melted butter and cover the dish with aluminum foil. Bake the lasagne in a preheated 350° F. [180° C.] oven for about 25 minutes, removing the foil after about 12 minutes to let the top crisp. Leave the dish at room temperature to firm for a few minutes before serving it in squares.

Meat-filled Cylinders Coated with Sauce

Individual Lasagne Rolls

Pastas such as manicotti or conchiglie provide ready-made hollows for filling, but it is equally easy to shape small, tidy packages from squares or strips of pasta—commercial or homemade. Save for the shaping, the cooking method is the same as for lasagne *(pages 52-53)*: The pasta is parboiled, rolled around a filling, covered with a sauce, and baked.

The choice of fillings and sauces includes the full range of meats, vegetables, cheeses and other ingredients found in dishes such as macaroni and cheese or layered lasagne. Be sure, however, that the consistency of a filling is such that the mixture can be spread onto the pasta without tearing it. The meats that compose the hearty filling at right *(recipe, page 162)* are ground fine. A lighter combination fills the rolled pasta squares, or cannelloni, opposite; it consists of thin slices of prosciutto and a rich mixture of eggs, ricotta cheese and flavorings.

1 Cooking meats. Prepare white sauce and tomato sauce *(pages 12-13)*. Stew chopped onion in oil until soft. Increase the heat, add sausage meat and fry it until it loses its pink color, breaking up lumps with a spatula *(left)*. Add ground veal *(right)* and brown it.

2 Draining the meats. Put the cooked meats in a strainer set over a bowl to drain the fat. Chop fresh parsley fine and grate lemon peel. Crumble dried rosemary between your fingers. Soak fresh bread crumbs heavy cream for three or four minute

5 Rolling the lasagne. Butter a baking dish and coat its bottom with a shallow layer of tomato sauce. Spread a little meat filling along the length of a strip of lasagne, roll the strip up around the filling, then place it seam side down in the pan. Fill and roll all of the lasagne strips in this manner and put them in the baking dish, placing them side by side in a single layer.

6 Adding the sauce. Prepare white sauce and, if desired, enrich it with a few spoonfuls of cream. Ladle enough sauce o the pasta rolls to coat them evenly. Sprinkle a generous layer freshly grated Parmesan cheese over the sauce.

Wrapping Cannelloni

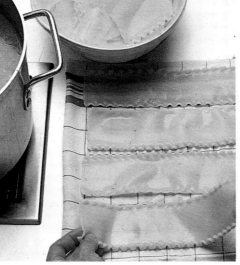

3 Finishing the filling. Stir the drained meat into the bread crumbs and cream, and beat the mixture until it is smooth. Beat eggs into the mixture, one at a time, then stir in the prepared parsley, rosemary and lemon peel. Season lightly with salt and pepper.

4 Cooking the pasta. Parboil strips of lasagne until they are flexible but still firm — about five minutes for the dried pasta shown here. Immediately plunge them into a bowl of cold water to stop the cooking. Lay the cooled strips side by side on a towel to drain.

1 Mixing a stuffing. Gradually add beaten whole eggs and egg yolks to ricotta cheese, stirring to blend them in evenly. Add some grated Parmesan cheese and chopped parsley. Season with salt, pepper and nutmeg.

2 Rolling the pasta. Parboil and drain pasta squares. For extra flavor, line each square with prosciutto. Spread filling on the prosciutto. Roll up the squares, brush these cannelloni with melted butter and put in a buttered baking dish.

7 Baking and serving the rolls. Transfer the dish to a preheated 350° F. [180° C.] oven and bake for half an hour, or until the sauce is bubbly. To produce a crisply browned surface, finish the dish by setting it under a preheated broiler for a few moments.

3 Serving the rolls. Pour tomato sauce between the cannelloni and then sprinkle them with grated Parmesan. Bake at 375° F. [190° C.] for 20 minutes. Cover the dish with foil for the first 10 minutes to prevent drying. Serve hot.

Pasta Cooked in Vegetable Cases

Whole Tomatoes Packed with Orzo

Mixtures of small pastas, sauces and flavorings may be encased in vegetable containers rather than in baking dishes, and the choice of containers is broad enough to satisfy any cook's need for variety.

Vegetables of the right size and shape to be filled whole include onions, peppers, zucchini, eggplants and tomatoes. None of these requires preparation more complex than hollowing out. For a more elaborate presentation, however, you can slice eggplant or zucchini lengthwise and form it into a molded casing *(below)*. The slices are fried to make them flexible enough to mold. For extra flavor, they may be coated with flour, egg and cheese, then fried again before baking.

All these vegetables lend distinctive tastes to baked assemblies; to balance them, season the fillings boldly. The tomatoes here encase orzo—a miniature pasta—cooked with onion and stock, and flavored with cheese *(recipe, page 128)*. The eggplant assembly consists of parboiled penne mixed with meats, peas and tomato sauce *(recipe, page 127)*.

1 **Preparing the containers.** Cut the tops from ripe tomatoes and use a spoon to scrape out their seeds and pulp. Sprinkle the interiors with a little sugar, salt, pepper and oregano, and set the tomatoes aside.

2 **Making the filling.** Sauté chopped onion in butter until it is soft; stir in the orzo. Add chicken stock, increase the heat, and simmer for about 10 minutes, until the liquid is absorbed. Remove the pan from the heat and s[...] in grated Parmesan cheese, cubed mozzarella cheese if desired, and sal[...]

Sliced Eggplant Molded around Penne

1 **Preparing eggplant.** Fry eggplant slices in olive oil over high heat until tender — about three minutes on each side. Drain on paper towels. Flour the slices and dip them in beaten egg mixed with grated Parmesan cheese. Fry again for about a minute on each side.

2 **Preparing the case.** Cut a circle from an eggplant slice and place the circle in the center of a deep, buttered baking dish. Lay three quarters of the remaining eggplant slices in the dish in an overlapping radial pattern that completely covers the bottom and sides of the dish *(above)*.

3 **Preparing the filling.** In a bowl, mix parboiled penne with chopped cooked tongue, chicken, sautéed chicken livers and chopped hard-boil[...] egg. Add fried sausage meat, parboiled peas and grated cheese — here, mozzarella and Parmesan. Stir in tomato sauce *(page 13)*.

3 **Stuffing and baking.** Pour out any liquid that has accumulated in the tomatoes and place a few mozzarella cubes in each one. Spoon in the stuffing *(above)*, place the tomatoes in a baking dish and pour a little stock around them to prevent sticking. Cover the dish and bake in a preheated 400° F. [200° C.] oven for about 25 minutes, uncovering the dish after 15 minutes so that the stuffing will develop a crisp golden crust *(right)*.

4 **Filling the case.** Pack the eggplant-lined baking dish with the filling *(above)*. Smooth the top of the filling and arrange the remaining eggplant slices over it in an overlapping radial pattern. Tuck the ends of the topmost eggplant slices inside the slices that line the side of the mold.

5 **Topping with sauce.** With a spoon, spread tomato sauce over the top of the eggplant. Sprinkle the sauce with Parmesan cheese. Cover the dish with foil and bake it in a preheated 375° F. [190° C.] oven for 30 to 40 minutes to heat the filling.

6 **Serving the assembly.** Remove the baking dish from the oven and let the contents settle for 10 minutes. Remove the foil and run a knife around the edge of the assembly to loosen it. Turn out the eggplant mold onto a serving platter. Pour tomato sauce around the mold *(above)* and serve it hot.

A Colorful Pasta Pie

An appealing way to display a selection of creamy pastas is to bake them in a crisp pastry casing. The pie in this demonstration is filled with different-colored pastas *(pages 20-21)* that have been precooked, then moistened with cream and flavored with grated Parmesan cheese and chopped ham.

Mixtures of pasta and long-simmered meat sauce *(pages 12-13)* would make an equally suitable filling, or you could combine the pasta with sautéed vegetables—mushrooms, zucchini or quartered artichoke bottoms, for example. If you like, you can include stuffed pasta in the pie. Here, tortellini filled with spinach are mixed with the noodles to add an extra dimension of flavor.

All kinds of pastry are suitable for the crust, from a butter or lard short crust to the olive-oil dough used in this demonstration. The dough's ingredients are the same as those of the pasta: flour, eggs and

oil. However, a higher proportion of olive oil is included *(recipe, page 165)*, giving the pastry a fruity taste and a pleasantly crumbly texture.

For a freestanding pie such as the one shown here, the pastry should be rolled out thick enough to make a sturdy case that will stand unsupported; ⅛ inch [3 mm.] is about the right thickness. Bake the pie in a spring-form pan, whose sides can be unclipped and separated from the case at the end of cooking *(Step 8)*.

To ensure that the pastry case does not become soggy and does provide a crisp contrast to the soft pasta, cook it partially before adding the moist filling. For the preliminary baking, weigh down the case with dried beans to prevent air bubbles from forming blisters and buckling the pastry. Prebake a lid for the pie at the same time as the case; then put the lid in place after adding the filling, so that the creamy pasta will not dry out in the oven.

1 Mixing the dough. Sift flour into a large mixing bowl; add an egg, salt and olive oil. Pour in a little tepid water *(above)* and mix the ingredients with a fork until they are bound loosely.

5 Trimming the base. Assemble the spring-form pan and close the spring clip. Brush the inside of the pan with oil. Roll out the remaining dough into a large circular shape. Roll the dough loosely around the rolling pin and transfer it to the pan. Gently press the dough into the pan. Trim the edge of the dough with a knife, leaving a 1-inch [2½-cm.] overhang.

6 Weighting the dough. Fold in the overhanging dough, pressing the double thickness of dough onto the rim of the pan and fluting it with your thumb. Line the pastry case with wax or parchment paper and fill it to the rim with dried beans *(above)*. Bake the case and lid in a preheated 350° F. [180° C.] oven for 15 minutes, or until lightly colored. Remove the paper and beans from the case, prick the bottom with a fork to prevent buckling and return the case to the oven briefly until the pastry looks dry.

2 **Kneading the dough.** Knead the dough with your knuckles *(above)*, sprinkling in more flour if the dough becomes sticky. Shape the dough into a ball. Cover it and refrigerate it in the bowl for about an hour to make the dough easier to roll out.

3 **Making the lid.** Remove slightly less than half of the dough from the bowl. On a smooth, floured surface, roll out the dough; lay the base of a spring-form pan in the middle. Trim the dough to make a circle, cutting about 1 inch [2½ cm.] outside the rim of the base *(above)*.

4 **Completing the lid.** Remove the pan base. To form a double-thickness rim that will make the lid less fragile, fold in the margin of the circle so that the edge aligns with the impression left by the lip of the pan base. For a decorative effect, flute the folded rim with your thumbnail or a fork. Slide the lid carefully onto an oiled baking sheet.

7 **Filling the case.** Boil tortellini *(page 37)* and green, orange and yellow pastas separately until they are tender but firm. Drain each pasta and mix it with heavy cream and chopped, cooked ham. Arrange the pasta mixtures in the pastry case, adding freshly grated Parmesan cheese *(above)*. Dribble a little more cream over the mixtures. Brush the rims of the case and lid with olive oil so that they will brown readily. Put the lid on the case *(inset)*. Bake the pie in a preheated 350° F. [180° C.] oven for about 20 minutes.

8 **Serving the pie.** Take out the pie when it is a rich, golden brown color. Remove the lid. Release the spring clip and lift off the sides of the pan *(above)*. Leaving the case on the base of the pan, transfer it to a serving plate. Replace the lid for serving, but remove it before cutting the pie into portions *(page 48)*.

Surprising Ingredients for Soufflés

Baked pasta soufflés are of two types: those in which pasta forms the basis of the mixture, and those in which pasta is used as a filling. To make the first type of soufflé, you will need homemade grated pasta shreds *(page 17)*. When the shreds are cooked in milk, they create a creamy sauce with enough thickening power to play the role performed by white sauce in a conventional soufflé. However, the pasta retains its shred shape during cooking, giving the finished soufflé a pleasantly rough texture.

In the grated-pasta soufflé that is demonstrated here, the cooked pasta, enriched with egg yolks, is combined with beaten egg whites—these expand during the cooking to inflate the assembly—and then transferred to a soufflé dish. A flavoring then is placed in its center. The flavoring used here *(recipe, page 130)* is boiled, ground beef heart; you could substitute any cooked ground meat—calf's liver, for instance, or veal. Or you could use lightly cooked, sliced or puréed vegetables, such as mushrooms or peas.

A topping of sour cream provides a foil for the piquant filling. As the soufflé bakes, the sour cream partly penetrates it and the surface of the sour cream turns a light biscuit color.

A soufflé that is filled with pasta rather than based on it can include ribbon-like varieties such as fettucini, boiled in advance and well drained. In the demonstration opposite *(box)*, fresh, thin green pasta, together with ham and grated cheese, is blended into a conventional white-sauce base *(recipe, page 166)*. The final step in the preparation of the soufflé is to fold in the beaten egg whites.

For either soufflé, the oven must be preheated and the mold buttered in advance. No time must be lost between folding the beaten whites into the other ingredients and baking the soufflés; delay might cause the airy whites to collapse.

1 **Making a meat filling.** Remove any veins or membranes from a beef heart. Cut up the heart, simmer for about an hour, drain and cool it. Put it through the medium disk of a meat grinder. In a skillet, melt lard and in it sauté finely chopped onion until translucent. Remove the pan from the heat, add the ground heart, and stir in lightly beaten eggs to bind the mixture.

2 **Cooking pasta shreds.** Prepare a stiff pasta dough and shred it *(page 1* Bring milk to a boil in a heavy pan, add the pasta shreds and reduce the heat. Stirring frequently, simmer for about 30 minutes, or until the past absorbs most of the milk.

3 **Adding the egg yolks.** Stir chopped parsley into the pasta mixture. Remove the pan from the heat and cool the mixture to lukewarm. Separate egg yolks from whites, and blend the yolks into the pasta mixture, stirring well to incorporate them thoroughly.

4 **Folding in the egg whites.** Whisk the egg whites until they stand in stiff peaks. Stir a large spoonful of beaten white into the pasta mixture to lighter Then add the pasta mixture to the remaining whites and, with a wooden spatula, fold it in gently but quickly.

Adding Substance with Green Noodles

1 **Adding flavorings.** Parboil fresh green pasta, such as the tagliatelle shown at top. With a wooden spoon, stir egg yolks into a thick white sauce (page 12). Add grated Parmesan cheese (above), chopped ham and the pasta. Season with salt, freshly ground pepper and grated nutmeg.

2 **Folding in egg whites.** Whisk egg whites until they form stiff peaks. Stir some of the beaten egg whites into the sauce to lighten it. Add the sauce to the remaining egg whites, folding it in quickly but gently to avoid deflating the whites or breaking the noodles.

3 **Serving the soufflé.** Spoon the mixture into a buttered soufflé dish. Bake the soufflé in a preheated 375° F. [190° C.] oven for about 40 minutes. Remove it when its surface is well browned (above), and serve at once.

Adding sour cream. Transfer the soufflé mixture to a buttered baking dish and spoon the beef heart into the center: The meat will sink. Cover the soufflé with a generous layer of sour cream. Put the soufflé in an oven preheated to 375° F. [190° C.].

Serving the soufflé. The soufflé will be ready in about 45 minutes, when well risen and lightly colored. Use a large spoon to serve it; each portion should include both the meaty filling and the lighter-textured soufflé (right).

A Caramel Finish for a Vermicelli Dessert

Because of its neutral taste, pasta lends itself to sweet baked dishes as well as to savory, or unsweetened, ones—and except for differences in flavorings, the methods of assembly are the same. As it is for savory dishes, the pasta is partly cooked, moistened with liquids, bound with eggs, flavored and finally baked to blend the elements. And also as for savory dishes, the basic ingredients may be varied to make a number of markedly different desserts *(recipes, pages 155-161)*.

Tiny pieces of orzo, for instance, mixed with cream and eggs, and flavored with sugar and vanilla, produce a dish with the smooth, custardy texture of rice pudding. Larger pastas, such as broad egg noodles, are mixed with cream or sour cream and eggs, and flavored with such ingredients as cream cheese, lemon or orange peel, and fresh or dried fruits to make the dense, colorful *kugeln*—the Yiddish word for puddings—of Middle European cookery.

For visual interest, a sweet pasta dish may include pasta that has been precooked in butter, as here *(recipe, page 160)*, to give it a pleasant sheen. The texture of the dish may be lightened by incorporating beaten egg whites, which puff up during baking. Furthermore, to provide a crackly contrast to the creamy center, the assembly may be baked in a caramel-lined mold, as shown. To make the caramel, sugar is heated with water until the granules liquefy and the mixture browns. After cooking, the pasta is turned out of its dish: The caramel will coat the surface of the molded assembly with a crisp golden glaze.

1 **Making caramel.** In a heavy saucepan, stir sugar and water over low heat until the sugar dissolves and the mixture boils. Stop stirring, increase the heat, and allow the syrup to boil for about five minutes, until it turns a pale amber. To stop the cooking, set the pan in cold water for a moment.

2 **Coating the dish.** While the caramel cooks, rinse a soufflé mold with hot water to warm it so that the caramel will spread easily. Dry the mold. Pour the prepared caramel into the mold and rotate the mold to coat the bottom and sides. Smear soft butter on any uncoated interior surfaces of the dish.

6 **Incorporating eggs.** Beat egg yolks until they are creamy and stir them into the vermicelli mixture. Beat egg whites until they form stiff peaks. Stir about a quarter of the whites into the pasta to lighten it, then pour the mixture over the remaining whites. Using a spatula, fold the whites into the pasta until the mixture is evenly colored.

3 **Preparing the vermicelli.** Break vermicelli into pieces 1½ inches [4 cm.] long. Heat butter in a heavy skillet until it melts, but is not yet sizzling.

4 **Cooking the vermicelli.** Add the vermicelli to the butter and stir over high heat until it browns. Pour in a little water and boil the pasta until tender — about five minutes. Add crushed cloves, grated lemon peel, salt and sugar. In a separate pan, heat heavy cream until bubbles form around the edges.

5 **Simmering the vermicelli.** Add the scalded cream to the skillet. Stir the ingredients with a spatula until they are well blended, then put the mixture in a bowl and let it cool for a few moments.

7 **Baking the pudding.** Transfer the vermicelli mixture to the prepared soufflé dish and place it in a preheated 325° F. [160° C.] oven. Bake the pudding for about 55 minutes or until it is puffed and the top is golden brown *(above)*. Unmold the hot pudding onto a plate *(right)* and serve it hot or warm, either plain or with a topping of whipped cream.

4

Frying

A Range of Unexpected Textures

bed of soft egg pasta, gently fried
th butter and cheese, is enlivened with
contrasting garnish: some of the
me sort of pasta fried over high heat
til it becomes crisp and golden. A
rinkling of chopped fresh parsley adds
lor and piquancy to this classic
satian dish (pages 68-69).

For unexpected alterations in texture, pasta can be fried, either at relatively low temperatures in a shallow pan in only a little fat or oil, or at high heats in deep fat or oil. Both methods can be used to quite different effect—depending on the type of pasta, its preliminary preparation and the ingredients chosen to complement it.

Almost all pasta to be pan fried, for example, must first be moistened and tenderized by preliminary boiling; otherwise, even fresh pasta would dry out and harden during frying. Once ready for the pan, the pasta lends itself to a wide range of finishes. The most common treatment—used from China to Hungary—is to fry such complementary ingredients as meats, vegetables or seafood alone, then add the parboiled pasta to them along with flavorings, and fry everything together just long enough to brown the pasta (pages 66-69). For textural contrast and a garnish, some of the pasta may be fried over very high heat so that it is crunchy (opposite; demonstration, pages 68-69).

In most pan frying, the pasta must be tossed constantly during cooking to prevent it from sticking together in clumps. Pasta's adhesive qualities are exploited, however, in certain dishes. If the pasta is pressed in a mass into a hot pan, its starch will bind it into a cake that may be fried on both sides, crisp on the surface but delectably soft and tender within—a perfect pillow for servings of highly seasoned stews (pages 70-71).

Because of the high temperatures and brief cooking times involved, deep frying presents different requirements from pan frying—and offers different opportunities. Any pasta used to give substance to a croquette or fritter mixture (pages 74-75) must be parboiled first; insulated from the oil's heat by other ingredients, the pasta would not cook to doneness. With rare exceptions (recipe, page 143), dried pasta that is deep fried without such a coating must also be rehydrated by a preliminary boiling; fried raw, the pasta would dry out further in the hot oil. Fresh pasta, however, can be fried alone without parboiling. Because it already contains moisture, it will cook to the right state—crusty outside, tender inside—during a short immersion in the bubbling oil or fat. And fresh pasta is versatile: It may be cut into ribbons and deep fried until crisp, or cut into squares or circles, then sealed around a stuffing to make savory, deep-fried packages (pages 72-73).

A Golden Finish in a Skillet

Fried in a little fat or oil, pasta makes a golden nest for ingredients ranging from meat, poultry and shellfish to vegetables. The play of textures is such an appealing invitation that dishes of this type appear in cuisines around the world *(recipes, pages 140-145)*.

Before it is fried, the pasta must be softened, lest frying harden its surface without cooking the interior to tenderness. The dried Chinese egg noodles used in this demonstration are parboiled in large quantities of water; because they are so thin, these noodles will become properly tender—yet still quite firm to the bite—within about three minutes. Thicker dried pasta may need up to seven or eight minutes of parboiling to become flexible. Dried rice-stick or cellophane noodles are precooked and need not be boiled; instead they are soaked in water *(page 38)* to soften them for frying.

The softened pasta must be thoroughly drained to prevent spattering when it is put into hot oil. Set it aside in a colander while you prepare the other ingredients for the dish. For the assembly shown here, pork was first cut into very small cubes; Boston shoulder was used in this demonstration, but any lean, boneless pork—loin, for instance—could be substituted for it. In addition, fresh shrimp were shelled raw, and a live crab was boiled and the flesh extracted from its body and claws. The pork could be replaced by other meats—chicken or ham, for example—and lobster could replace the shrimp or crab.

The meat and shellfish are first fried separately from the pasta; the rapid stirring and turning necessary to cook the small pieces evenly would break up the fragile pasta. During frying, the pasta must be stirred gently with a wooden spoon or spatula. It must be kept moving so that it does not burn on the bottom of the pan. As soon as the pasta is well colored, the other ingredients are mixed with it, reheated and coated with seasonings—in this case, sesame-seed oil and vinegar. The assembly must be served immediately to prevent the sauce from making the noodles too soft.

1 **Parboiling noodles.** Over high heat, bring a large pan of salted water to a rolling boil. Immerse the noodles in the water. Keep the water at a vigorous boil: The constant motion will keep the noodles from sticking to the bottom of the pan and to one another.

2 **Testing for doneness.** After about three minutes, lift a few of the noodles from the boiling water; let them cool briefly before biting into the. The noodles are done when they seem barely tender to the bite. Drain th parboiled noodles in a colander, rinse under cold running water to stop the cooking, drain again and set aside.

6 **Seasoning.** Dribble sesame-seed oil over the contents of the skillet *(above, left)*. Add a dash of vinegar. Stir, taste and add salt if needed. Quickly, but carefully, toss the ingredients until they are all flavored with the seasonings *(right)*; the sesame-seed oil would become acrid if it were heated for too long.

3 **Frying meats.** In a skillet over high heat, bring lard to a sizzle. Stirring constantly, fry shelled raw shrimp for one minute, or until they are pink, then set them aside. Fry cooked crab meat for about a minute and set it aside. Then fry cubes of pork *(above)* over medium heat for about 10 minutes, until they are well browned. Set the pork aside.

4 **Frying the noodles.** Add enough lard to bring the level in the skillet to about ¼ inch [6 mm.] deep. When the oil is sizzling hot, add the drained noodles. Fry them for about three minutes, or until they are golden brown, turning them frequently with a spatula.

5 **Adding the meats.** Using the spatula, add the crab, shrimp and pork to the skillet. Gently fold them into the mass of fried noodles, and heat all of the ingredients together for about three minutes, stirring occasionally, until the mixture is warmed through.

7 **Serving.** Without delay, use the spatula and a large spoon to transfer the noodle assembly onto a warmed serving dish *(right)* or into warmed individual bowls. Serve at once, while the noodles are piping hot.

Variations of Time and Heat

With slight variations, the basic technique of frying pasta—first parboiling it, then tossing it with flavorings in hot oil or fat—can produce a range of effects. Parboiled pasta may, for instance, be added to a dish of lightly fried vegetables, such as the cabbage and onions shown at right *(recipe, page 141)*. Heated briefly in this moist environment, the pasta retains its soft, tender texture.

For a dish that also provides crispness, parboiled pasta is divided into two batches that are fried separately using different techniques as shown below *(recipe, page 140)*. One batch is gently heated in butter with cheese: The cheese melts and coats the pasta as a sauce. The second batch of pasta is fried in hot oil in another skillet—butter would burn at the high temperatures required to crisp the pasta—until it is golden brown. The two batches are then combined to pro-

duce a dish that has particularly tempting contrasts of color and texture and is appropriately called "double noodles."

Either type of dish may be made with almost any kind of pasta, from ribbons, such as tagliatelle or fettucini, to the more substantial squares shown in the demonstration at right. Plain pasta is suitable, but so is pasta flavored by spinach, saffron or, as here, beets *(page 21)*. The pasta may be dried or homemade— even leftover pasta if it was served with a coating of butter. (In this case, of course, you would eliminate the parboiling step.)

The ingredients that are used for flavoring may also be varied. The cabbage used at right could be replaced by sorrel, chard or spinach. The cheese used in the demonstration below is Gruyère; Parmesan or Fontina could be substituted. And either dish could be augmented by slivers of cooked ham, corned beef or bacon.

A Cabbage and Pasta Sauté

1 **Preparing the vegetables.** Make beet-flavored pasta dough *(page 21)*, cut the dough into ½-inch [1-cm.] squares, parboil the squares *(page 31)* and drain them thoroughly. Chop onion fine. Cut a head of green cabbage in half, cut out the core and slice each half into fine shreds.

Egg Noodles Treated Two Ways

1 **Frying pasta in butter.** Parboil and drain pasta—egg noodles are used here. Divide it into two batches. In a skillet over medium heat, melt butter until it sizzles. Stir in half of the noodles. Season with salt and pepper, then add shredded Gruyère cheese and stir until it melts. Transfer the pasta to a warmed serving dish.

2 **Crisping pasta in oil.** Add a thin layer of olive oil to a clean skillet and heat it until a haze forms above the surface. Stir the remaining parboiled pasta into the hot oil, turning and tossing the noodles to coat them evenly.

2 **Frying the vegetables and pasta.** Melt lard in a skillet over medium heat, add the chopped onion and stir until the onion is soft and translucent. Add the shredded cabbage *(left)* and stir to coat it with the lard *(center)*. Season with paprika and salt, and add just enough water to coat the bottom of the skillet. Cover the skillet and steam the vegetables for 10 to 20 minutes, or until they are tender. Add the drained pasta squares *(right)* and, stirring constantly, fry them for a moment to heat them through.

3 **Serving the pasta.** Transfer the pasta mixture to a warmed serving bowl at once. If you like, add a traditional garnish: sour cream thinned with a little milk to make it spread easily. Then sprinkle paprika over the sour cream.

3 **Finishing the pasta.** Increase the heat to high and fry the pasta, tossing it briskly to prevent sticking. After about five minutes, when the pasta is golden brown in color and crisp in texture, remove the skillet from the heat and taste the pasta for seasoning.

4 **Serving the pasta.** Immediately spoon the crisp pasta over the bed of tender, cheese-flavored noodles. Garnish the top of the pasta with finely chopped fresh herbs — in this case, parsley — and serve the double noodles right away.

A Crusty Chow Mein

Packed into a skillet rather than stirred during cooking, pasta will mass into a thick cake, held together by its own surface starch. Almost any type of pasta can be treated in this way; in China, a crisp-surfaced pasta cake forms the base of the original chow mein *(recipe, page 142)* — literally, "fried noodles," a dish quite different from its American versions.

As is true for any pan-fried pasta, the noodles must be softened before frying by parboiling. In addition, the parboiled pasta should be sorted through *(Step 4, opposite)* to remove tangled clumps; tangles produce a lumpy cake.

A well-prepared pasta cake provides a fine platform for highly seasoned, stew-like mixtures whose ingredients can be chosen to suit the cook's taste. In this demonstration, strips of beef are combined with mushrooms, snow peas and scallions in a sauce flavored with ginger, garlic and oyster sauce. Chicken, pork or shrimp could replace the beef; peppers, peas or celery could substitute for the vegetables shown here.

1 **Making the marinade.** In a deep bowl, stir together soy sauce, hot-pepper oil *(page 72)* and oyster sauce. Stir in sesame-seed oil, dry sherry, chopped fresh ginger and chopped scallions.

2 **Marinating the beef.** Use a sharp knife to slice lean beef — in this instance round steak — into strips about ⅛ inch [3 mm.] thick. Mix the beef strips with marinade in the bowl, cover the bowl with plastic wrap or aluminum foil and the beef strips marinate at room temperature for about one hour.

5 **Making the cake.** In a skillet, heat oil to sizzling. Pack the noodles into the skillet. Cover and cook over medium heat for five to seven minutes. Lift one edge of the cake *(left)*. If the bottom is golden, cover the skillet again and invert it so that the cake slides onto the lid. Slide the cake back into the skillet, crust side up *(right),* and fry uncovered for five minutes. Drain the noodle cake on a rack covered with paper towels.

6 **Cooking sauce.** In a pan — in this demonstration, a Chinese wok — heat oil to sizzling. Add salt, the ginger and the garlic. Dr[...] and add the marinated beef, then fry for half a minute, stirring rapidly. Remove the beef, and stir fry the mushrooms, scallions a[...] celery. Add the sherry, then stir in sugar, cornstarch, oyster sauce and chicken stock. When the liquid thickens, return the b[...] to the pan, add the snow peas, then turn off the heat.

Preparing the vegetables. Quarter mushrooms. Cut celery hearts and snow peas, trimmed of their strings, into strips about ⅛ inch [3 mm.] wide. Cut scallions diagonally into 2-inch [5-cm.] lengths. Peel and chop a garlic clove and a ⅛-inch [3-mm.] slice of fresh ginger root. Set the vegetables and flavorings aside.

Preparing the pasta. Parboil and drain Chinese egg noodles. Spread the cooled noodles in a thin layer in a shallow baking pan. Using your fingers, gently remove and discard any noodles that are twisted into knots or stuck together.

Serving the cake. Slide the noodle cake onto a heated platter. Ladle the beef, vegetables and plenty of the cooking liquid over it. Serve the sauced cake immediately, cut into wedges.

Crisping in Deep Hot Oil

Any pasta, properly prepared, can be deep fried to a delicious crispness. Although dried pastas should be parboiled, fresh pastas are so moist that they need no precooking. Small fresh pastas—ravioli or the won tons shown here—may be sealed around a filling before frying; the result is airy enough to justify won ton's name, which means "swallow a cloud."

Dough for won tons should be freshly made to ensure maximum flexibility. Fresh or frozen won-ton wrappers are available at Oriental markets; for the very best results, however, prepare the wrappers at home (box, below).

Fillings for the wrappers may include meat, fowl, seafood or vegetables (recipes, pages 138 and 140); the filling here is a combination of pork, shrimp and watercress. Any filling should be composed of ingredients that have been chopped fine, so that it may be enfolded easily and

heated through in the brief time it takes to fry the pasta. Long-cooking ingredients such as pork should be precooked.

To make the filled won tons properly crunchy, fry them in oil that has been heated until its temperature registers 360° F. [185° C.] on a deep-frying thermometer or until a bread cube dropped in the oil browns within a minute. Fry only a few won tons at a time, both to eliminate any possibility of sticking and to avoid lowering the oil temperature. If the oil is too cool, the cooking time will be prolonged and the pasta will absorb the oil and become soggy.

Like most pasta, won tons are accompanied by sauce. Because the packets are meant to be eaten as snacks, the sauce usually is a thin, spicy mixture intended for dipping: vinegar and soy sauce, for instance, or hot-pepper oil (box, below, right; recipe, page 138).

1 **Mixing the filling.** Fry ground pork in a little oil, tossing it until the pinkness disappears. Drain the meat and put it in a bowl. Add chopped raw shrimp and blanched, chopped watercress. Stir in sherry, soy sauce, a beaten egg, cornstarch dissolved in a little water, salt and pepper. Mix thoroughly.

Mixing Won-Ton Dough

1 **Making the dough.** Mix flour, salt, eggs and water, then knead the mixture until it is smooth. Cover the dough and allow it to rest for 30 minutes. Divide the dough in half and, on a floured board, roll each half into a rectangular sheet ¹⁄₁₆ inch [1½ mm.] thick. Alternatively, you can knead and roll the dough with a pasta machine (pages 18-19).

2 **Cutting the wrappers.** With a sharp knife or pastry wheel, cut one sheet of dough into 3-inch [8-cm.] squares. Sprinkle flour over the squares to prevent them from sticking to one another, then stack them. Cover the stack with a dry towel while you cut the remaining sheet of dough into squares.

A Pungent Dipping Sauce

Preparing the sauce. Heat Szechwan and black peppercorns and salt for about five minutes. Cool, crush with a rolling pin and sieve. Heat flavorless vegetable oil until it smokes; cool for 30 seconds, then stir in the sieved spices, cayenne pepper and paprika. When the solids settle, pour the oil through a paper-towel-lined strainer.

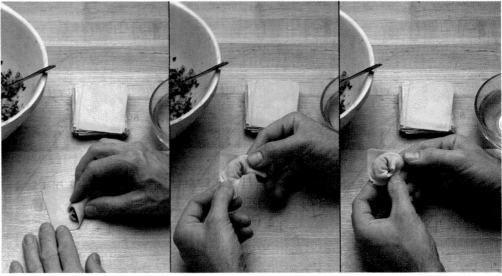

Filling the wrappers. Moisten one corner of each won-ton wrapper with a little cold water. Place a teaspoonful of the filling just inside the moistened corner of the wrapper.

3 **Shaping the won ton.** Fold the corner of the wrapper over the filling and roll toward the center *(left)*, stopping 1 inch [2½ cm.] from the opposite corner. Pull back the two ends of the rolled won ton, away from the exposed corner *(center)*, until they meet. Moisten one end, press the other over it and pinch the ends together to seal them *(right)*.

4 **Frying and serving.** Pour oil to a depth of about 3 inches [8 cm.] into a deep pan or, as shown, into a wok. Heat the oil. Fry the won tons in the oil in small batches for two to three minutes, until they are golden *(left)*. Transfer the won tons to a plate lined with paper towels to drain. Serve the won tons as shown below, with dipping sauces — here, vinegar, soy and hot-pepper oil *(box, opposite, bottom right)*.

Fritters and Croquettes: Soft-centered Morsels

Pasta not only can be deep fried on its own *(page 73)*, it also can lend body to such deep-fried dishes as croquettes and fritters. For fritters *(top right)*, parboiled pasta is mixed with a liquid batter and fried by the spoonful. Croquettes *(bottom)* are much more substantial concoctions. The pasta is first simmered in milk to produce a thick, pasty binder similar to that used as a soufflé base *(page 60)*. Combined with meats, cheese and vegetables, then chilled, the pasta mixture becomes firm enough to shape into cylinders or spheres that can be coated with egg and bread crumbs, then deep fried so that the exterior crisps into a brown envelope around its creamy interior.

Fritters and croquettes can be made with either dried or fresh pasta. To give both fritters and croquettes the right texture, the pasta—and any ingredients mixed with it—should be chopped fine.

Any of a broad range of flavoring ingredients can enhance both fritters and croquettes. In this demonstration, spaghetti fritters are flavored by chopped scallion; herbs such as parsley, chives or tarragon would also taste good. The croquettes shown are made with chopped ham, parsley and grated Parmesan, but they could equally well be prepared with bits of leftover chicken and raw celery, or poached-and-flaked salmon brightened with lemon juice.

Because of their varying compositions, fritters and croquettes are fried somewhat differently. Fritter mixtures are light and liquid: If they are to have any shape, the oil must be hot enough to firm the batter instantly—375° F. [190° C.]. Croquettes, on the other hand, are fried at a slightly lower temperature—350° F. [180° C.]—for a slightly longer period. This is because croquettes are larger and denser than fritters and are chilled before cooking; fried at a high temperature, croquettes would burn on the outside before the interior cooked through.

A Batter for Binding Chopped Spaghetti

1 Making the batter. In a bowl, stir together flour and salt. Whisk in egg yolks, oil and a little cayenne pepper, then whisk in beer, stirring just until this batter is smooth *(recipe, page 165)*. Cover and let it rest at room temperature for one hour to thicken it and ensure an even coating for the pasta.

2 Preparing the pasta. Chop scallions fine. Parboil pasta—spaghetti is shown—drain it thoroughly and chop it into small pieces. Stir the pasta and scallions into the batter. Whisk egg whites until they form soft peaks and, just before frying, fold them into the fritter mixture.

A Bread-Crumb Coating for Noodles and Meat

1 Cooking the noodles. Heat milk in a saucepan until bubbles form at the edges; use about 3 cups [¾ liter] of milk for each ½ pound [¼ kg.] of pasta. Add pasta—here, egg noodles—and simmer, uncovered, for about 30 minutes, until the pasta absorbs the milk. Transfer the pasta to a bowl.

2 Mixing the filling. Chop parsley and cooked ham. Add them to the paste along with grated Parmesan cheese, salt and pepper. Cover the bowl and chill for one hour to firm the mixture. Beat eggs; set them aside. In a food processor or grinder, reduce fresh bread to fine crumbs; set the crumbs aside.

3 | **Frying the fritters.** In a deep pan, heat about 3 inches [8 cm.] of vegetable oil until it reaches 375° F. [190° C.] on a deep-frying thermometer. Layer paper towels on a rack for draining the fritters. Lift a teaspoonful of the fritter mixture and, with another teaspoon, push the mixture into the hot oil.

4 | **Finishing the fritters.** Fry only a few fritters at a time to avoid reducing the oil temperature, and thus making the fritters soggy. After 20 to 30 seconds, when the fritters are golden brown, remove them with a perforated spoon or skimmer and drain on the paper towels.

5 | **Serving the fritters.** Transfer the cooked fritters to a warmed platter. Garnish them with lemon wedges and parsley — in this case, the parsley also has been fried in the hot oil. Serve immediately, squeezing a little lemon juice over each fritter.

3 | **Shaping the croquettes.** To form each croquette, lightly roll a few spoonfuls of the chilled pasta mixture between your palms until it forms a cylinder. To prevent any sticking, you can rub your palms with oil, then rinse them with cold water.

4 | **Breading the croquettes.** As each croquette is molded, dip it into the beaten eggs, then into the bread crumbs, turning it to coat all sides. Place the croquette on a layer of paper towels set on top of a rack. When all the croquettes are molded and coated, refrigerate them for an hour to firm them.

5 | **Frying.** Heat oil in a deep pan until it reaches 350° F. [180° C.]. Fry each croquette in the oil for one or two minutes on each side. When they are brown *(above),* use a skimmer to transfer the croquettes to a rack covered with paper towels to drain. Serve as soon as all of the croquettes are fried.

Dumplings
Ensuring a Proper Puff

Like pasta, dumplings begin with a flour-based dough and are cooked in large quantities of water. But while pasta doughs are dried and flattened, dumpling doughs are moist and loosely compacted. During the cooking, dumplings expand from the steam that forms in the dough and, in some instances, from the action of other leavenings that have been added to the mixture.

The exact ingredients, their proportions and the ways the dough is handled can all be varied to produce dumplings in a range of textures and tastes. Thin, batter-like doughs produce the lightest of dumplings, among them the airy "noodles" demonstrated on page 78. At the other end of the spectrum are dumplings made from a firm, heavy dough, such as the potato dumplings demonstrated on page 79.

Between these extremes lie numerous possibilities: fluffy dumplings made from a chou paste flavored with grated Parmesan cheese and puréed spinach, spongy dumplings studded for textural contrast with crisp croutons, bready concoctions made either from a baking-powder biscuit mixture or from a yeast dough.

The method used to shape the dumplings is determined by the consistency of the dough. Batter doughs can be squeezed from the tube of a pastry bag into simmering water; the batter settles into cylindrical shapes on contact with the liquid. Soft doughs can simply be dropped from a spoon into the cooking medium. Soft dough can also be cooked suspended in an over-sized linen napkin *(pages 82-83)*—an ingenious technique that molds the dumpling into a large ball while preventing it from settling on the bottom of the pan and sticking or burning. Still firmer doughs can be rolled by hand into small balls or egg shapes or even formed into miniature shells.

No matter how they are made, dumplings should be cooked in a large vessel in an ample quantity of liquid. But because they are less compact—and thus more fragile—than pasta, dumplings must be simmered rather than boiled. Whether the cooking medium is salted water, soup or stew, it should be kept at a bare tremble so the dumplings do not break apart during cooking. And unless the dumplings are to be served immediately in a soup or stew, they should be removed from the cooking medium as soon as they are done to prevent them from becoming soggy.

eamed to perfection atop a simmering
w, plump and parsley-flecked
mplings are gently lifted from the pot.
e dumplings can be dished up
parately or served with the stew
aight from the pot—a presentation in
cord with the rustic nature of the dish.

Thick Noodles Made from Batter

The chubby, noodle-shaped dumplings demonstrated here begin, as does pasta, with a mixture of flour, egg and oil. But because the dough contains a higher proportion of eggs *(recipe, page 145)*, it has a batter-like consistency. Too liquid to be rolled and cut, the dough is shaped at the moment of cooking, setting in the form in which it enters the simmering liquid. As the batter cooks, moisture in it turns to steam and the dough puffs up, developing a soft, springy texture that earns it a place in the dumpling category.

To shape the batter, you can squeeze it from a pastry bag *(Step 3, below)* or trickle it—a few tablespoons at a time—through a colander. With either method, the water must be kept at a simmer so that the dumplings do not break.

The dumplings have a subtle, eggy flavor that is best paired with a similarly delicate sauce. The dumplings can, for example, be bathed in heavy cream and grated cheese, or tossed with butter and herbs. The bread-crumb topping shown here adds complementary crispness.

1 **Whisking the batter.** Put flour into a large bowl. Mix eggs and olive oil in another bowl. Whisking constantly, slowly pour the egg-and-oil mixture into the flour *(above, left)*. Continue whisking until bubbles appear and the batter is smooth. Whisk in more flour until the mixture is thick and creamy *(above, right)*, but will still trickle from the whisk when it is lifted.

2 **Filling a pastry bag.** Fit a plain ¼-inch [6-mm.] tube tip into a pastry bag. To prevent the batter from running through as you fill the bag, fold up the tip against the side of the bag. Turn down the upper half of the bag to make it easier to handle and spoon the batter into the lower half. Unfold the bag and twist the top to enclose the batter.

3 **Piping the dumplings.** Holding the top of the pastry bag closed, position the tip of the tube just above a broad pot of lightly salted, simmering water. Squeezing the bag gently, pipe out the batter in strips about 3 to 5 inches [8 to 13 cm.] long, making sure that the strips do not touch. Cover the pot to bring the water quickly back to a simmer; cook the dumplings for no more than a minute, until they are firm.

4 **Serving the dumplings.** Drain the dumplings in a colander and put them in a warmed serving dish. To make a sauce, sauté fresh bread crum in a large quantity of butter until they are golden brown. Pour the butter an the bread crumbs over the dumplings

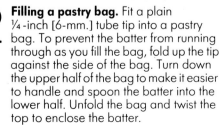

Firm Dough for Molding

...mplings that are to be shaped before ...king require a firm dough—whether ...le with the same ingredients as pasta ...with a mixture in which some of the ...r is replaced with another starch, ...h as cornmeal or potatoes *(recipes, ...es 150-151)*. Typically, the dough is ...ed into tiny balls or into cylinders ...t are sliced into segments. For a more ...gant presentation, the segments can ...ormed into miniature shells and giv-...a decorative embossed surface, as in ...demonstration.

...nlike dumplings made from batter, ...ch float on the surface of the cooking ...id, firm dumplings contain such a ...h proportion of starch that they sink ...he bottom of the pot. As the dump-...s cook, moisture in the dough turns to ...m, lightening the dumplings so that ...y rise to the surface of the liquid. The ...to dumplings demonstrated on this ...e can be topped simply with melted ...ter, browned bread crumbs or a sprin-...ng of cheese—or, for a more robust ...a, with a hearty meat or tomato sauce.

1 Preparing the potatoes. Boil potatoes, drain them well and peel them. With a pestle, force the potatoes through a strainer set over a bowl, or purée them through a food mill or with a potato masher. Add butter, as here, or lard and stir it in; the heat of the potatoes will melt it. Stir in flour, beaten egg, salt and pepper. Add flour, if needed, to form a stiff but malleable dough.

2 Rolling the dough. In the bowl, lightly knead the dough for about two minutes to incorporate the flour thoroughly. On a floured board, cut off fist-sized portions of dough. Roll each portion into a cylinder about as thick as a finger. Slice each cylinder into dumplings about 1 inch [2½ cm.] wide.

3 Shaping the dumplings. Place each dumpling near the tip of the tines of a fork. Press the center of the dumpling with your finger *(above, left)*, then fold the dumpling in half toward the fork handle. Roll the dumpling along the tines of the fork, pressing lightly to give the surface decorative ridges *(right)*.

4 Cooking the dumplings. Bring a large pan of salted water to a simmer. Drop dumplings into the water in batches of 20 or so to avoid crowding the pan. Cook the dumplings, uncovered, over low heat for about 10 minutes, or until they rise to the surface. Drain them in a colander or with a perforated skimmer *(above)*. Transfer the cooked dumplings to a warmed baking dish.

5 Covering with sauce. Pour a sauce—in this case, meat sauce *(pages 12-13)*—over the heaped dumplings *(above)*. Serve the dumplings immediately, or sprinkle the sauce with grated cheese and bake the dish in a preheated 400° F. [200° C.] oven for five to 10 minutes, or until the cheese has melted and browned lightly.

A Light Paste Rich in Eggs

Chou paste, more commonly baked to make cream puffs and éclairs, also can be simmered to produce the delicate, bite-sized dumplings that the Italians term "gnocchi"—meaning bumps or lumps. While chou paste is made with the conventional dumpling ingredients—flour, liquid, butter and eggs—the proportions and the preparation are altered radically to make an elastic dough that puffs spectacularly when poached. The flour, liquid and butter are cooked together to blend the ingredients and make the mixture absorbent. Then eggs are beaten in to give the paste resilience.

The paste can be flavored with grated cheese or, as shown, with both cheese and a spinach purée (recipe, page 147). After the spinach is boiled and drained, it must be squeezed dry before it is puréed; otherwise, it would make the paste too thin to trap the steam and rise successfully.

Though firmer than batter dumpli (page 78), chou paste is also shaped in cooking water. The paste can be for through a pastry tube to form cylindr shapes or, as demonstrated here, it ca rounded into balls with the aid of spoons, and dropped immediately i the water to set. The cooked dumpli can be served with a topping of gra cheese, as shown, or with a tomato sa or cheese-enriched white sauce.

1 **Mixing the paste.** In a saucepan, bring liquid—water is used above—butter and seasonings to a boil. As soon as the butter melts, reduce the heat to low and blend in spinach purée. Add sifted flour all at once and beat until the dough forms a paste that pulls away in a mass from the sides of the pan.

2 **Adding the eggs.** Remove the pan from the heat and let the paste cool slightly. Make a well in the center of the paste and beat in one egg at a time, stirring until each is absorbed. Stir grated cheese—Parmesan is shown in this demonstration—into the dough.

3 **Shaping dumplings.** Dip a teaspoon in hot water, fill it with paste, then smooth the paste with the concave side of another dampened spoon. Use the second spoon to push the shaped dumpling gently into a large pot of simmering water. Poach uncovered for about 15 minutes, turning the dumplings once so they cook evenly. When the dumplings are fluffy and nearly double in size, remove them with a slotted spoon and drain them.

4 **Preparing the gratin.** Arrange the dumplings in a single layer in a buttered gratin dish. Dot the dumplings with bits of butter and coat them with a generous topping of grated cheese, such as Parmesan or the Fontina shown here.

5 **Baking the dumplings.** Preheat the oven to 350° F. [180° C.]. Set the gratin dish with the dumplings on the middle shelf and bake for 10 to 15 minutes to permit the butter and cheese to mingle and brown the tops of the dumplings.

6 **Serving the dumplings.** Slide the dish under the broiler for a few final minutes to give the topping a delicate crust. Serve the dumplings from the baking dish as a first course or as an accompaniment to cooked meats.

An Outsized Dumpling in a Napkin Wrapper

Instead of being subdivided into small shapes, a batch of soft dough can be formed with the aid of a napkin into a single, large dumpling. If the napkin is gathered around the dough and tied at the top, as shown in the demonstration on these pages, the dumpling will develop a spherical shape during cooking. Alternatively, the napkin can be rolled around the dough and tied at both ends to form a cylindrical, or sausage, shape.

In any case, precautions must be taken to prevent the dumplings from sticking to the bottom of the pan: The spherical dumpling is cooked suspended from a spoon; the sausage-shaped dumpling is set on a perforated rack inside a roasting pan or fish poacher.

To keep the large mass from becoming heavy, the dumpling dough *(recipe, page 147)* is lightened by creaming the butter to aerate it. In addition, the eggs are separated and the whites beaten to incorporate more air, which will expand during cooking. Adding croutons provides a crisp textural contrast for the otherwise soft dumpling. For a sweeter version, sugar, nuts and raisins can replace the croutons *(recipe, page 160)*.

A white linen or cotton napkin is the traditional support for the dough, but a long strip of muslin or cheesecloth, folded double to give it a square shape and extra strength, may be substituted. The cloth is soaked and wrung out before use to soften it and thus make it easier to shape

and tie. If the napkin is gathered tight around the dough, the dumpling w develop a firm, compact texture. For softer texture, gather the napkin mo loosely so that the dough will have mo room to puff up.

The cooked dumpling may be slic with a knife that has been moistened that the blade does not stick to the dum ling's moist interior. Alternatively it c be sliced by sliding a piece of string u derneath the dumpling, then drawi the string up through the dumpling wi a gentle sawing motion. Either way, t dumpling should be sliced and serv while it is still piping hot—topped wi melted butter, perhaps, or as an acco paniment to a stew.

4 **Incorporating egg whites.** Stir the croutons into the dough. In a separate bowl, whisk the egg whites until they form stiff peaks. Stir a few spoonfuls of the whites into the mixture to lighten it, then gently fold in the remaining whites.

5 **Wrapping the dumpling.** Wet and wring out a large cloth napkin and place it in a bowl or colander. Spoon the dough into the cloth. Gather the napkin around the dough *(above, left)*. To hold the napkin closed, tie a piece of string around it just above the mound of dough *(above, right)*. Tie two opposite corners of the loose napkin top in a knot, positioned 3 to 4 inches [8 to 10 cm.] above the string closing. Tie the two remaining corners of the napkin around the string closing to reinforce it.

Making croutons. Trim the crusts from slightly stale bread and cut the bread into ½-inch [1-cm.] cubes. Melt butter in a skillet and add a layer of cubes. Sauté the cubes over medium heat, turning them often, until brown — about three minutes. Drain on paper towels; sauté the remaining cubes.

2 **Creaming the butter.** Place butter that has been allowed to soften at room temperature in a large mixing bowl. Cream the butter by beating it against the sides of the bowl with a spoon until it is light and fluffy. Separate the eggs. Stir the yolks, one at a time, into the butter, mixing thoroughly after each addition.

3 **Adding flour and milk.** Sift a small portion of flour into the butter-and-egg mixture and stir to incorporate it. Add a little milk. Continue adding the flour and milk alternately, until the dough is smooth and well combined.

6 **Cooking and serving the dumpling.** Slip a wooden spoon between the knots at the top of the napkin and suspend the spoon across the rim of a pot of boiling water *(left)*. Adjust the height of the upper knot, if necessary, so that the dumpling is completely immersed but does not touch the bottom of the pot. Cover the pot and simmer the dumpling for an hour. Then lift out the dumpling and unwrap it onto a cutting board. Cut the dumpling into slices about ¾ inch [2 cm.] thick and serve them immediately, perhaps with a stew, as shown above.

Baking-Powder Mixtures for Steaming and Poaching

While steam provides some leavening in all dumplings, mixtures that have a high proportion of starch are sometimes given an extra lift through the addition of another leavening. The dumplings shown on these pages, for example, contain baking powder and are made with flour, liquid and butter *(recipe, page 147)*. Baking powder consists of acid and alkaline materials that interact with the moisture in the dough to form carbon-dioxide gas; during cooking, the gas expands and the dough puffs up into mild-flavored, porous dumplings that make an excellent sop for a tangy soup or stew.

If you like, the dumpling ingredients can be flavored with snippets of parsley, as here, or a pinch of grated nutmeg or a spoonful of chopped onions. Or you can add a mixture of cayenne and sugar, producing a sweet-peppery dumpling that reinforces a spicy stew *(recipe, page 154)*.

Formed into a soft dough, dumplings made with baking powder will cook by steaming on top of a stew as demonstrated above. The addition of more flour produces a firmer dough that can be poached in water, in soup or—as below—in the hearty broth that results when a large chunk of meat is poached with vegetables. The firmer version can be shaped into balls or cut into rounds with a biscuit cutter; in either instance, the dumplings should be chilled before cooking to ensure that they maintain their shape. When the dough is formed into rounds or balls, it should not be compressed too much; a loosely packed dumpling will expand and lighten better as steam and carbon dioxide form inside.

Soft dumplings should be added to stew when it is nearly done so both stew and dumplings will be finished at the same time. Firmer dumplings are immersed in cooking liquid *(Step 3, bottom)*. The meat and vegetables are cooked, then removed before the dumplings are added.

Practical meats for both stewing and poaching are relatively tough cuts such as veal shoulder or breast, or beef flank, chuck or round (the last is shown on these pages). These tougher cuts profit from slow simmering and have flavor to spare for the broth, which may be served as a soup or thickened to a sauce for the meat, vegetables and dumplings.

Soft Complements to a Stew

1 **Browning the beef.** Fry diced salt pork in a deep, heavy pot to render the fat, then discard the pork. Fry sliced onions in the fat until translucent, then set aside. Lightly coat beef cubes with flour, brown them in the fat, then remove them. Pour in a cup [¼ liter] of water, bring it to a boil and loosen the browned deposits from the pot bottom.

2 **Making the stew.** Return the onions and beef to the pot. Add water cover them, and seasonings. Bring the liquid to a boil, reduce the heat, cov tightly and simmer for an hour. Skim off surface fat. Add cubed vegetables in this case, potatoes, carrots and rutabagas. Cover, and simmer an additional 30 minutes.

Firm Spheres for Cooking in Broth

1 **Poaching the meat.** Put the meat in a deep pot, immerse in water and bring to a boil, skimming the scum from the surface. Simmer, partly covered, for 40 minutes. Add seasonings and aromatic carrots and onions, and cook for 40 minutes. Add rutabagas and potatoes and cook for 30 minutes, or until tender.

2 **Shaping the dumplings.** Prepare parsley dumplings as demonstrated ir Step 3 above, adding enough extra flour to produce a stiff dough. Lightly flc your hands and drop a spoonful of dough into one palm *(left)*. Lightly sha the dough into a ball *(right)*. Chill the dumplings for 20 minutes to firm them

Making the dumplings. Chop fresh parsley fine and set it aside. Sift flour, baking powder and salt into a mixing bowl. Add pieces of softened butter and with your fingers work the butter into the dry ingredients until the mixture is flaky. Add milk *(left)* and the parsley. Beat the mixture until it is smooth *(right)*.

4 **Cooking the dumplings.** When the stew is almost finished cooking, drop tablespoonfuls of dumpling batter onto the surface *(above)*. Cover tightly and simmer for about 10 minutes, or until the dumplings are puffy *(inset)* and a cake tester or skewer inserted in a dumpling comes out clean. Serve the dumplings and stew right from the pot.

3 **Cooking.** Remove the meat and vegetables from the pot and set them aside, covered with foil. Bring the broth to a simmer. With a slotted skimmer, carefully lower a few dumplings at a time into the liquid *(left)*. Do not overcrowd the pot. Cover tightly and simmer for about 15 minutes; drain the dumplings on a towel. Carve the meat and arrange the vegetables around it on a platter. Top with the dumplings *(inset)*.

Pillowy Accompaniments Leavened with Yeast

Yeast-leavened dumplings develop a fine texture, delicate flavor and bready aroma *(recipes, pages 148 and 161)* and need only a few more steps than other types.

Yeast is composed of living organisms that feed on the starch in dough and leaven it by producing carbon dioxide as they grow. Unlike the other leavenings, yeast must be activated in tepid liquid to begin its work. The dry, granular type of yeast grows best in liquids ranging in temperature from 105° to 115° F. [40° to 46° C.]; fresh, compressed-cake yeast should be activated at about 80° F. [26° C.].

After the dough is made, it must be kneaded to develop the gluten in the flour and produce an elastic mixture capable of rising as the yeast organisms multiply. Once the dough has risen, it is punched down and kneaded again briefly to redistribute the gas bubbles even[ly].

The risen dough can then be shap[ed] into plain dumplings, as here, or pieces [of] the dough can be wrapped around bits [of] soft fruit. Yeast dumplings can simply [be] dropped into simmering water; as th[ey] cook, they will rise to the surface a[nd] be steamed. For a firmer texture, pl[ace] them on a rack that holds them above t[he] water, as shown below.

1 Activating the yeast. Sprinkle dry yeast and a bit of sugar into a bowl of lukewarm water *(left)*. Let the mixture stand for a few minutes, then stir to dissolve the yeast. Cover the solution *(right)* and set it in a warm place for five minutes, or until doubled in volume.

2 Making the dough. In a large bowl, combine an egg with nutmeg, and beat until smooth. Stir in melted butter. Add lukewarm milk, salt and the yeast solution. Stir in flour, half a cup [125 ml.] at a time, until the dough pulls away from the sides of the bowl in a mass.

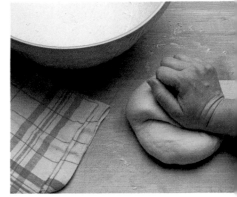

3 Kneading the dough. Gather the dough into a ball and place it on a lig[htly] floured surface. Knead the dough by repeatedly pushing it down with the h[eel] of your hand and pressing it forward for approximately 10 minutes, or until [the] dough is smooth and elastic.

4 Letting the dough rise. Place the dough in a buttered bowl, cover and set it in a warm, draft-free place to rise for an hour, or until doubled in volume. Punch down the dough, then knead it briefly. Pinch off pieces of dough and shape them into 1½-inch [4-cm.] balls.

5 Steaming the dumplings. Pour water into a roasting pan to a depth of about 1 inch [2½ cm.]. In the pan, set a wire rack that is high enough so its grid is above the water. Cover the rack with a damp towel and set the dumplings on it. Bring to a boil, then cover.

6 Serving the dumplings. Steam the dumplings for 20 minutes, or until doubled in size. Break open one dumpling to see if it is firm throughou[t;] not, steam the batch for a few more minutes. Serve the dumplings hot, wi[th] stew or, as shown, fruit compote.

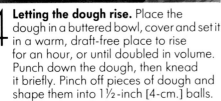

Anthology of Recipes

awing upon the literature of more than 20 countries, the itors and consultants for this volume have selected 192 published recipes for the Anthology that follows. Most pasta dishes isist of many components—doughs, sauces, fillings and toppings—any one of which can be used in other combinations. thin the recipes are instructions for creating more than 60 of ese components, thus providing a grand total of 255 recipes. e selections range from the familiar to the unique—from six riations of homely macaroni and cheese to wine-flavored pastriangles, filled with chard, borage and cheese, and smothed with walnut sauce.

Many of the recipes were written by world-renowned exponts of the culinary art, but the Anthology also includes selecns from rare and out-of-print books and from works that have t been published in English. Whatever the source, the recipes phasize fresh, natural ingredients that blend harmoniously.

Since many early recipe writers did not specify amounts of gredients, sizes of pans or even cooking times, the missing ormation has been judiciously added. In some cases, instrucns have been expanded and clarifying introductory notes suped. Modern terms have been substituted for archaic lanage, but to preserve the character of the original recipes the thors' texts have been changed as little as possible.

In keeping with the organization of the first half of the book, st of the recipes are categorized according to their cooking ethods. For easy reference, sweet pastas and dumplings are uped together, as are separate recipes for sauces and fillings.

Recipes for standard preparations—basic pasta dough and nato sauce among them—appear at the end of the Anthology. familiar cooking terms and uncommon ingredients are examined in the combined General Index and Glossary.

Apart from the primary components, all ingredients are listwithin each recipe in order of use, with both the traditional nited States measurements and metric measurements provided. The metric quantities reflect the American practice of easuring such solid ingredients as flour or sugar by volume ther than by weight, as in Europe.

To make the quantities simpler to measure, many of the ures have been rounded off to correspond to the gradations on S. metric spoons and cups. (One cup, for example, equals preely 240 milliliters; however, wherever practicable in these cipes, a cup's equivalent appears as a more readily measured 0 milliliters—¼ liter.) Similarly, the weight, temperature d linear metric equivalents have been rounded off slightly. us the American and metric figures do not precisely match, t using one set or the other will produce the same good results.

Boiled and Steamed Pasta

Recipes for basic pasta doughs appear in Standard Preparations, pages 164-165.

Japanese Udon

The techniques of folding pasta dough and cutting it into strips are shown on page 23.

To make about 1 1/2 pounds [3/4 kg.] fresh noodles, 10 to 12 ounces [300 to 350 g.] dried noodles

4 cups	all-purpose or whole-wheat flour	1 liter
1 tsp.	salt	5 ml.
1	egg yolk	1
1/2 to 2/3 cup	cold water	125 to 150 ml.

Sift the flour and salt together into a large bowl. Add the egg yolk and enough cold water to make a stiff dough. Knead thoroughly. Cover the dough with a damp cloth kitchen towel and let it stand for 30 minutes. Sprinkle a board and rolling pin with additional flour. Roll out the dough until it is paper-thin. Fold the dough into a long, loose roll and cut it crosswise into strips, 1/10 inch [2 mm.] wide. When unrolled, the dough strips should be at least 12 inches [30 cm.] long. Cook for three or four minutes in boiling salted water.

KAREN GREEN
THE GREAT INTERNATIONAL NOODLE EXPERIENCE

Homemade "Little Ears"

Orecchiette Casalinga

Orecchiette dry very well and can be kept for a month or so in a dry, cool cupboard.

To make about 1 1/2 pounds [3/4 kg.] fresh pasta, 10 to 12 ounces [300 to 350 g.] dried pasta

1 cup	semolina	1/4 liter
2 cups	unbleached flour	1/2 liter
1/4 tsp.	salt	1 ml.
about 3/4 cup	lukewarm water	about 175 ml.

Combine the semolina, unbleached flour and salt, and mound it on a large work surface. Make a well in the center with your finger and pour in 3 or 4 tablespoons [45 or 60 ml.] of the water. Begin pulling the flour from the inner wall of the well into the liquid. Add more water and continue forming a paste until the flour has absorbed as much water as possible without becoming hard or dry. The perfect consistency is softer than the basic flour-and-egg pasta, but not at all sticky. Knead vigorously on a lightly floured board until the dough is smooth and elastic. This may take 20 minutes or so. Form the dough into a ball and cover.

To make the "little ears," pull off a scant handful of the dough (keep the remaining dough covered). On a lightly floured board, roll the dough into a rope about 3/4 inch [2 cm.] in diameter. Cut the rope into slices no more than 1/8 inch [3 mm.] thick to form small circles of dough. Now put one of these circles into the cupped palm of your hand and, with the thumb of the other hand, press and turn the circle at the same time to form a dent in the center that will spread the dough a little on each side. It should look like a small ear, with slightly thicker ear lobes. Repeat with all of the remaining dough, placing the orecchiette on a lightly floured cloth as they are made.

The orecchiette are cooked in the same manner as fresh flour-and-egg pasta, although they take longer to cook. Watch them carefully and taste frequently for doneness.

GERTRUDE HARRIS
PASTA INTERNATIONAL

Whole-Wheat Noodles

Gluten flour is obtainable from health-food stores.

To make about 1 1/2 pounds [3/4 kg.] fresh noodles, 10 to 12 ounces [300 to 350 g.] dried noodles

2 cups	whole-wheat flour	1/2 liter
1/2 cup	gluten flour plus 1/2 cup [125 ml.] all-purpose flour, or 1 cup [1/4 liter] bread flour	125 ml.
4	eggs, lightly beaten	4
2 tsp.	salt	10 ml.
	water	

Combine the flours in a bowl. Mix together the eggs and salt, then add to the flours and mix. If the mixture is too dry to make a ball of dough, you may have to sprinkle in a few drops of water; if it is too moist, dust on more flour. Knead by hand on a floured board until the dough is smooth and elastic.

Divide the dough into portions of a good handful each and work with one portion at a time, keeping the other portions covered with plastic wrap or an inverted bowl so they will not dry out.

Flour a big pastry board and a rolling pin. Roll one portion of dough out from the center in every direction, stretching it with your hands from time to time, until you can see through it. When the sheet is thin enough, dust it again and set it aside for a few minutes to dry slightly, but not to the point of brittleness. Roll the remaining portions of dough in the same way.

To cut the noodles, either accordion-pleat each sheet of dough into a neat stack about 2 inches [5 cm.] wide, or roll it up into a cylinder. Use a very sharp serrated-edged knife to cut noodles of the width you prefer. Shake the noodles out onto a floured cloth and proceed to dry them partly or completely, and/or freeze them.

To cook the noodles, bring 6 or 7 quarts [6 or 7 liters] of water to a boil and salt generously. When the water boils again, sprinkle in the pasta, stir occasionally with a long fork and watch the pot—the pasta will be done very quickly. Dried pasta will take slightly longer to cook than fresh, but it requires less cooking time than the store-bought. Test a strand every half minute or so by biting. Stop the cooking by pouring in 2 cups [½ liter] of cold water the instant the pasta is done to your taste.

To remove the pasta from the water, use tongs or a spaghetti lifter instead of draining it in a colander. Put it into a warmed bowl and add butter, seasonings or sauce.

HELEN WITTY AND ELIZABETH SCHNEIDER COLCHIE
BETTER THAN STORE BOUGHT

Fettucini with Butter, Cream and Parmesan Cheese

Fettucini all' Alfredo

To serve 4 to 6

1 lb.	narrow egg noodles	½ kg.
8 tbsp.	unsalted butter, softened and cut into pieces	120 ml.
¼ cup	heavy cream	50 ml.
1 cup	freshly grated Parmesan cheese	¼ liter
	freshly ground pepper	

Boil the noodles in a large pot of salted water until tender but still firm (about eight minutes should do it). Drain the noodles and dry them in a hot napkin.

Place the noodles on a heated platter or bowl, add the butter, cream and half of the Parmesan cheese, and use two forks to toss until well mixed.

Serve topped with pepper and the remaining cheese.

ARTHUR HAWKINS
COOK IT QUICK

Spaghettini with Cream and Whiskey Sauce

Spaghettini al Whisky e Panna

To serve 4 or 5

1 lb.	spaghettini	½ kg.
1½ cups	heavy cream	375 ml.
¾ cup	Scotch or rye whiskey	175 ml.
2 oz.	dried mushrooms, soaked in warm water for 30 minutes and drained	60 g.
3 tbsp.	butter	45 ml.
½ cup	chopped fresh parsley	125 ml.
1	garlic clove, chopped	1
	salt and pepper	
¼ cup	freshly grated Parmesan cheese (optional)	50 ml.

Soak the mushrooms in the whiskey for at least one hour, longer if possible.

Melt the butter in a saucepan and, when bubbly, add the chopped parsley and garlic. Let cook for a minute or two (no more, or the garlic will burn).

Take the mushrooms out of the whiskey and drain well, reserving the whiskey. Cut the mushrooms into small pieces and add to the simmering parsley and garlic. Add salt and pepper to taste. Allow the mushrooms to cook for a minute or two, add the reserved whiskey, reduce the heat, then simmer, uncovered, until most of the whiskey has evaporated.

Put the spaghettini into boiling salted water, let it come to a boil again, stir well with a fork to separate the strands and cook for a few minutes. Taste one strand to see if it's ready, and drain when *al dente*—cooked but still firm—reserving 2 tablespoons [30 ml.] of the cooking water. Put the spaghettini in a preheated bowl with the reserved water.

When most of the whiskey has evaporated, taste the mushrooms. They should be soft; if not, add small amounts of hot water until they are cooked through. Add the cream, let it heat through, and pour this sauce over the spaghettini. Toss well. If you like, sprinkle with the grated Parmesan.

WILMA PEZZINI
THE TUSCAN COOKBOOK

Spaghettini with Curry-Yogurt Sauce

To serve 4

½ lb.	spaghettini, boiled and drained	¼ kg.
2 tsp.	curry powder	10 ml.
2 cups	plain yogurt, at room temperature, or 1 cup [¼ liter] each yogurt and sour cream	½ liter
2 tbsp.	butter	30 ml.
1	large onion, finely chopped	1
1	large garlic clove, finely chopped	1
1 tbsp.	flour	15 ml.
	salt and freshly ground white pepper	

In a medium-sized, heavy saucepan melt the butter over medium heat. Add the onion and garlic and sauté until golden and soft, stirring frequently. Add the curry powder and cook, stirring, for half a minute. Add the flour, and salt and pepper to taste, and cook, stirring, for one or two minutes. Stir in the yogurt or yogurt and sour cream, and cook gently just until heated through.

Place the pasta in a heated serving dish and cover with the curry-yogurt sauce. Toss gently until the pasta is well coated with the sauce. Serve at once.

SONIA UVEZIAN
THE BOOK OF YOGURT

Rigatoni with Butter, Cream and Eggs

Rigatoni con Burro, Crema e Uova

Rigatoni are large grooved pasta tubes similar to commercial manicotti but smaller.

It is essential that this sauce be made at the last moment. In fact, the safest thing to do is to start it when the rigatoni go into the colander.

To serve 6

1½ lb.	rigatoni	¾ kg.
12 tbsp.	butter	180 ml.
5	egg yolks	5
½ cup	heavy cream	125 ml.
1⅓ cups	freshly grated Parmesan cheese	325 ml.
	salt	
	white pepper	

Cook and drain the rigatoni in the usual way. They should be a shade more *al dente* than the normal.

In a frying pan, big enough to eventually hold the cooked rigatoni, put the butter. The butter should be melted in a separate pan; otherwise the big pan would become too hot and the egg yolks would set as soon as they were added.

To the melted butter, add the egg yolks, the cream, all of the grated Parmesan, and season with salt and pepper to taste. Mix all of the ingredients well together. Only now do you put the pan on the stove, over very low heat.

Cook as gently as possible, stirring all the time, until the mixture becomes tepid. Take the pan off the stove and add the rigatoni, which must be very hot still, to the butter, egg and cheese mixture.

Mix the whole lot well together, transfer to a serving dish and send to the table.

ENRICA AND VERNON JARRATT
THE COMPLETE BOOK OF PASTA

Lenten Spaghetti

Spaghetti di Quaresima

During Lent, Sicilians eat meat only a few times a week. Eggs are an economical substitute providing protein and sustenance. This combination of wholesome ingredients, cooked in a unique way, has made Lenten spaghetti a popular winter's meal.

To serve 4 to 6

1 lb.	spaghetti	½ kg.
6	eggs, hard-boiled	6
Egg croquettes		
6	eggs	6
1 cup	bread crumbs	¼ liter
⅓ cup	finely chopped fresh parsley	75 ml.
1	small onion, finely chopped	1
⅓ cup	freshly grated Parmesan cheese	75 ml.
½ tsp.	salt	2 ml.
¼ tsp.	black pepper	1 ml.
¼ cup	olive oil	50 ml.
Winter's tomato sauce		
14 oz.	canned tomato paste	400 g.
3 tbsp.	olive oil	45 ml.
1	large onion, finely chopped	1
3	garlic cloves, cut into halves	3
3 cups	water	¾ liter
1 tbsp.	dried mint, crumbled	15 ml.
1 tsp.	salt	5 ml.
¼ tsp.	pepper	1 ml.

First prepare the tomato sauce. In a large saucepan, heat the oil, and sauté the onion and garlic until the onion is soft. Add the tomato paste and sauté for three or four minutes. Pour in the water; season with the mint, salt and pepper. Bring to a boil; cover and simmer slowly for 30 to 45 minutes. Discard the garlic and correct the seasoning, if necessary.

To make the croquettes, using a fork beat the six eggs in a bowl until the yolks and whites are mixed. Add the bread crumbs, parsley, onions, cheese, salt and pepper, and mix until the ingredients are combined. Drop rounded table-spoons of the mixture into hot oil and fry until golden on both sides. (Flatten the croquettes slightly with a spatula before turning them.)

Add the croquettes and hard-boiled eggs to the sauce and simmer slowly for 20 minutes; the croquettes will absorb some of the sauce and almost double in size.

Cook the spaghetti in boiling salted water until *al dente.* Drain, and portion it into individual serving bowls. Cover each portion with sauce and top it with one hard-boiled egg and two croquettes.

ANNA MUFFOLETTO
THE ART OF SICILIAN COOKING

White or Green Noodles with Four Cheeses

Tagliatelle ai Quattro Formaggi

Fontina is a semisoft to hard, slightly yellow cheese, obtainable at most supermarkets. Gorgonzola, also known as Stracchino di Gorgonzola, is a pungent, blue-green veined Italian cheese obtainable at cheese specialty stores.

To serve 4 to 6

1½ lb.	medium or fine white or green noodles	¾ kg.
¼ lb.	Fontina cheese, cut into ¼-inch [6-mm.] cubes	125 g.
¼ lb.	Gorgonzola cheese, cut into ¼-inch [6-mm.] cubes	125 g.
¼ lb.	mozzarella cheese, cut into ½-inch [1-cm.] cubes	125 g.
1 cup	freshly grated Parmesan cheese	¼ liter
6 tbsp.	butter	90 ml.
1 cup	heavy cream	¼ liter
	salt and freshly ground pepper	

In a large casserole that can go to the table, heat the butter. Add the Fontina, Gorgonzola and mozzarella cheeses. Cook over low heat, stirring constantly, until the cheeses melt. Keep the sauce mixture warm over the lowest possible heat.

Cook the noodles in plenty of boiling salted water, stirring often, for five to 10 minutes, or until barely tender. The

cooking time depends on the kind and quality of the noodles you use: Imported Italian noodles take longer to cook, but do not overcook them.

While the noodles are cooking, stir the Parmesan cheese into the sauce, stirring until it is melted. Stir in the cream and heat through thoroughly, but do not boil. Check the seasoning; if necessary, add salt and pepper to taste.

Drain the noodles and put them into the casserole with the sauce. Toss and serve very hot.

NIKA HAZELTON
THE REGIONAL ITALIAN KITCHEN

Trahana with Cheese

Liuta Trahana

Trahana, a leavened pasta with a pleasantly sour flavor, is one of the most ancient grain products. It is served as an accompaniment to meat, fish or cheese throughout the Balkans and the countries of the former Ottoman Empire. Trahana takes at least two weeks — and a dry, sunny climate — to prepare. A purée made from such vegetables as zucchini, green peppers and sometimes hot chilies, is mixed with flour to form a dough; ground sesame seeds and sour dough (flour and water left for a few days in a warm place to ferment naturally) are added. The dough is then set in a warm place for a few days. When doubled in bulk, the dough is sieved or chopped into small pieces the size of peas and left to dry out completely — at least a week. Fortunately, trahana can be bought ready-made from Greek, Cypriot or Turkish grocers. Store it in a cloth bag to aerate it and keep it dry.

The original version of this recipe calls for sirene cheese, a salty white cheese not available in the United States. Greek feta cheese is similar and is substituted for sirene cheese here.

To serve 4

9 oz.	trahana	280 g.
¼ lb.	feta cheese, crumbled with a fork	125 g.
½	medium-sized onion, sliced	½
4 tbsp.	butter	60 ml.
1 tsp.	paprika	5 ml.
2½ quarts	boiling water	2½ liters
4 tsp.	salt	20 ml.

Fry the onion in the butter until brown. Remove the pan from the heat and stir in the paprika.

Add the salt to the boiling water and drop in the trahana. Boil briskly, uncovered, for three minutes, or until the trahana is just soft on the outside. Drain immediately and serve on hot plates. Spoon the onion mixture over the trahana and sprinkle with the cheese.

L. PETROV, N. DJELEPOV, E. IORDANOV AND S. UZUNOVA
BULGARSKA NAZIONALNA KUCHNIYA

Hungarian Noodles and Cottage Cheese

Herb salt is obtainable from health-food stores. The techniques of rolling out and cutting pasta dough to make noodles are demonstrated on page 17.

	To serve 6	
3 cups	cake flour	¾ liter
1	sprig each of basil, thyme, marjoram and costmary, finely chopped	1
3	chive stems, finely cut	3
3	sprigs parsley, finely chopped	3
1½ tsp.	baking powder	7 ml.
¾ tsp.	salt	4 ml.
2 tbsp.	butter	30 ml.
6	eggs, beaten	6

Cottage-cheese sauce

1 lb.	creamed cottage cheese	½ kg.
4 tbsp.	butter	60 ml.
1	onion, thinly sliced	1
1	garlic clove, finely chopped	1
2 cups	sour cream	½ liter
1 tsp.	herb salt	5 ml.

To make the noodles, mix together well the flour, herbs, chives, parsley, baking powder and salt. Add the butter and mix the ingredients to the consistency of cornmeal.

Make a well in the flour mixture and add the eggs. Mix well to form a dough.

Have ready a kettle of boiling salted water. Put about one third of the dough on a floured board and roll it out into a thin sheet. Roll up the sheet and cut crosswise slices about ⅔ inch [2 cm.] wide. Roll and slice all of the dough in this way. Unroll the slices and drop them, a few at a time, into the boiling water to cook for about five minutes. (If all are put in at once the water will stop boiling and the noodles will not be as good.) If the noodles are to be kept a while before serving, melt plenty of butter in a pan of adequate size, add the noodles and shake them around until they are coated with the butter. This will prevent them from sticking together and they can be kept for as long as an hour before serving.

Cook together the butter, onion and garlic until just done, but not mushy. Mix together the cottage cheese, sour cream and herb salt, and add to the cooked onions and garlic. The cottage cheese and sour cream will cool the mixture. Add the noodles and mix them in well, then warm the mixture again—but only to serving temperature. More heat will make the cheese stringy.

ALAN HOOKER
VEGETARIAN COOKERY

Noodles with Roquefort

Nouilles au Roquefort

	To serve 4	
10 oz.	noodles	300 g.
¼ lb.	Roquefort cheese, softened at room temperature	125 g.
¼ cup	heavy cream, at room temperature	50 ml.
	freshly ground pepper	

Cook the noodles in plenty of rapidly boiling salted water until just tender. Meanwhile, crush the Roquefort with a fork, then gradually incorporate the cream. Season to taste with pepper. Drain the noodles, add the Roquefort-cream mixture, and mix gently over low heat for two or three minutes. Serve very hot.

MYRETTE TIANO
PÂTES ET RIZ

Noodles Alsatian-Style with Mustard Butter

Senfnudeln

	To serve 6	
4 cups	flour	1 liter
5	eggs	5
4	egg yolks	4
1½ tsp.	salt	7 ml.

Mustard butter

16 tbsp.	butter (½ lb. [¼ kg.])	¼ liter
⅓ cup	strong Dijon mustard	75 ml.
¼ cup	chopped fresh parsley	50 ml.
2 tbsp.	finely cut fresh chives	30 ml.
2	garlic cloves, mashed to a paste	2

To prepare the noodles, first make a well in the flour. Add four of the eggs and the egg yolks as well as the salt. Beat the eggs and egg yolks with a fork until liquid. Using one hand only, gradually incorporate the flour into the egg. When the dough cannot absorb any more flour, beat the fifth whole egg and add it, a tablespoon [15 ml.] at a time, until all of the flour has been incorporated. Knead without interruption until the dough is smooth, elastic and soft, and—when cut through the center—the bubbles imprisoned in the dough are tiny. Cut into eight pieces of equal size. Let stand under a bowl for half an hour.

Roll out the dough into sheets ⅟₂₀ inch [1 mm.] thick. Flour each sheet of dough evenly; roll it into a cigar shape and cut across into ¼-inch [6-mm.] bands. Unroll and set the noodles to dry for about 30 minutes.

Meanwhile, bring a large pot of water to a boil. Salt the water only when you are ready to cook the noodles.

To prepare the mustard butter, first cream the butter. Add the mustard, parsley, chives and garlic. Mix well.

Cook the noodles *al dente*. Put one third of the mustard butter into a sauté pan and add half of the noodles; then add another third of butter and the remaining noodles; finally add the remainder of the butter and toss together. Serve the noodles piping hot.

MADELEINE M. KAMMAN
WHEN FRENCH WOMEN COOK

Trenette with Pesto

The technique of making pesto is demonstrated on page 35. Trenette are flat egg noodles, similar to fettucini but narrower. Pecorino Romano is the variety of Italian sheep's-milk cheese most commonly obtainable at cheese specialty stores. The author suggests that one tablespoon [15 ml.] of pine nuts may be added to the pesto at the end.

There is a lot of argument about what goes to make good pesto and it varies from one household to the next, most of all in its native Genoa. The most ancient and traditional recipes contain basil, garlic and Sardinian pecorino Romano. Basil rules supreme in Ligurian cooking, which is always well endowed with fresh herbs. It is claimed that sea breezes produce the finest basil, even the breezes blowing through the narrow streets or *carrugi* of Genoa that nurture the little pots of basil growing on every window sill. Garlic is the dominant flavor in the pesto; if you reduce the quantity the pesto is no longer genuine. All these are indisputable facts: The arguments begin when it comes to the cheese. Once, only pecorino Romano was used, but gradually Parmesan has crept into pesto. Some purists say that adding even the smallest amount of Parmesan is sacrilege, whereas others claim that a mixture of Parmesan and pecorino Romano has been common for a long time and that the combination of flavors is an advantage.

	To serve 4 to 6	
1 lb.	trenette	½ kg.
2 cups	fresh basil leaves, wiped with a cloth	½ liter
3 or 4	garlic cloves, chopped	3 or 4
	coarse salt	
1 cup	grated pecorino Romano cheese	¼ liter
	olive oil	

Tear the basil leaves into pieces over the mortar, add the garlic and start pounding them together with a pestle, gradually adding more garlic and basil and a little coarse salt. Add more of the ingredients only when you have obtained a good pulp. When all of the garlic and basil are incor-

porated, continue pounding with a circular movement and start to add the grated pecorino Romano so that all of the ingredients blend to form a fairly thick sauce. Dilute with a little olive oil, preferably a characteristic clear, light Ligurian variety. The pesto is then ready.

Cook and drain the trenette, and serve with the pesto.

VINCENZO BUONASSISI
PASTA

Whole-Wheat Noodles with Mixed Herbs
Nouilles Bis aux Fines Herbes

Raw sour cream is unpasteurized, but is certified by the American Association of Medical Milk Commission. Herb salt is composed of sea salt, organically grown herbs and marine kelp, and is used in this recipe as a substitute for salt and pepper. Raw sour cream, herb salt and cold-pressed safflower oil are obtainable at health-food stores.

	To serve 4	
1 lb.	whole-wheat noodles	½ kg.
3 tbsp.	cold-pressed safflower oil	45 ml.
2 tsp.	sea salt	10 ml.
4 tbsp.	raw sour cream, or substitute regular sour cream	60 ml.

	Herb mixture	
1 tbsp.	finely chopped fresh tarragon	15 ml.
1 tsp.	finely chopped fresh thyme, or ½ tsp. [2 ml.] crumbled dried thyme	5 ml.
2 tbsp.	finely chopped fresh parsley	30 ml.
¼ tsp.	ground sage	1 ml.
¼ tsp.	ground rosemary	1 ml.
6 tbsp.	cold-pressed safflower oil	90 ml.
2 tsp.	very finely chopped white onion	10 ml.
½ tsp.	herb salt	2 ml.
¼ tsp.	dry mustard	1 ml.

To make the herb mixture, put all of the ingredients in a blender and purée them.

Fill a large pan three quarters full with water and add the safflower oil and sea salt. Bring the water to a rolling boil and put in the noodles. Cook the whole-wheat noodles no more than 10 minutes. Drain immediately in a colander or wire strainer, and transfer them to a hot serving dish.

Put the sour cream on top of the noodles with about half of the herb mixture, and toss lightly but well with two forks. Add only enough of the remaining half of the herb mixture to coat the noodles lightly.

MARION GORMAN AND FELIPE P. DE ALBA
THE DIONE LUCAS BOOK OF NATURAL FRENCH COOKING

Baker's Wife's Pasta

Pastasciutta alla Fornaia

To serve 5 or 6

1 lb.	spaghetti	½ kg.
2½ tsp.	salt	12 ml.
30 to 35	fresh basil leaves, wiped clean with a soft cloth	30 to 35
½ cup	freshly grated Parmesan cheese	125 ml.
1 cup	shelled walnuts, coarsely chopped	¼ liter
⅓ cup	olive oil	75 ml.

Put 5 quarts [5 liters] of water into a large pot, add 2 teaspoons [10 ml.] of the salt and heat to the boiling point. Put the basil, cheese, the remaining ½ teaspoon [2 ml.] of salt and the nut meats into a large mortar and pound them to a pulp. Slowly add the olive oil, stirring.

When the water boils, add the spaghetti. Wait until it boils again, then stir, separating the spaghetti strand by strand. Allow to cook until *al dente*, drain, then put the spaghetti into a large bowl and season with the sauce. Mix well and serve at once.

WILMA PEZZINI
THE TUSCAN COOKBOOK

Spaghetti with Nut Sauce

To serve 4

1 lb.	spaghetti, boiled and drained	½ kg.
2 cups	toasted walnuts	½ liter
½ cup	olive oil	125 ml.
½ cup	salad oil	125 ml.
½ cup	freshly grated Parmesan cheese	125 ml.
1 tbsp.	chopped fresh oregano or 2 tsp. [10 ml.] dried oregano	15 ml.
1 tbsp.	chopped fresh chervil or 2 tsp. [10 ml.] dried chervil	15 ml.
¼ cup	chopped onion	50 ml.
1	garlic clove	1
½ tsp.	salt	2 ml.
¼ tsp.	freshly ground black pepper	1 ml.
2 tbsp.	chopped fresh flat-leafed parsley	30 ml.
1 cup	sliced zucchini, parboiled for 3 minutes and drained	¼ liter

Combine all of the ingredients except the spaghetti in the container of an electric blender, and blend until smooth.

Pour this sauce into a saucepan, and heat to just below a boil.

Place the spaghetti in a deep platter. Pour the hot sauce over it and toss.

JEAN HEWITT
THE NEW YORK TIMES WEEKEND COOKBOOK

Almond-Poppy Seed Noodles

To serve 6

1 lb.	egg noodles	½ kg.
1½ cups	almonds, sliced	375 ml.
½ cup	poppy seeds	125 ml.
16 tbsp.	butter (½ lb. [¼ kg.])	¼ liter
1 tsp.	salt	5 ml.

Melt the butter; add the almonds and poppy seeds; sauté until the almonds are lightly browned. Cook the noodles in boiling salted water until *al dente*. Drain; turn into a serving dish. Pour the warm butter-and-almond mixture over the noodles. Toss and serve.

THE JUNIOR LEAGUE OF FAYETTEVILLE, INC.
THE CAROLINA COLLECTION

Noodles with Poppy Seed

If fresh noodles are used, the cooking time should be reduced to two or three minutes.

To serve 4

½ lb.	broad egg noodles	¼ kg.
2 tbsp.	poppy seeds, washed and drained	30 ml.
½ cup	slivered, blanched almonds	125 ml.
2 tbsp.	rendered chicken fat	30 ml.
	salt and pepper	

Break the noodles into 2-inch [5-cm.] pieces. Cook them in a large amount of boiling salted water for eight to 10 minutes or until tender, but not mushy. Drain.

In a frying pan, toast the poppy seeds with the almonds in the chicken fat. Pour over the noodles, dusting with salt and pepper. Toss and serve very hot.

FANNIE ENGLE AND GERTRUDE BLAIR
THE JEWISH FESTIVAL COOKBOOK

Tagliatelle with Broad Beans

To skin broad beans, split the protective skin on each broad bean lengthwise, then pull away the skin in one piece.

To serve 4

1 lb.	tagliatelle	½ kg.
2 lb.	fresh broad beans, shelled and skins removed	1 kg.
1	onion, chopped	1
3 tbsp.	olive oil	45 ml.
	salt	
⅔ to 1 cup	freshly grated Parmesan cheese	150 to 250 ml.

Put a large pot of water on to boil for the pasta.

Fry the onion in the oil until soft. Add the beans, a pinch of salt and enough water to barely cover the beans. With the lid slightly ajar, boil the beans rapidly until the water has nearly evaporated.

Meanwhile, salt the pot of boiling water and cook the pasta in it. When the pasta is cooked, drain it and put it on a warmed serving dish. Mix in the beans and grated Parmesan, and serve.

ROSEMARY CROSSLEY
THE DOLE COOKBOOK

Fusilli with Cauliflower

Fusilli con Cavolfiore

To serve 4 to 6

1 lb.	fusilli	½ kg.
1	small head cauliflower	1
4 tbsp.	olive oil	60 ml.
1	large onion, diced	1
3	oil-packed anchovy fillets, rinsed and patted dry	3
20 oz.	canned Italian-style tomatoes, with the liquid reserved	625 g.
1 tbsp.	pine nuts	15 ml.
1 tbsp.	currants	15 ml.
	salt and pepper	
	freshly grated Romano cheese (optional)	

Wash and break or cut the cauliflower into small pieces. Cook in rapidly boiling water for 12 minutes, or until tender but not soft. Drain; set the cauliflower aside.

Heat the oil in a saucepan; add the onion; cook for three minutes or until soft. Cut up the anchovies; add to the onion and stir for about two minutes or until the anchovies dis-

solve. Add the tomatoes and their liquid; cover and simmer for about 20 minutes. Add the cauliflower, pine nuts, currants, and a little salt and pepper. Mix well; keep hot over very low heat.

Cook the fusilli in 4 quarts [4 liters] of rapidly boiling salted water for 15 minutes or until tender. Drain; place in a hot bowl; add the cauliflower and sauce.

Serve very hot in individual plates. If desired, sprinkle with grated Romano cheese just before serving.

MARIA LO PINTO AND MILO MILORADOVICH
THE ART OF ITALIAN COOKING

Fettucini with Asparagus and Peas

Primavera

The techniques for rolling out pasta dough and cutting it into noodles are demonstrated on pages 16-19 and 22-23.

To serve 4 or 5

¾ to 1 lb.	pasta dough (recipe, page 164), cut into flat noodles	⅓ to ½ kg.
½ lb.	thin fresh asparagus	¼ kg.
1 cup	freshly shelled peas	¼ liter
3	large eggs	3
	salt and freshly ground black pepper	
6 tbsp.	freshly grated Parmesan cheese	90 ml.
3 tbsp.	butter	45 ml.
½ cup	diced smoked ham	125 ml.

Scrape the asparagus stalks. Tie them into bundles of equal size and set aside. Beat the eggs until smooth, and season with salt and pepper. Add 2 tablespoons [30 ml.] of Parmesan cheese and set aside.

In a casserole, bring salted water to a boil, add the asparagus bundles and cook for five minutes, or until just tender; do not overcook. Untie the asparagus, drain it and rinse under cold running water. Cut each stalk into 1-inch [2½-cm.] pieces and set them aside.

In a saucepan, again bring salted water to a boil. Add the peas and cook until just tender, or for about five minutes. Drain and set aside.

In a cast-iron skillet, melt the butter over low heat. Add the ham and simmer until just heated through. Add the asparagus and peas, and simmer the mixture gently for two or three minutes. Keep warm.

In a large casserole, bring plenty of salted water to a boil. Add the fettucini and cook for five minutes, or until just tender; do not overcook. Drain and add to the skillet.

Remove the skillet from the heat. Pour the egg mixture over the fettucini and toss with two forks. Add the remaining Parmesan cheese and a large grinding of pepper. Serve immediately, right from the skillet.

PERLA MEYERS
FROM MARKET TO KITCHEN COOKBOOK

Orecchiette with Broccoli

Orecchiette "chi Vruoccoli Arriminata"

Pecorino is the Italian word for sheep's milk. The most common pecorino cheese is pecorino Romano, obtainable at cheese specialty stores.

This is a famous traditional Sicilian dish. The Sicilians make it with either orecchiette (literally "little ears," so called because of the shape) or spaghetti—but never with any other pasta. Don't ask us why.

To serve 6

1½ lb.	orecchiette or spaghetti	¾ kg.
1 cup	freshly grated pecorino or Parmesan cheese (optional)	¼ liter
	Broccoli sauce	
2 lb.	broccoli, the stalks peeled and sliced, the tops divided into florets	1 kg.
	salt	
½ cup	olive oil	125 ml.
2	garlic cloves, peeled but left whole	2
1	small piece fresh red hot chili	1
8	medium-sized tomatoes, peeled, seeded and chopped, or 1½ lb. [¾ kg.] canned tomatoes, drained and chopped	8
¼ lb.	salt anchovies, filleted, soaked in water for 30 minutes, rinsed, patted dry and chopped	125 g.
¼ cup	finely chopped onion	50 ml.
⅓ cup	seedless white raisins, soaked in warm water for 15 minutes and drained	75 ml.
¼ cup	pine nuts	50 ml.
	freshly ground black pepper	

Into the pan in which you intend to cook the pasta, put an appropriate quantity of water. Bring to a boil and add salt. Put in the broccoli and cook for about three minutes, boiling briskly. Remove the broccoli with a perforated ladle and set it aside. Keep the pan and the water available.

Put half of the oil into a skillet. Add one garlic clove and the chili. Fry fairly briskly until the garlic turns golden. Then remove and discard the garlic clove, and add the chopped tomatoes and anchovies. Season with a little salt. Bring to a boil and cook for 15 minutes. If at the end of this time the sauce seems to be thin, boil briskly for a few minutes until you reach the desired consistency.

Put the rest of the oil into a second skillet. Add the chopped onion and second garlic clove. Cook over medium heat until the garlic turns golden. Discard the garlic. Then add the cooked broccoli, the raisins and the pine nuts. Season

with a very little salt and a fair amount of pepper. Cook for about two minutes over medium heat, stirring with two forks to lessen the risk of breaking the florets. Then add the contents of this skillet to that with the anchovies and tomatoes. Mix gently and keep the sauce hot.

Bring the water used for cooking the broccoli back to a boil, add the orecchiette or spaghetti, and cook until firm to the bite. Drain the pasta and arrange it in a deep, heated serving dish in layers, alternating with layers of the sauce. In this way the pasta and the sauce can be mixed well together with less risk of breaking the broccoli florets. If you are using grated cheese, this too should go in layers.

ENRICA AND VERNON JARRATT
THE COMPLETE BOOK OF PASTA

Flemish Noodles

The author suggests that 15 scallions may be substituted for the leeks; the scallions need only be boiled for 10 minutes.

To serve 4

½ lb.	broad noodles	¼ kg.
4 or 5	leeks (1 lb. [½ kg.])	4 or 5
1½ tsp.	salt	7 ml.
1 tbsp.	butter	15 ml.
	White sauce with cheese	
2 tbsp.	butter	30 ml.
3 tbsp.	flour	45 ml.
2 cups	milk	½ liter
½ cup	heavy cream	125 ml.
	nutmeg	
	salt and pepper	
½ cup	freshly grated Parmesan cheese	125 ml.

Bring a pot of water to a boil while preparing the leeks. Trim off the roots and cut away all the green leaves. Rinse the leeks well; they can stubbornly hold onto a lot of sand between the layers. Add 1 teaspoon [5 ml.] of salt and the leeks to the water; cook for 15 to 20 minutes, or until the leeks are soft. Drain at once and rinse the leeks under cold water. Drain again, very well. Refill the pot with water, put it back on the heat and bring to a boil.

While the leeks are cooking, prepare the white sauce. Heat 2 tablespoons [30 ml.] of butter in a saucepan until it is hot and foamy; stir in the flour and cook for one minute while stirring. Slowly add the milk while stirring with a wire whisk, then add the cream. Season with a large pinch of nutmeg, and salt and pepper to taste. Add the cheese and stir until it melts.

When the water in the pot comes to a boil, add the remaining ½ teaspoon [2 ml.] of salt and the noodles, and cook them for just three minutes or until *al dente*. Do not over-cook. Drain very well. Transfer the noodles to a deep bowl and add the 1 tablespoon [15 ml.] of butter; toss to melt the butter and prevent the noodles from sticking together.

Put the cooked noodles back in the pot. Separate the leeks into their natural layers and add them to the noodles. Pour in the sauce and mix together well so that all of the noodles and leeks are coated with the sauce. Reheat slowly for a few minutes. Transfer to a deep serving bowl and use a large spoon and fork for serving.

CAROL CUTLER
THE SIX-MINUTE SOUFFLÉ AND OTHER CULINARY DELIGHTS

Pasta and Eggplant
Pasta alla Norma

Vincenzo Bellini was born in Catania, Sicily. His most fa-mous opera was *Norma*. Small wonder that wherever you go in Trinacria you can obtain this most delectable pasta with eggplant, or *Pasta alla Norma*. It has become one of my fa-vorite ways of preparing pasta.

To serve 4

1 lb.	spaghetti, or other pasta	½ kg.
2	small eggplants, sliced into rounds ½ inch [1 cm.] thick	2
1 tsp.	salt	5 ml.
½ cup	olive oil	125 ml.
2	garlic cloves, crushed	2
1 lb.	fresh plum tomatoes, plunged into boiling water for 2 minutes, peeled, seeded and coarsely chopped, or 4 cups [1 liter] canned Italian-style tomatoes, drained	½ kg.
½ tsp.	dried red pepper flakes	2 ml.
	fresh basil sprigs	
	freshly ground black pepper	
4 tbsp.	freshly grated Romano cheese	60 ml.

Place the sliced eggplant in a colander, sprinkle with ½ tea-spoon [2 ml.] of salt, weigh the slices down with a heavy plate and leave them for 30 minutes to drain out their natu-ral bitterness.

Heat ¼ cup [50 ml.] of the olive oil in an iron skillet and add the crushed garlic. When the garlic begins to color, add the tomatoes, pepper flakes, basil, the remaining salt and a generous grinding of pepper, and sauté for 15 minutes. Set aside and keep warm. Now blot the eggplant slices dry.

Meanwhile, begin cooking the spaghetti or other pasta.

While the pasta cooks, sauté the eggplant—a few slices at a time—in a separate skillet in the remaining olive oil,

flipping the slices to brown both sides. Remove with a slotted spatula to a warm plate.

When the pasta is just barely *al dente*, drain and place it in a heated serving bowl. Add the sauce and toss lightly. Top with the eggplant slices and toss again to mix well. Serve while very hot. Pass the grated Romano cheese for each guest to sprinkle to taste.

STENDAHL
SPICY FOOD

Springtime Spaghetti
Spaghetti Primavera

To serve 4

1 lb.	spaghetti	½ kg.
1	medium-sized onion, quartered and cut into thin slices	1
⅔ cup	thinly sliced fresh mushrooms	150 ml.
1	medium-sized carrot, cut into thin strips	1
1	celery rib, cut into thin strips	1
3	small ripe tomatoes, peeled, quartered, seeded and cut into thin strips	3
¾ cup	freshly shelled peas, boiled in salted water for 2 minutes and drained	175 ml.
4 tbsp.	oil	60 ml.
2	basil leaves, finely chopped or ⅛ tsp. [½ ml.] dried basil	2
2	thin slices cooked ham, cut into thin strips	2
	salt and pepper	
¾ cup	freshly grated Parmesan cheese	175 ml.

Allow the onion to soften—not brown—in the oil over medi-um heat. Add the mushrooms and cook for two minutes over low heat. Add the carrot, celery, basil leaves, tomatoes and the peas. Next add the ham, and salt and pepper to taste. Simmer this sauce slowly for 15 minutes.

Cook the spaghetti in abundant boiling salted water for eight minutes and drain. Turn onto a large preheated serv-ing dish. Pour the sauce over the spaghetti, add the Parme-san, mix well, and serve.

JACQUES HARVEY
365 WAYS TO COOK PASTA

Spaghetti with Spinach, Mushrooms and Cream
Spaghetti Primaverile

To serve 2 or 3

½ lb.	spaghetti	¼ kg.
4 cups	spinach, stemmed, shredded, parboiled and drained	1 liter
½ lb.	mushrooms, trimmed and sliced	¼ kg.
1 cup	heavy cream	¼ liter
⅓ cup	freshly grated Parmesan cheese	75 ml.
3 tbsp.	fresh lemon juice	45 ml.
4 tbsp.	butter	60 ml.
1	garlic clove, finely chopped	1
2 tbsp.	Marsala wine	30 ml.
	salt	
	freshly ground black pepper	

Add the lemon juice to the mushrooms and mix well. Melt the butter in a skillet; add the garlic and Marsala. Cook for three minutes; add the mushrooms. Cook for five minutes more. Add the heavy cream and bring the mixture to a boil. Add some salt, then pepper liberally. Remove from the heat.

Cook the spaghetti *al dente*. Drain the pasta and return it to the pan in which it was cooked. Add the spinach and the mushroom mixture to the pasta. Put the spaghetti onto individual serving plates and top each with grated Parmesan.

JOE FAMULARO & LOUISE IMPERIALE
THE FESTIVE FAMULARO KITCHEN

Spaghetti or Vermicelli with Uncooked Tomato Sauce

To serve 4

1 lb.	spaghetti or vermicelli, boiled and drained	½ kg.
6	medium-sized tomatoes, peeled, seeded, chopped and the juices retained	6
8 tbsp.	olive oil	120 ml.
2	garlic cloves, finely chopped	2
	basil	
	salt and pepper	

Put the olive oil (a fruity oil from Southern Italy is the best) in a deep serving dish with the tomatoes, the garlic and a little basil, and marinate for at least two hours.

Season the sauce with salt and pepper, and stir the sauce gently. Mix with the hot pasta and serve immediately.

VINCENZO BUONASSISI
PASTA

Pasta Primavera

To serve 8

1 lb.	pasta	½ kg.
3 or 4	medium-sized zucchini, trimmed but not peeled, and cut into small pieces	3 or 4
½ lb.	broccoli, trimmed and cut into small pieces	¼ kg.
½ lb.	fresh green beans, trimmed and cut into small pieces	¼ kg.
2 tbsp.	vegetable oil	30 ml.
6	shallots	6
1	garlic clove	1
¼ cup	chopped fresh flat-leafed parsley	50 ml.
2 tbsp.	finely chopped fresh basil	30 ml.
	salt and pepper	
¼ cup	freshly grated Parmesan cheese	50 ml.

Fill a large pot with water and start heating it for the pasta. Heat the oil in a large skillet and add the green vegetables. Chop the shallots into the pan and push the garlic through a press into the mixture. Cover and oil-steam for five minutes. Uncover, stir to mix well, and add the parsley and basil. Cover again and continue to cook, until the vegetables are done to your taste; they should still be crunchy.

Meanwhile cook the pasta until *al dente*. When the sauce is ready, season with salt and pepper to taste. Toss with the pasta and sprinkle with cheese.

ELISA CELLI & INEZ M. KRECH
NATURALLY ITALIAN

Pasta Shells with Peppers

To serve 4 or 5

1 lb.	small pasta shells	½ kg.
3	green, red and/or yellow sweet peppers, halved, seeded, deribbed and cut into strips	3
	oil	
	butter	
1	onion, thinly sliced	1
4	small tomatoes, peeled, seeded and diced	4
1	large bunch basil	1
	salt and pepper	
	freshly grated Parmesan cheese	

Cover the bottom of a frying pan with oil and a little butter. Sauté the onion slices until they turn pale gold. Add the peppers and cook over fairly high heat, stirring frequently. When the peppers begin to become tender, add the tomatoes, the basil, and salt and pepper to taste. Reduce the heat. Cover the pan and cook for about 15 minutes. Remove the lid and let the water from the tomatoes evaporate.

While the pepper and tomatoes are simmering, cook the pasta shells *al dente* and drain them well. Combine the cooked shells with the pepper-and-tomato mixture. Sprinkle generously with grated Parmesan.

NAOMI BARRY & BEPPE BELLINI
FOOD ALLA FLORENTINE

Chilled Buckwheat Noodles with Cucumbers and Mushrooms

Japanese rice vinegar is a mild, slightly sweet vinegar available where Oriental foods are sold.

To serve 4 to 6		
½ lb.	buckwheat noodles, boiled, drained, rinsed and chilled	¼ kg.
2	large cucumbers, peeled, halved, seeded and cut into thin shreds 3 inches [8 cm.] long	2
4	large dried mushrooms, soaked in warm water for 15 minutes, drained, stems removed, and caps shredded	4
½ cup	rice vinegar	125 ml.
1 tsp.	vegetable oil	5 ml.
⅔ cup	soy sauce	150 ml.
½ cup	beef stock *(recipe, page 167)*	125 ml.
4 tbsp.	sugar	60 ml.
2	scallions, chopped	2

Combine the vinegar, oil, ½ cup [125 ml.] soy sauce, ¼ cup [50 ml.] of the stock and 2 tablespoons [30 ml.] of the sugar in a saucepan. Simmer this sauce for five minutes, then place in the refrigerator.

Put the shredded mushrooms in a saucepan with the remaining stock, soy sauce and sugar. Heat the liquid, stir for three minutes, remove the mushrooms and set them aside. Add the mushroom liquid to the chilled sauce.

Heap the chilled noodles in a large serving bowl. Arrange the shredded cucumbers and mushrooms decoratively on top. Pour the sauce over the noodles. Garnish the center with the chopped scallions.

KAREN GREEN
THE GREAT INTERNATIONAL NOODLE EXPERIENCE

Noodles with Uncooked Tomato Sauce

Nouilles à la Sauce Tomate Crue

To serve 4		
10 oz.	noodles	300 g.
6	medium-sized tomatoes, parboiled for 1 minute, peeled, seeded and diced	6
1	bunch basil, the leaves washed and chopped	1
6	garlic cloves, crushed with the back of a knife and peeled	6
	salt and pepper	
¾ cup	olive oil	175 ml.

Mix the basil with the tomatoes and add the crushed garlic. Season the mixture with salt and pepper, add the oil, cover, and put in a cool place.

Cook the noodles in plenty of rapidly boiling salted water until just done. Drain. Discard the garlic cloves and toss the tomato sauce with the noodles. Serve immediately.

MYRETTE TIANO
PÂTES ET RIZ

Spaghettini with Fried Zucchini

Pasta chi Cucuzzeddi Fritti

To serve 4		
1¼ lb.	spaghettini	⅔ kg.
6 or 7	small zucchini, sliced into rounds	6 or 7
2	garlic cloves	2
½ cup	olive oil	125 ml.
	salt	
½ cup	pecorino pepato or hard ricotta salata cheese, grated	125 ml.
	freshly ground black pepper	

Soften the garlic cloves for a moment in hot but not smoking oil, then add and fry the zucchini. Drain the zucchini, reserving the oil and discarding the garlic. Season the zucchini, transfer it to a plate and keep it hot.

Cook the spaghettini in boiling salted water until *al dente*, then drain the spaghettini and add to it the cheese, the zucchini and the oil. Serve with freshly ground black pepper.

PINO CORRENTI
IL LIBRO D'ORO DELLA CUCINA E DEI VINI DI SICILIA

Spaghetti with Zucchini

Pâtes aux Courgettes

To serve 4

10 oz.	thin spaghetti	300 g.
3	zucchini, thinly sliced into rounds	3
⅓ cup	olive oil	75 ml.
	salt and freshly ground pepper	
6	basil leaves, finely chopped	6
1 cup	freshly grated aged Gruyère or Parmesan cheese	¼ liter

Sauté the zucchini in 2 tablespoons [30 ml.] of the oil over high heat for eight to 10 minutes. Add salt and pepper.

Cook the spaghetti for seven minutes in plenty of rapidly boiling salted water. Drain. Add the zucchini with their cooking juices, the rest of the oil and the chopped basil. Season with freshly ground pepper. Mix well. Serve hot, with the grated cheese in a separate dish.

MYRETTE TIANO
PÂTES ET RIZ

The Stew That Is Always Good

Minestra Sempre Buona

The original version of this recipe calls for paternostri, another name for anellini rigati, which are small, ridged rings, or for avemarie, more commonly known as anellini, which are smaller unridged rings. Orzo or stelline may be substituted. If bean broth (the cooking liquid from dried beans) is not available, use meat stock (recipe, page 167).

To serve 4

¾ lb.	small pasta	⅓ kg.
⅓ cup	oil	75 ml.
1	onion, finely chopped	1
1	carrot, finely chopped	1
3 or 4	celery leaves, finely chopped	3 or 4
1	garlic clove, finely chopped	1
	freshly grated nutmeg (optional)	
1¼ quarts	bean broth, brought to boiling point	1¼ liters

Pour the oil into a heavy saucepan, heat, and add the onion, carrot, celery, garlic and nutmeg, if desired. Fry slowly. This mixture is known as a battuto. When the battuto is nicely browned, add the pasta and stir until it begins to brown. Then gradually pour in the bean broth, stirring constantly until the pasta is cooked. The result should resemble a risotto in consistency.

MARIÙ SALVATORI DE ZULIANI
LA CUCINA DI VERSILIA E GARFAGNANA

Soba with Zucchini and Mushrooms

To serve 2 to 4

3 oz.	soba, boiled and drained	90 g.
½ lb.	zucchini, cut into 2-inch [5-cm.] shreds	¼ kg.
3	dried Chinese mushrooms, soaked in warm chicken stock for 30 minutes, drained, stems removed, caps shredded	3
1 tbsp.	oil	15 ml.
2	garlic cloves	2
1 tbsp.	soy sauce	15 ml.

Heat a wok over high heat; add the oil and garlic. Stir fry the garlic for a few seconds, then add the zucchini and mushrooms and continue to fry, stirring constantly, for another few seconds. Add the soba; continue stirring for two minutes. Add the soy sauce; stir for another minute; serve at once.

KAREN GREEN
THE GREAT INTERNATIONAL NOODLE EXPERIENCE

Vermicelli with Onions and Peas

Vermicelli con Cipolline e Piselli

To serve 4 to 6

1 lb.	vermicelli	½ kg.
10	small onions, finely chopped	10
1 cup	shelled fresh peas	¼ liter
6 tbsp.	butter, 3 tbsp. [45 ml.] melted	90 ml.
2	slices bacon, diced	2
½ tsp.	sugar	2 ml.
	salt and pepper	
2 tbsp.	puréed tomato (recipe, page 167)	30 ml.
½ cup	hot meat stock (recipe, page 167)	125 ml.
⅔ cup	freshly grated Parmesan cheese	150 ml.
	chopped fresh parsley	

In a saucepan, sauté the onions lightly with 3 tablespoons [45 ml.] of butter and the diced bacon. Cover and cook slowly, adding some water if necessary. Add the peas, sugar, pepper to taste, and the puréed tomato and the hot stock. Cook over medium heat for about 20 minutes. To keep the peas tender and preserve their color, add salt after they are cooked.

Cook the vermicelli in plenty of boiling salted water until it is *al dente* (firm to the bite). Drain, and mix it with the melted butter, together with a few tablespoons of the Parmesan cheese and a little of the onion-and-pea sauce. Arrange on a warm serving dish and pour on the remaining sauce. Garnish with parsley and serve with the remaining cheese.

FEAST OF ITALY

Tortiglioni with a Brandy Sauce

Tortiglioni is another name for rotelle.

To serve 4 to 6		
1 lb.	tortiglioni	½ kg.
½ cup	brandy	125 ml.
⅓ cup	olive oil	75 ml.
2 or 3	small mild onions, coarsely chopped	2 or 3
	coarsely chopped fresh parsley	
4	ripe tomatoes, peeled and coarsely chopped	4
1 tsp.	sugar	5 ml.
	salt	
12	ripe black olives, pitted and chopped	12
	freshly ground black pepper	

First prepare the sauce. Heat the oil, add the onions and parsley to taste, and simmer until the onions begin to soften, but do not let them brown. Add the tomatoes, sugar and salt to taste. Stir and cook over low heat until the tomatoes are soft and the sauce is thick and smooth.

Start cooking the tortiglioni in a pan of boiling salted water. While the pasta is cooking, add the brandy and olives to the sauce. Stir and simmer for 10 minutes. Drain the pasta and return it to the pan or turn it out into a warmed serving dish. Stir the sauce into the tortiglioni, mix well and serve. Black pepper should be ground over each plateful.

ROBIN HOWE
THE PASTA COOKBOOK

Spaghetti with Tripe

The honeycomb tripe sold at most butchers and supermarkets is parboiled to tenderize it and reduce its cooking time.

To serve 4		
1 lb.	spaghetti, boiled and drained	½ kg.
1 to 1½ lb.	precooked tripe	½ to ¾ kg.
2	onions, chopped	2
1	garlic clove, finely chopped	1
3 tbsp.	olive oil	45 ml.
34 oz.	canned Italian-style tomatoes in purée	1 kg.
1 tsp.	oregano	5 ml.
1 tsp.	sugar	5 ml.
	salt and freshly ground pepper	
	freshly grated Parmesan cheese	

Wash the tripe, put it into a pan, cover it with cold water, and bring to a boil. Drain, and cut the tripe into strips or squares.

Sauté the onions and garlic in the oil until the onions are limp. Add the tomatoes, rinsing out the cans with a little water and adding the water to the pan. Add the seasonings and the tripe.

Cook slowly with the pan partially covered until the sauce is rich and thick, about two to three hours. Serve on a bed of spaghetti, and pass grated Parmesan cheese.

HARRIET HANDS
MORE TASTE THAN MONEY

Spaghetti with Veal Dumplings

Spaghetti Piatto Unico

To serve 4		
1 lb.	spaghetti, boiled and drained	½ kg.
3 tbsp.	butter	45 ml.
2 tbsp.	dry vermouth	30 ml.
4	medium-sized tomatoes, peeled, seeded and chopped	4
¼ tsp.	freshly ground black pepper	1 ml.
1 tsp.	salt	5 ml.
	freshly grated Parmesan cheese	
Veal dumplings		
½ lb.	lean ground veal	¼ kg.
2 oz.	prosciutto or cooked ham, finely chopped (about ½ cup [125 ml.])	60 g.
2 tbsp.	freshly grated Parmesan cheese	30 ml.
½ tsp.	salt	2 ml.
1	egg, beaten	1
½ cup	dry bread crumbs	125 ml.

To make the dumplings, first mix together the veal, ham, cheese, salt and egg. Shape teaspoonfuls of the mixture into little balls. Roll them in the bread crumbs.

Melt the butter in a saucepan; brown the balls in it. Add the vermouth; cook until the vermouth has been absorbed. Add the tomatoes, pepper and salt. Cook over low heat for 30 minutes. Taste for seasoning.

Pour the dumplings and sauce over the hot spaghetti and serve with grated cheese.

ROMEO SALTA
THE PLEASURES OF ITALIAN COOKING

Somen with Ground Beef

To prepare the onion-flavored oil called for in this recipe, pour 3 tablespoons [45 ml.] of hot, but not smoking, vegetable oil over two or three chopped scallions; then strain the oil. The volatile oils in hot chilies may make your skin sting and your eyes burn; wear rubber gloves when handling them and avoid touching your face.

To serve 4

½ lb.	somen	¼ kg.
½ lb.	lean ground beef	¼ kg.
1 tbsp.	oil	15 ml.
1	small onion, finely chopped	1
1	medium-sized Chinese yam, peeled and finely chopped	1
	black pepper	
2 cups	lettuce, cut into 1-inch [2½-cm.] squares	½ liter
½	medium-sized cucumber, peeled, seeded and cut into julienne	½
½ cup	fresh bean sprouts, washed well and drained (optional)	125 ml.
	fresh mint leaves, coarsely chopped	
	fresh coriander sprigs, coarsely chopped	
4 tbsp.	onion oil	60 ml.
4 tbsp.	roasted peanuts	60 ml.

Nuoc mam sauce

4 tbsp.	*nuoc mam*	60 ml.
1	small fresh red chili, stem removed, halved, seeded and chopped	1
1	garlic clove	1
1 tsp.	sugar	5 ml.
½	lime, peeled, halved and seeded	½
1 tbsp.	vinegar	15 ml.
1 tbsp.	water	15 ml.

If you are not sure how hot you want the *nuoc mam* sauce, start with very little of the chili. It is easy to add more. Crush the chili and garlic together in a mortar with the sugar. Mash the lime pulp in the mortar with the chili and garlic. Add the vinegar and water, and mix well. Add the *nuoc mam* last. If it is added before the other ingredients, the pieces of garlic, pepper and lime pulp will all sink to the bottom and it is preferable to have them in suspension or floating on top. Set the sauce aside.

Heat the oil in a skillet over high heat and sauté the chopped onion and yam with the ground beef, stirring con-stantly until done (about five minutes; do not overcook). Sprinkle black pepper on top. Set aside.

Cook the noodles in 1 quart [1 liter] of boiling water for about five to eight minutes. When tender, drain the noodles in a colander and rinse with cold water until the noodles are cool and not sticky. Set aside to cool.

Mix the lettuce, cucumber, bean sprouts, mint and cori-ander like a salad. Chop the peanuts coarse just before serv-ing. Be sure to reserve the peanut "dust," since that contains much of the flavor and aroma.

In each of four individual medium-sized bowls, put one fourth of the mixed vegetables. Divide the cold noodles into four portions and put on top of the salad. Put the cooked-meat mixture on top of the noodles. The meat mixture may be served hot or cold. Pour 1 tablespoon [15 ml.] of *nuoc mam* sauce over each serving. Pour about 1 tablespoon of onion oil over each serving. Sprinkle the peanuts over the top, and serve. Each person stirs his bowlful before eating. If not salty enough, add more *nuoc mam* sauce—never add salt.

JILL NHU HUONG MILLER
VIETNAMESE COOKERY

Skillet Meatballs and Noodles

To serve 6

7 or 8 oz.	egg noodles	200 or 250 g.
1 lb.	lean ground beef	½ kg.
1	egg	1
½ cup	fine dry bread crumbs	125 ml.
¼ cup	finely chopped fresh parsley	50 ml.
1½ tsp.	salt	7 ml.
½ tsp.	pepper	2 ml.
1¼ cups	water	300 ml.
2 tbsp.	oil	30 ml.
28 oz.	canned tomatoes, drained and cut into small pieces, and their liquid reserved	875 g.
1	garlic clove, finely chopped	1
½ tsp.	basil	2 ml.
	oregano (optional)	

Combine the beef, egg, bread crumbs, parsley, 1 teaspoon [5 ml.] of the salt, ¼ teaspoon [1 ml.] of the pepper and ¼ cup [50 ml.] of the water. Mix lightly but thoroughly. Shape the mixture into balls about 1½ inches [4 cm.] in diameter.

Heat the oil in a large skillet. Add the meatballs and cook over medium heat until browned, turning carefully with tongs or two forks to brown all sides. Remove the meatballs and keep them warm. Drain off most of the drippings from the pan, leaving only the browned bits and a thin film of fat.

Add the tomatoes, 1 cup [¼ liter] of water, the remaining salt and pepper, the garlic, basil and a pinch of oregano, if using. Bring to a boil.

Add the noodles a few at a time. Cook for eight minutes or until the noodles are tender, stirring often to keep them from sticking. Add the meatballs and cook for three or four minutes longer to heat them through.

JEANNE A. VOLTZ
THE FLAVOR OF THE SOUTH

Ants Climb a Tree

Mayi Shang Shu

To serve 4 or 5

½ lb.	dried cellophane noodles	¼ kg.
1 lb.	lean ground pork or beef	½ kg.
⅓ cup	soy sauce	75 ml.
1 tbsp.	sesame-seed oil	15 ml.
6	scallions, white and green parts, finely sliced crosswise	6
5 tbsp.	peanut oil	75 ml.
½-inch	slice fresh ginger, peeled and finely chopped	1-cm.
6	garlic cloves, finely chopped	6
2 tbsp.	hot-pepper paste	30 ml.
⅔ cup	water	150 ml.
	salt	
	freshly ground black pepper	

Put the cellophane noodles in a large bowl and cover them with about 1 quart [1 liter] of boiling water. Set them aside to soak for at least 20 minutes.

Put the ground pork in a bowl and add to it 2 tablespoons [30 ml.] of soy sauce and the sesame-seed oil. Add half of the scallions to the pork or beef and mix well; set the rest of the scallions aside.

When the cellophane noodles have become nice and soft, rinse them several times under cold running water and then drain them well.

Heat your wok or a large pan over high heat for 15 seconds, then pour in the peanut oil. It will be hot enough to cook with when the first tiny bubbles form and a few small wisps of smoke appear. When the oil is ready, toss in the chopped ginger and garlic and add the hot-pepper paste. Stir fry these ingredients together for 30 seconds, using your cooking shovel or a spoon to keep everything moving around in the hot oil. Add the meat and continue to stir fry for about one minute, taking particular care to break up any large chunks of meat. Now pour in the remaining soy sauce and stir fry everything for 30 seconds longer. Add the cellophane noodles to the pan and cook for about one minute, turning the noodles over occasionally and taking several cuts at them with your shovel or spoon while they cook so that they won't be too long to eat.

After you have fried the noodles for about one minute, add the water and the rest of the scallions. Taste for salt and add as much as you need to give a rich, clear taste to the noodles. Then cover the pan and let simmer over medium heat for three or four minutes.

Just before you are ready to serve the noodles, sprinkle some regular black pepper over them. This adds a pleasantly sharp flavor to the dish.

ELLEN SCHRECKER
MRS. CHIANG'S SZECHWAN COOKBOOK

Boiled Beef Potpie

To serve 8

2 cups	flour	½ liter
3 tbsp.	shortening	45 ml.
1 tsp.	salt	5 ml.
1	small egg, beaten	1
¼ to ½ cup	milk	50 to 125 ml.

Boiled beef

1½ to 2 lb.	stewing beef, cut into cubes	¾ to 1 kg.
about 2 quarts	boiling water	about 2 liters
2	onions, quartered	2
2 tbsp.	finely chopped fresh parsley	30 ml.
1½ tsp.	salt	7 ml.
1 tsp.	marjoram	5 ml.
4	medium-sized potatoes, peeled and cut into ¼-inch [6-mm.] slices	4
	black pepper	

Cook the meat in the water until tender, about one and a half hours. Add the onions, parsley, salt and marjoram.

Meanwhile, prepare the potpie. Cut the shortening into the flour and salt. Beat the egg and add it to the dry ingredients with enough milk to make a soft dough. Roll out half of the dough very thin. Cut it into 2-inch [5-cm.] squares.

Drop into the meat broth a layer of potatoes, using half of them, and then drop in the potpie squares for the next layer. Let the broth come to a boil; stir. Roll out the remainder of the dough and cut it into squares. Add these potpie squares and the remaining potatoes to the broth. Sprinkle with pepper. Add boiling water, if necessary, to keep the broth boiling up through the potpie squares. Cover and cook for 20 minutes without removing the lid.

EDNA EBY HELLER
THE ART OF PENNSYLVANIA DUTCH COOKING

Straw and Hay Tagliatelle

Tagliatelle Paglia e Fieno

The techniques of making plain pasta dough and colored pasta dough are shown on pages 16-17 and 20-21 respectively. The cutting of pasta dough to make tagliatelle is shown on pages 22-23. Pancetta is a cut of pork belly that is similar to bacon but cured with salt and pepper. It is obtainable from Italian delicatessens.

To serve 4

¾ lb.	pasta dough *(recipe, page 164)*	⅓ kg.
¾ lb.	spinach-pasta dough *(recipe, page 165)*	⅓ kg.

Beef, pork and mushroom sauce

3½ oz.	boneless lean beef, finely chopped	100 g.
3½ oz.	boneless pork loin, finely chopped	100 g.
½ oz.	dried mushrooms, soaked in warm water for 30 minutes, drained and the water reserved	15 g.
1	small celery rib, finely chopped	1
1	carrot, finely chopped	1
1	onion, finely chopped	1
2 oz.	*pancetta,* or salt pork with the rind removed, blanched in boiling water for 5 minutes, drained and finely chopped	60 g.
2 tbsp.	olive oil	30 ml.
7 tbsp.	butter, cut into pieces	100 ml.
⅓ cup	dry white wine	75 ml.
1 cup	puréed tomato *(recipe, page 167)*	¼ liter
1	whole clove	1
1	bay leaf	1
	salt	
3	chicken livers, trimmed and coarsely chopped	3
	pepper	
⅓ cup	freshly grated Parmesan cheese	75 ml.

Make plain and green tagliatelle from the pasta dough and allow them to dry.

In a heavy casserole, mix the chopped vegetables with the *pancetta* or salt pork, and add the oil and about 2 tablespoons [30 ml.] of the butter. Fry the vegetables lightly over medium heat, stirring frequently. When the *pancetta* or salt pork has rendered all of its fat and the vegetables are soft, add the beef and pork. Continue cooking, moistening the mixture with the wine. When the wine has evaporated, add the mushrooms. Add the puréed tomato, season with the clove, bay leaf and salt to taste, stir, cover and simmer for about one hour, stirring occasionally. If the mixture becomes

dry, add a little of the reserved mushroom water, pouring it in carefully to avoid disturbing the bed of meat and vegetables that will have formed in the bottom of the casserole. At the end of the cooking time, set the chicken livers on top of the meat and vegetables, and cook for five minutes. Add salt and pepper to taste, and remove this sauce from the heat.

Bring two large pans of salted water to a boil. Put the plain tagliatelle into one pan and the green tagliatelle into the other. Stir the pastas and boil them both over high heat for about 10 minutes or until cooked through. Then drain the plain tagliatelle and tip it into a warmed bowl. Melt the remaining butter, and pour half of it over the pasta. Sprinkle on 2 tablespoons [30 ml.] of the cheese. Toss, and arrange the pasta on a warmed serving dish. Drain the green tagliatelle and toss it with the remaining butter and 2 tablespoons of cheese. Add it to the serving dish.

Stir the sauce and serve it in a warmed sauceboat, sprinkled with the rest of the cheese.

FERNANDA GOSETTI
IN CUCINA CON FERNANDA GOSETTI

Spaghetti with Prosciutto and Basil Sauce

To serve 4 to 6

1 lb.	spaghetti, boiled and drained	½ kg.
¼ lb.	thinly sliced prosciutto, cut into shreds	125 g.
½ cup	fresh basil leaves, chopped	125 ml.
4 tbsp.	butter	60 ml.
1	onion, chopped	1
1	garlic clove	1
2	large tomatoes, cut into thin wedges	2
6	sprigs fresh parsley, the leaves chopped	6
½ cup	dry red wine	125 ml.
	freshly ground pepper	
	freshly grated Parmesan cheese	

Toss the prosciutto in hot butter until it is browned. Add the onion, and the garlic clove speared on a toothpick for easy removal later. Add the tomatoes, parsley, basil, wine and pepper. Simmer for five to 10 minutes. Remove the garlic and discard it. Add the sauce to the cooked spaghetti and toss together. Serve with grated Parmesan cheese.

HARRIET HANDS
MORE TASTE THAN MONEY

Tagliatelle with Prosciutto

Tagliatelle al Prosciutto

To serve 6

1½ lb.	tagliatelle	¾ kg.
5 oz.	thinly sliced prosciutto, cut into strips ¼ inch [6 mm.] wide	150 g.
8 tbsp.	butter	120 ml.
½ cup	freshly grated Parmesan cheese	125 ml.
	freshly ground black pepper	

Bring a pan of lightly salted water to a boil and add the tagliatelle. Meanwhile, put the butter in a small saucepan over very low heat. As soon as the butter is just melted, add the strips of prosciutto. The prosciutto must simply be heated—it must not fry.

When the tagliatelle is cooked, drain and place on a warmed serving dish. Sprinkle the tagliatelle with the grated Parmesan, grind a fair amount of pepper over it, add the ham and butter, mix, and send to the table.

ENRICA AND VERNON JARRATT
THE COMPLETE BOOK OF PASTA

Sausages and Sea Shells

Maruzelle, also called conchigliette, are the smallish shells you'll be looking for among the spirals, bows, rings and ruffled pastas to be found in almost any supermarket. If you can't find shells, use some other pasta—for instance, farfalle (bows) or the little springs called fusilli.

To serve 4

1 lb.	maruzelle	½ kg.
6	Italian sweet or hot sausages	6
2 tbsp.	butter or olive oil	30 ml.
1	onion	1
1	garlic clove, finely chopped	1
	chopped fresh parsley	
2	fresh tomatoes, seeded and chopped	2
	freshly grated Parmesan cheese	

Prick each of the sausages with a sharp fork, cover them with cold water, and bring to a boil. Simmer, uncovered, for about 10 minutes, drain and dry, and slice them into rounds ¼ inch [6 mm.] thick. Heat the butter or oil in a skillet and add the sausage, onion, garlic and 2 tablespoons [30 ml.] of parsley. Stirring often, cook until the meat and vegetables

are golden brown; then add the tomatoes, cover and simmer while you prepare the pasta.

Cook the maruzelle until its texture is *al dente;* drain in a colander but do not rinse it. Mix the sausage and its sauce with the hot pasta, sprinkle with more parsley and serve at once on hot plates. Pass the cheese at the table.

MIRIAM UNGERER
GOOD CHEAP FOOD

Vermicelli Catalan-Style

Fideos a la Catalana

Chorizos are spicy, garlic-flavored Spanish sausages, obtainable where Spanish or Latin American foods are sold.

To serve 4

1 lb.	vermicelli or spaghetti	½ kg.
10 oz.	pork spareribs, chopped into small chunks with a cleaver	300 g.
2 tbsp.	lard	30 ml.
1	onion, chopped	1
2	medium-sized tomatoes, peeled, seeded and chopped	2
2 tbsp.	chopped fresh parsley	30 ml.
3½ oz.	*chorizos* or other spicy garlic-flavored frying sausages, cut in pieces	100 g.
1 quart	boiling water	1 liter
	salt	

In a large saucepan, fry the spareribs in the lard over medium heat. When the spareribs are lightly browned, add the onion. When the onion begins to brown, add the tomatoes and parsley. Add the sausages and cook, stirring occasionally, for five or six minutes.

Break the vermicelli or spaghetti into lengths to fit the saucepan. Stir them into the meat mixture, then pour in the boiling water. Season with salt, cover the pan and simmer for 10 minutes, or until the pasta is cooked and most of the water is absorbed.

VICTORIA SERRA
TIA VICTORIA'S SPANISH KITCHEN

Fettucini with Garlic, Tomatoes and Garlic Sausages

Tagliatelle alla Romagnola

The authors suggest that you may use either commercial or homemade pasta.

To serve 4 to 6

1 lb.	fettucini	½ kg.
3	garlic cloves, chopped	3
14 to 16 oz.	canned Italian-style tomatoes, with the liquid reserved	400 to 500 g.
12	small fresh garlic sausages, each pricked in 2 or 3 places with a fork	12
3 tbsp.	olive oil	45 ml.
	chopped fresh parsley	
	salt and pepper	

Cook the pasta in boiling salted water until just soft.

Meanwhile make the following sauce with sausages: Heat the olive oil in a heavy frying pan. In it gently fry the garlic, some parsley and the sausages. When the sausages are nearly cooked, add the tomatoes and their liquid. Season with salt and pepper to taste. Let the sauce and sausages stew for 10 minutes.

Drain the fettucini and lay it in a dish, making a well in the middle. Arrange the sausages in the middle, pour in the sauce and sprinkle with grated Parmesan. Serve very hot.

JANET ROSS AND MICHAEL WATERFIELD
LEAVES FROM OUR TUSCAN KITCHEN

━━━━━◆━━━━━

Fresh Noodles with Pork and Tomato

Nouilles au Lard

The techniques of rolling out pasta dough and cutting it into noodles are demonstrated on pages 16-19 and 22-23.

To serve 4

¾ lb.	pasta dough (recipe, page 164), cut into noodles	⅓ kg.
½ lb.	fresh pork belly	¼ kg.
6 or 7	medium-sized tomatoes (2 lb. [1 kg.])	6 or 7
2	garlic cloves, finely chopped	2
8	fresh mint leaves, or substitute fresh basil leaves	8
	coarse salt	
	freshly ground pepper	

Cut 1 ounce [30 g.] of the noodles into 1-inch [2½-cm.] pieces. Set them aside.

Remove the rind from the pork belly and cut the pork into

lardons—strips about 1 inch [2½ cm.] long and ¼ inch [6 mm.] thick. Place them in a saucepan, cover with cold water and bring to a boil. Blanch the lardons for three minutes, then drain them in a sieve.

Drop the tomatoes into boiling water. Count to 10, drain, and plunge them into cold water. Peel and seed the tomatoes, squeezing out excess water, then pass them through a fine sieve or a food mill. Turn the sieved tomatoes into a medium-sized saucepan, add the garlic and mint leaves, and bring to a boil. Cook the sauce for five minutes, then cool slightly and remove the mint leaves.

Lightly brown the pork lardons in a small skillet over low heat. Allow 20 to 30 minutes for this operation. Remove the lardons with half of their cooking fat and set them aside.

Fry the 1 ounce [30 g.] of cut noodles in the remaining fat for about three minutes, or until crisp and nicely browned. Set them aside.

Plunge the remaining noodles into a large kettle of boiling salted water. Cook for seven to eight minutes, or until just done *(al dente)*. Stop the cooking by adding a cup [¼ liter] of cold water and drain the noodles immediately in a colander. With fresh noodles the cooking time varies, depending upon their thickness; begin to check on their degree of doneness after three minutes.

While the noodles are cooking, warm the tomato sauce over very low heat. Do the same with the lardons.

As soon as the noodles have been well drained, return them to the hot kettle in which they were cooked. Pour the tomato sauce over the noodles and add the drained lardons with their extra fat. Add a liberal grinding of pepper, taste for salt, and mix well with a large fork. Turn the noodles into a wide heated serving bowl and sprinkle them with the crisp fried noodles. Serve at once.

JEAN & PIERRE TROISGROS
THE NOUVELLE CUISINE OF JEAN & PIERRE TROISGROS

━━━━━◆━━━━━

Spaghetti with Bacon and Eggs

Spaghetti alla Carbonara

To serve 4

¾ lb.	spaghetti	⅓ kg.
¼ lb.	*pancetta*, or substitute slab bacon with the rind removed, cut into small strips (about 1 cup [¼ liter])	125 g.
4	egg yolks	4
1 tbsp.	olive oil or butter	15 ml.
2 tbsp.	light cream	30 ml.
⅔ cup	freshly grated Parmesan cheese	150 ml.
	freshly ground black pepper	

Put the oil or butter into a fairly large skillet, add the *pancetta* or bacon, and fry it lightly over medium heat until the fat has melted. Remove from the heat and set aside, keeping the skillet warm.

Cook the spaghetti in plenty of boiling salted water. Meanwhile, beat the egg yolks in a bowl with a whisk. Then whisk in the cream and half of the Parmesan, and grind in a generous amount of black pepper (you can vary the amount to taste).

When the spaghetti is still very firm to the bite, drain it; transfer it to the skillet with the bacon, and place over medium heat. Stir the spaghetti so that it absorbs the flavor of the *pancetta* or bacon, then remove the skillet from the heat and pour the egg mixture over the spaghetti. Stir quickly and serve straight away on warmed individual plates. Serve the remaining Parmesan separately.

ANNA MARTINI (EDITOR)
PASTA AND PIZZA

Chicken-Liver Spaghetti Sauce

This dish is said to have been a favorite with the immortal tenor Enrico Caruso. Pine nuts, browned in olive oil, may be added to this dish for a wonderful variation.

To serve 4 to 6

1 lb.	spaghetti, boiled and drained	½ kg.
¼ lb.	raw chicken livers, cut into small pieces (1 cup [¼ liter])	125 g.
2	garlic cloves, crushed to a paste	2
2 tbsp.	olive oil	30 ml.
2 tbsp.	butter	30 ml.
¼ cup	finely chopped scallions	50 ml.
2	small tomatoes, peeled, seeded and chopped or 1 cup [¼ liter] drained, canned tomatoes	2
½ cup	sliced fresh mushrooms	125 ml.
½ cup	dry white wine	125 ml.
	salt and pepper	
	rosemary	
	melted butter	
	freshly grated Parmesan cheese	

Cook the garlic in the olive oil and butter until soft. Remove and discard the garlic, and to the pan add the finely chopped scallions and the raw chicken liver. Cook gently for four minutes or so, then add the tomatoes, mushrooms, white wine, salt, pepper and a little rosemary. Simmer the sauce slowly for 20 minutes, correct the seasoning, and serve with spaghetti that has been dressed with melted butter. Pass freshly grated Parmesan.

HELEN BROWN
HELEN BROWN'S WEST COAST COOK BOOK

Shells San Marino

Sardo is the Sardinian name for pecorino Romano, the most common of the Italian pecorino—or sheep's milk—cheeses.

To serve 8

1 lb.	pasta shells	½ kg.
3	chicken breasts, boned and skinned	3
2 tbsp.	flour	30 ml.
2 tbsp.	olive oil	30 ml.
2 tbsp.	butter	30 ml.
½ cup	dry white wine or dry vermouth	125 ml.
¾ cup	milk, heated to boiling	175 ml.
	salt and freshly ground white pepper	
2	egg yolks, beaten	2
1½ cups	freshly grated Parmesan cheese, or a mixture of Parmesan, Romano and Sardo cheeses	375 ml.
¾ cup	heavy cream, heated to lukewarm	175 ml.

Place the chicken breasts between sheets of wax paper, and with a heavy mallet or meat cleaver pound them to a thickness of about ½ inch [1 cm.]. Dust the breasts with 1 tablespoon [15 ml.] of the flour. Heat the olive oil and butter in a heavy sauté pan or skillet and sauté the breasts until golden. Remove the breasts from the pan, toss them with the rest of the flour and return them to the pan. Stir in the wine and cook over medium-high heat until the wine is reduced by half. Add the milk, and salt and pepper to taste, and stir to blend thoroughly. Remove the pan from the heat and carefully stir in the egg yolks. Return the pan to the heat, cover and simmer very gently for 25 minutes.

Meanwhile, cook the shells in 8 quarts [8 liters] of boiling salted water for about 15 minutes. They should be just *al dente*, or firm to the bite. Drain and put the shells in a preheated 4-quart [4-liter] serving bowl. Add all of the sauce and ¾ cup [175 ml.] of the grated cheese. Toss until thoroughly mixed. Add the heavy cream and toss again to mix. Cover with the remaining ¾ cup of grated cheese, and correct the seasoning, if necessary.

JUNIOR LEAGUE OF THE CITY OF NEW YORK
NEW YORK ENTERTAINS

Chicken Potpie

The technique of preparing chicken potpie is on page 40.

	To serve 6 to 8	
½ lb.	pasta dough *(recipe, page 164)*, cut into 2-inch [5-cm.] potpie squares	¼ kg.
5 to 6 lb.	roasting chicken, cut into 6 or 8 pieces	2½ to 3 kg.
4 quarts	water	4 liters
2	medium-sized celery ribs, including the green leaves, cut into 3-inch [8-cm.] pieces	2
¼ tsp.	crumbled saffron threads or ground saffron	1 ml.
5 tsp.	salt	25 ml.
6	whole black peppercorns	6
½ cup	coarsely chopped celery	125 ml.
2	medium-sized boiling potatoes, peeled and coarsely chopped	2
2 tbsp.	finely chopped fresh parsley	30 ml.
	freshly ground black pepper	

Combine the chicken and water in a heavy 6- to 8-quart [6- to 8-liter] casserole and bring to a boil over high heat, skimming off the foam and scum as they rise to the surface. Add the pieces of celery, the saffron, 3 teaspoons [15 ml.] of the salt and the peppercorns, and reduce the heat to low. Simmer partially covered for approximately one hour, or until the chicken shows no resistance when a thigh is pierced deeply with a small knife.

With a slotted spoon, transfer the chicken to a plate. Strain the stock through a fine sieve and return 2 quarts [2 liters] to the casserole. (Reserve the remaining stock for another use.) With a knife, remove the skin from the chicken and cut the meat from the bones. Discard the skin and bones; slice the meat into 1-inch [2½-cm.] pieces and set aside.

Add the chopped celery, potatoes and the remaining 2 teaspoons [10 ml.] of salt to the casserole and bring to a boil over high heat. Drop in the potpie squares and stir briefly, then cook briskly, uncovered, for about 15 minutes, until the noodles are tender.

Stir in the reserved chicken and the parsley, and cook for a minute or so to heat them. Taste and season with more salt, if desired, and a few grindings of pepper. To serve, ladle the potpie into heated individual bowls.

FOODS OF THE WORLD
AMERICAN COOKING: THE EASTERN HEARTLAND

Spaghetti with Cuttlefish in Its Ink

Pasta cu Niuru di Sicci

To prepare cuttlefish, slice the body pouch open carefully with a sharp knife, slitting along the back from head to tail; avoid damaging the ink sac. Remove the cuttlebone, cut out the ink sac and reserve it. Scoop out and discard the viscera. Remove and discard the tentacles and beaklike mouth. If the cuttlefish is fresh, the ink will be liquid. If frozen, it will have solidified; remove the granules from the sac and dissolve them in a tablespoonful [15 ml.] of boiling water, stock or wine. Pecorino is the Italian word for sheep's milk. The most common pecorino cheese is pecorino Romano, a very sharp grating cheese, obtainable at cheese specialty stores.

	To serve 4	
1¼ lb.	spaghettini, cooked	⅔ kg.
1¼ cups	grated aged pecorino cheese	300 ml.
	Cuttlefish sauce	
1 lb.	cuttlefish, boned and ink sacs reserved, sliced into thin strips	½ kg.
1	onion, thinly sliced	1
¼ cup	olive oil	50 ml.
¼ cup	chopped fresh parsley	50 ml.
4 or 5	plum tomatoes, peeled and coarsely chopped	4 or 5
	salt and pepper	

Open the ink sacs and carefully pour the ink into a bowl. Brown the onion in hot oil with the parsley, then add the tomatoes and cuttlefish. Stir the mixture constantly and cook over medium heat for about 15 minutes, or until the liquid is reduced slightly. Then add the ink and seasoning. The sauce will take on a brownish hue with topaz reflections, due to the mingling of the oil and the tomato with the ink. Pour this dark, savory sauce over the cooked spaghetti and sprinkle with the grated cheese.

PINO CORRENTI
IL LIBRO D'ORO DELLA CUCINA E DEI VINI DI SICILIA

Spaghetti with Clams and Tomato Sauce

Vermicelli alle Vongole con i Pelati

The Italian title of this classic recipe uses the colloquial Neapolitan term, "vermicelli" for spaghetti. To prepare clams for cooking, first examine each one and discard any that is open; grasp each closed shell in both hands and try to rotate the top and bottom halves in opposite directions; if the halves move, discard the clam. Scrub each clam vigorously with a stiff brush under cold running water, then wash the clams by soaking them in a pan of lightly salted water for several hours. Change the water if it becomes muddied.

	To serve 8	
1¼ lb.	spaghetti, boiled	⅔ kg.
48	live littleneck clams, scrubbed and drained	48
8	medium-sized tomatoes, peeled, seeded and chopped	8
⅔ cup	olive oil	150 ml.
2	garlic cloves, chopped	2
	pepper	
	chopped fresh parsley	

Pour 6 tablespoons [90 ml.] of the oil into a frying pan. Heat the oil and add the clams. When the shells open, remove the clams from the pan. Discard the shells and put the clams aside. Over medium heat, reduce the clams' cooking liquid to half its original volume. Strain the liquid through a fine sieve or a piece of muslin and let it cool.

In a saucepan, heat the remaining oil and fry the garlic in it until golden. Remove the garlic from the pan. Add the tomatoes to the pan and season with pepper. Boil for three or four minutes over high heat. Add the clams' cooking liquid and cook until the sauce is thick. Add the clams and the parsley and simmer for three or four more minutes.

Pour three quarters of the sauce over the freshly boiled and drained spaghetti and serve the rest in a sauceboat.

JEANNE CARÒLA FRANCESCONI
LA CUCINA NAPOLETANA

Linguini with White Clam Sauce

	To serve 6	
1½ lb.	linguini	¾ kg.
36	live small hard-shell clams	36
4 tbsp.	butter	60 ml.
4 tbsp.	olive oil	60 ml.
1	garlic clove, crushed to a paste	1
¼ tsp.	freshly ground black pepper	1 ml.
2 tbsp.	finely chopped fresh parsley	30 ml.
½ tsp.	dried oregano	2 ml.
¼ cup	dry white wine	50 ml.
1 tsp.	salt	5 ml.

Open the clams, cut out the flesh and discard the shells. Wash the clams thoroughly under cold running water.

Melt the butter with 2 tablespoons [30 ml.] of the olive oil in a small saucepan. Add the crushed garlic, the pepper, parsley, oregano, wine and the washed clams. Cover and cook gently over low heat for 15 minutes.

While the sauce is cooking, bring 4 quarts [4 liters] of water to a boil in a large stockpot or saucepan. Add the salt and the remaining 2 tablespoons of olive oil, then the linguini. The linguini should be added a little at a time so that the water continues to boil. Cook for exactly eight minutes, then drain in a colander.

Transfer the hot linguini to a serving dish or platter, pour the hot clam sauce over, and serve immediately.

PAUL RUBINSTEIN
JUST GOOD FOOD

Mussels with Green Pasta

Cozze con Pasta Verde

For the technique of cleaning mussels, see the editor's note for Spaghetti with Mussels, page 111.

	To serve 4 to 6	
1 lb.	spinach-pasta dough (recipe, page 165), cut into noodles	½ kg.
48 to 54	live mussels, cleaned	48 to 54
1	garlic clove, halved	1
1 cup	dry white wine	¼ liter
2 tbsp.	butter	30 ml.
⅓ cup	olive oil	75 ml.
¼ cup	fresh lemon juice	50 ml.
3	medium-sized fresh tomatoes, not too ripe, cored, blanched, peeled, seeded and chopped into ½-inch [1-cm.] pieces	3

Put the mussels in a large, covered saucepan. Add the garlic pieces and the wine. Cover the pan and steam the mussels over low heat until the shells open. Discard any unopened ones. Remove the mussels from their shells, being careful to capture all of the juices for the sauce. Discard the shells.

Cook the pasta until it is *al dente*. Drain it and return it to the saucepan in which it was cooked. Add the butter, olive oil, lemon juice and the juice from the steamed mussels. Also add half of the mussels and half of the fresh tomatoes, and toss the pasta well.

Empty the mixture of pasta and sauce into a large bowl or platter, or divide for individual servings. Arrange the remaining mussels and tomato pieces on top of the pasta. The cool tomato pieces, uncooked, contribute to a wonderful combination of textures and tastes.

JOE FAMULARO & LOUISE IMPERIALE
THE FESTIVE FAMULARO KITCHEN

Oysters with Spaghetti

To serve 4 to 6

1½ lb.	spaghetti	¾ kg.
about 48	freshly shucked live oysters (1 quart [1 liter]), well drained	about 48
8 tbsp.	butter	120 ml.
½ cup	olive oil	125 ml.
6	large garlic cloves, cut into large pieces	6
1 tsp.	basil	5 ml.
2 tbsp.	finely chopped fresh parsley	30 ml.
1 tsp.	freshly ground black pepper	5 ml.
½ tsp.	salt	2 ml.

Melt the butter over low heat in a large sauté pan or saucepan. Add the ½ cup [125 ml.] of olive oil and mix thoroughly. Continue cooking for three minutes, then increase the heat to medium and add the garlic. Cook for about four or five minutes, until the garlic just begins to turn brown. With a slotted spoon, quickly remove the garlic and discard it. Add the basil, parsley, pepper and ½ teaspoon [2 ml.] of salt to the butter and oil, and simmer for about four minutes. Add the drained oysters and cook over low heat for about five minutes, until the oysters just begin to curl at the edges. Remove the pan from the heat, cover loosely and set aside while you cook the spaghetti.

To cook the spaghetti, combine 6 quarts [6 liters] of water, 2 tablespoons [30 ml.] of salt and 1 tablespoon [15 ml.] of olive oil in a large saucepan or kettle. Bring to a rolling boil, then add the spaghetti. When the water boils up again, cook for eight to 10 minutes, checking for doneness after eight minutes. When the spaghetti is cooked, dump the contents of the pan into a large colander placed in the sink. Allow the spaghetti to drain thoroughly, then return it to the large pan and add the olive-oil-and-oyster mixture. Mix gently but thoroughly, using a long fork and a smooth circular motion. Cover the saucepan and allow to stand for about eight minutes before serving. If you have a heavy pan, no additional heat is required; if you do not, set the pan on a warming tray or in a 200° F. [100° C.] oven.

To serve, toss the spaghetti and oysters thoroughly with the long fork in order to distribute the sauce, which tends to settle to the bottom of the pan. Serve in preheated, wide soup or spaghetti bowls, taking care to place a generous quantity of oysters on top of each portion.

RIMA AND RICHARD COLLIN
THE PLEASURES OF SEAFOOD

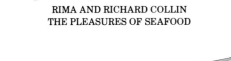

Spaghettini with Shrimp Tasca

The volatile oils in hot chilies may make your skin sting and your eyes burn; wear rubber gloves when handling them and avoid touching your face.

To serve 5 or 6

1 lb.	spaghettini	½ kg.
½ lb.	raw small shrimp, shelled and diced	¼ kg.
2 tbsp.	olive oil	30 ml.
1	dried hot chili	1
	salt and freshly ground black pepper	
3	garlic cloves, finely chopped	3
3 tbsp.	finely chopped fresh parsley	45 ml.
1 cup	finely diced green pepper	¼ liter
½ cup	green peas, cooked	125 ml.
Tomato sauce		
5 or 6	large ripe tomatoes, peeled, seeded and chopped, or 35 oz. [1 kg.] canned Italian-style tomatoes, drained and chopped	5 or 6
3 tbsp.	olive oil	45 ml.
2 tbsp.	finely chopped shallots	30 ml.
2 tbsp.	finely chopped fresh parsley	30 ml.
1 tsp.	finely chopped garlic	5 ml.
1 tsp.	tomato paste	5 ml.
	salt and freshly ground black pepper	
2 tbsp.	finely chopped fresh basil or 1 tsp. [5 ml.] dried basil	30 ml.
2 tbsp.	finely chopped fresh oregano or 1 tsp. [5 ml.] dried oregano	30 ml.
1	bay leaf	1

Start by making the sauce. In a 10-inch [25-cm.] heavy cast-iron skillet, heat the olive oil over low heat. Add the shallots, parsley and garlic, and cook the mixture for one or two minutes without browning it. Add the tomato paste and tomatoes. Season with salt and pepper, the basil and oregano, and add the bay leaf. Bring to a boil, reduce the heat, and simmer the tomato sauce, partially covered, for 25 to 30 minutes. When the tomato sauce is done, set it aside.

In another 10-inch cast-iron skillet, heat the 2 tablespoons [30 ml.] of olive oil, add the chili and cook until the chili turns dark. Discard the chili.

Add the shrimp to the oil and sauté over high heat until they turn bright pink. Season with salt and pepper, reduce the heat, and add the garlic, parsley, green pepper and peas. Toss the mixture and cook for two minutes without letting the parsley or garlic burn. Immediately add the tomato sauce and heat the mixture. Taste and correct the seasoning, then keep the shrimp-and-tomato sauce warm.

In a large, heavy casserole, bring 3 or 4 quarts [3 or 4 liters] of salted water to a boil. Add the spaghettini and cook, stirring with a wooden spoon to prevent the spaghettini from sticking to the bottom of the casserole. Cook for seven or eight minutes, or until the spaghettini is barely tender. Drain and return it to the casserole.

Add the shrimp-and-tomato sauce to the casserole, and toss the sauce and spaghettini with two forks. Add a generous grinding of black pepper and serve hot.

PERLA MEYERS
PERLA MEYERS' FROM MARKET TO KITCHEN COOKBOOK

Ziti with Cauliflower, Sardine and Anchovy Sauce

Pasta Palina o a la Paulata

To serve 6

1¼ lb.	ziti	⅔ kg.
1	large head cauliflower (about 2 lb. [1 kg.]), cored and separated into florets	1
	olive oil	
3½ oz.	fresh sardines or anchovies, filleted	100 g.
2 oz.	salt anchovies, filleted, soaked in water for 30 minutes, rinsed and patted dry	60 g.
½	medium-sized onion, sliced	½
1	garlic clove	1
4	whole cloves, crushed	4
	ground cinnamon	
1 cup	puréed tomato *(recipe, page 167)*	¼ liter
	freshly ground black pepper	

Boil the cauliflower florets in salted water for about five minutes. Drain, reserving the cooking water. In a large saucepan, lightly fry the florets in oil together with the fresh sardine or anchovy fillets, onion and garlic. Add the cloves, a pinch of cinnamon and the puréed tomato. Simmer for 10 to 15 minutes, then add the salt anchovy fillets and cook until these disintegrate into the sauce—about five minutes.

Boil the pasta in the cauliflower water until firm to the bite. Drain, and stir the pasta into the pan with the sauce. Add freshly ground pepper at the moment of serving.

PINO CORRENTI
IL LIBRO D'ORO DELLA CUCINA E DEI VINI DI SICILIA

Spaghetti with Mussels

Vermicelli alle "Cozze" in Bianco

The Italian title of this classic recipe uses the colloquial Neapolitan term, "vermicelli," for spaghetti. To prepare mussels for cooking, first examine each one and discard any that is open. Grasp each closed shell in both hands and try to rotate the top and bottom halves in opposite directions; if the halves move, discard the mussel. Scrape each mussel to remove its beard and any other growths from the shell, then scrub the mussels with a brush and soak them in lightly salted water for several hours. Change the water if it becomes muddied.

To serve 6

1¼ lb.	spaghetti, boiled, drained and kept hot	⅔ kg.
about 40	live mussels, scrubbed and debearded	about 40
2	garlic cloves, whole or chopped	2
3 tbsp.	oil	45 ml.
	freshly ground black pepper	
	chopped fresh parsley	

In a large frying pan, lightly fry the garlic in the oil. If you put the cloves in whole, remove them as soon as they brown; if you have chopped them, cook them until they sizzle but do not remove them. Add pepper to taste and the mussels. Stir the mixture. Cover the pan. As the mussels open, remove them one by one from the pan and put them in a bowl. When all of the mussels have been removed from the pan, after about five minutes, continue simmering the remaining liquid to reduce its volume.

Shell the mussels and return them to the frying pan. Add the chopped parsley and cook over medium heat for two or three minutes.

Moisten the freshly boiled and drained spaghetti with some of the juices from the frying pan. Present the mussels with the cooking liquid in a large sauceboat so that each diner can serve himself.

JEANNE CARÒLA FRANCESCONI
LA CUCINA NAPOLETANA

Linguini with Capers, Olives and Anchovies

Linguine Capperi Olive e Acciughe

To serve 6

1¼ lb.	linguini or spaghetti	⅔ kg.
¾ cup	salted capers, rinsed	175 ml.
⅔ cup	Mediterranean black olives, pitted	150 ml.
3½ oz.	salt anchovies, filleted, soaked in water for 30 minutes, rinsed, patted dry and thinly sliced	100 g.
2	garlic cloves	2
⅔ cup	olive oil	150 ml.
2 tbsp.	water	30 ml.
⅓ cup	chopped fresh parsley	75 ml.
	pepper	

Lightly fry the garlic in the oil. Add the capers, olives, water, parsley and pepper. Cook for four or five minutes. Remove the pan from the heat. Add the anchovies and stir until they disintegrate. Bring a pan of lightly salted water to a boil. Throw in the pasta and cook until it is *al dente*. Drain the pasta and serve very hot with the sauce poured over it.

JEANNE CARÒLA FRANCESCONI
LA CUCINA NAPOLETANA

Carinthian Cheese Dumplings

Käsenockerln nach Kärnter Art

The amount of flour used in the dough is approximate because it depends on the potatoes' mealiness. Start with half of the stated amount and add to produce a firm, dry dough.

To make 25 to 30 dumplings

2	large potatoes (1 lb. [½ kg.])	2
2½ cups	flour	625 ml.
¼ tsp.	salt	1 ml.
1	egg, beaten	1
	freshly grated Parmesan cheese	
2 tbsp.	butter	30 ml.

Cottage-cheese-and-mint filling

½ cup	creamed cottage cheese	125 ml.
1 tbsp.	chopped fresh mint	15 ml.
	salt and pepper	
4 tbsp.	butter, melted	60 ml.

Cook the whole potatoes in unsalted water; while still hot, peel and rice them. Combine the flour, salt, egg and ¼ cup

[50 ml.] grated Parmesan. Cut in the butter and knead to make a firm, dry dough. Roll out the dough ⅛ inch [3 mm.] thick on a floured board. Cut it into 3-inch [8-cm.] squares.

Beat together the cottage cheese, mint, salt and pepper to taste, and 2 tablespoons [30 ml.] of melted butter. Place about 1 teaspoon [5 ml.] of mixture in the center of each potato-dough square; fold the square into a triangle, pressing the edges firmly together. Cook, covered, for 10 minutes in gently boiling salted water. Drain; run under cold water and drain again. Swirl the remaining melted butter in the emptied but still hot pan used for boiling the dumplings. Gently toss the dumplings in the butter until they are glossy and hot. If desired, sprinkle with additional grated Parmesan. Serve as a main luncheon course with a green salad.

MARCIA COLMAN MORTON
THE ART OF VIENNESE COOKING

Cottage Cheese Vareniki

An additional egg or egg yolk, or some thick sour cream, may be used in the filling if the cottage cheese is very dry.

To serve 6

2 cups	flour	½ liter
1 tsp.	salt	5 ml.
1 lb.	cottage cheese	½ kg.
1	egg, lightly beaten	1
about ⅓ cup	milk	about 75 ml.
	melted butter	
	bread crumbs, browned in butter	
	sour cream (optional)	
	fried bacon, crumbled (optional)	

Cottage-cheese filling

1 lb.	dry cottage cheese	½ kg.
1	egg, lightly beaten	1
	salt	

For the dough, first mix the flour with the salt. Press the cottage cheese through a sieve and combine it with the egg and milk. Stir in the flour and knead to make a soft dough. Cover and let the dough stand for 10 minutes.

To make the filling, combine the cottage cheese with the egg, and season to taste with salt. The filling should be thick enough to hold its shape in a spoon.

Roll the dough quite thin on a floured board. Cut rounds with a large biscuit cutter or with the rim of a glass. For speedier work, the dough may be cut into 2- to 2½-inch [5- to 6-cm.] squares. Put a round or square of dough on the palm of your hand. Place a spoonful of the cheese filling on the dough, fold it over to form a half circle or triangle, and press the edges together with your fingers. The edges should be free of filling. Be sure that the edges are sealed well to prevent the filling from running out. Place the vareniki on a floured board or a cloth kitchen towel without crowding them. Cover with a towel to prevent drying.

Drop a few vareniki at a time into a large quantity of rapidly boiling salted water. Do not attempt to cook too many at a time. Stir very gently with a wooden spoon to separate the vareniki and to prevent them from sticking to the bottom of the pot. Continue boiling rapidly for three or four minutes. The cooking period will depend on the size of the vareniki and the thickness of the dough. Vareniki are ready when they are well puffed. With a perforated spoon or skimmer, remove them to a colander and drain thoroughly. Place in a deep dish, sprinkle generously with melted butter, and toss very gently to coat the vareniki evenly with butter and prevent them from sticking. Cover and keep them hot until all are cooked. Serve in a large dish without piling or crowding them. Top with bread crumbs. The traditional accompaniment is sour cream or crumbled bacon, or both.

SAVELLA STECHISHIN
TRADITIONAL UKRAINIAN COOKERY

Cheese and Spinach Ravioli
Raviolis

Broccio is a Corsican cheese, very similar to ricotta and made from goat's or sheep's milk, or a combination of both. It is creamy when newly made and becomes a grating cheese when aged. It is unavailable in the United States but you may substitute fresh ricotta or farmer cheese for creamy broccio, and pecorino Romano or Parmesan for aged broccio.

To serve 4 to 6

1½ lb.	pasta dough (recipe, page 164)	¾ kg.
1¼ cups	tomato sauce (recipe, page 166)	300 ml.
⅔ cup	grated aged *broccio*	150 ml.
Cheese-and-spinach filling		
14 oz.	creamy *broccio*	400 g.
1 lb.	spinach, parboiled for 3 minutes, drained, squeezed dry and finely chopped	½ kg.
10 oz.	corn salad, finely chopped	300 g.
1	fennel bulb, parboiled for 10 minutes, drained and finely chopped	1
5 to 10	fresh mint leaves, finely chopped	5 to 10
5 to 10	fresh sage leaves, finely chopped	5 to 10
	salt	

Mash the creamy *broccio,* mix it thoroughly with all of the greens and season with salt. Roll out the dough as thin as possible, and cut it into rectangles about 1¼ by 1½ inches [3

by 4 cm.]. Place a little of the stuffing mixture on each rectangle; fold the rectangle over and pinch the edges together.

Poach the ravioli in boiling salted water for about five minutes. Drain, and serve with the tomato sauce and the grated cheese on top.

CHRISTIANE SCHAPIRA
LA CUISINE CORSE

Tortellini with Cream Sauce
Tortellini alla Panna

The square shapes referred to as tortellini in this recipe are more commonly known as ravioli. The technique of making ravioli is demonstrated on page 25.

To serve 6

1 lb.	pasta dough (recipe, page 164)	½ kg.
Spinach filling		
½ lb.	spinach, parboiled for 3 minutes, drained, squeezed dry and chopped	¼ kg.
½ lb.	ricotta or farmer cheese	¼ kg.
1 cup	freshly grated Parmesan cheese	¼ liter
2	eggs, beaten	2
	ground allspice	
	salt and freshly ground black pepper	
Cream sauce		
2 cups	heavy cream	½ liter
2 tbsp.	butter	30 ml.
3 tbsp.	freshly grated Parmesan cheese	45 ml.

Mix together the spinach, ricotta or farmer cheese, the cup [¼ liter] of grated Parmesan, the eggs and a pinch of allspice, and season with a little salt and pepper.

On a floured board, roll out the pasta dough into one thin sheet. Put small spoonfuls of the spinach-and-cheese mixture in straight rows about 2 inches [5 cm.] apart on half of the sheet. Fold over the remaining half of the pasta and press, quite firmly, between the mounds of stuffing. Cut the ravioli with a pastry wheel and allow them to stand for a short while. Then cook them in boiling salted water for five minutes or until tender.

Remove the cooked ravioli with a perforated spoon and place them in a warmed serving dish. Cover them with a cream sauce made by swirling the cream, butter and grated Parmesan over medium heat until the mixture thickens. Serve very hot and pass more grated Parmesan and a mill of black pepper at the table.

FRANCO LAGATTOLLA
THE RECIPES THAT MADE A MILLION

Green Roll

Rotolo Verde

The technique of making a pasta roll is shown on pages 36-37. In this recipe, the mixture is halved to make two rolls.

To serve 4		
2 cups	flour	½ liter
2	eggs	2
1 tbsp.	water	15 ml.
7 tbsp.	butter	100 ml.
⅓ cup	freshly grated Parmesan cheese	75 ml.
	Spinach-and-ricotta-cheese filling	
2 lb.	spinach, washed	1 kg.
½ lb.	ricotta cheese	¼ kg.
3 tbsp.	butter	45 ml.
3 tbsp.	freshly grated Parmesan cheese	45 ml.
	salt and pepper	

To make the filling, cook the spinach in the water remaining on the leaves after washing. Drain the spinach, squeeze it dry and then chop it. In a skillet, brown the butter, add the spinach and stir over low heat for about five minutes. Sieve the ricotta. Remove the spinach from the heat, add the ricotta, the grated Parmesan cheese, some salt and pepper. Mix well and set aside to cool.

To make the pasta dough, sift the flour onto a board, make a well in the flour and into it break the eggs. Add the water, and knead the flour and eggs for about 10 minutes until the pasta dough is firm. Divide the mixture in half. Put one half in a plastic bag to keep it from drying out, and roll out the other half into a strip about 10 inches by 20 inches [25 cm. by 50 cm.], or to fit the length of the oval casserole or fish poacher in which the roll is to be cooked.

Using a spatula, spread half of the spinach mixture evenly over the rolled-out pasta. Then, starting from one of the short sides, roll up the pasta, enclosing the spinach filling. Wrap the roll in a piece of cheesecloth. Tie the cloth at both ends and in the middle. Repeat the same process to roll and fill the other piece of pasta dough.

Fill a deep oval casserole or fish poacher with salted water. When the water boils, add the pasta rolls and cook for 40 minutes to one hour. The rolls must remain immersed in the water throughout the cooking period; add more boiling water if necessary.

Melt the butter over low heat. Take one roll at a time from the water, remove the cloth and slice the roll into ½-inch [1-cm.] rounds with a sharp knife. Put each slice into a casserole as you cut it. When you have made one layer, sprinkle it with a little of the melted butter and with grated Parmesan cheese. Add a second layer, and so on, repeating the process until both pasta rolls have been used up.

Stand the casserole containing the sliced pasta rolls in a bain-marie containing boiling water. Make sure no water gets into the casserole. Cover and simmer for a few minutes to let the pasta absorb the flavors of the butter and cheese. The dish may be kept warm this way for up to 30 minutes.

FERNANDA GOSETTI
IN CUCINA CON FERNANDA GOSETTI

Pierogi with Potato and Cheese Stuffing

Pierogi z Ziemniakami i Serem

To serve 4		
3 cups	flour	¾ liter
1	egg	1
	water	
4 tbsp.	butter	60 ml.
	Potato-and-cheese stuffing	
4	medium-sized potatoes, boiled, peeled and mashed	4
¼ lb.	farmer cheese, crumbled	125 g.
⅔ cup	chopped onion	150 ml.
2 tbsp.	butter	30 ml.
1 tsp.	salt	5 ml.
	pepper (optional)	
1	egg (optional)	1

To make the pasta, place the flour on a board, add the egg and a little water, and work into a dough with your finger tips. Knead the dough, adding water little by little so that the dough does not become too thin. Its final consistency should be such that the dough neither falls apart nor sticks to your fingers. Roll the dough out to the thickness of a knife blade and cut out rounds about 2 inches [5 cm.] in diameter.

To prepare the stuffing, place the mashed potatoes and crumbled cheese in a mixing bowl. Fry the onion in the 2 tablespoons [30 ml.] of butter and add it to the potatoes and cheese. Add salt, and pepper if desired. An egg may also be added to improve the taste and nutritional value of the stuffing. Mix all of these ingredients well.

Spoon the potato-and-cheese mixture onto the rounds of dough. Then, holding each pierogi lightly between your fingers so that it remains plump and does not squash, moisten the edges with water and pinch them together to seal them.

Bring a pan of salted water to a boil, throw in the pierogi and cook for three minutes. Drain the pierogi. Melt the remaining butter until slightly browned. Place the pierogi on a serving dish, pour over the melted butter and serve at once.

MARIA DISSLOWA
JAK GOTOWAĆ

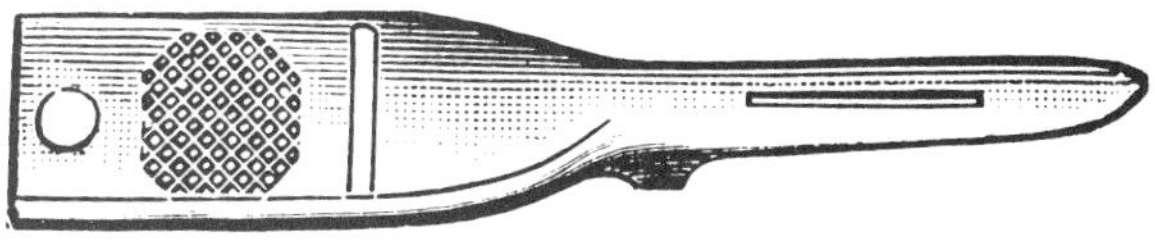

Tortellini with Fresh Peas and Beans
Tortelle di Piselli e di Faggioli Freschi

The technique of making pasta dough is shown on pages 16-19; the techniques of filling and shaping tortellini are demonstrated on pages 26-27. To skin broad beans, split the protective skin on each broad bean lengthwise, then pull away the skin in one piece and discard it.

To serve 4

¾ lb.	pasta dough *(recipe, page 164)*	⅓ kg.
2 tbsp.	freshly grated Parmesan cheese	30 ml.
1 tbsp.	sugar	15 ml.
1 tsp.	ground cinnamon	5 ml.
	Pea-and-broad-bean filling	
½ lb.	fresh peas, shelled	¼ kg.
½ lb.	fresh broad beans, shelled and skins removed	¼ kg.
2 quarts	meat stock *(recipe, page 167)*	2 liters
6	scallions, chopped	6
2 tbsp.	butter	30 ml.
2	egg yolks	2
½ tsp.	ground cinnamon	2 ml.
¼ tsp.	ground cloves	1 ml.
½ tsp.	grated nutmeg	2 ml.
1 tbsp.	sugar	15 ml.
	pepper	
⅓ cup	freshly grated Parmesan cheese	75 ml.
¼ cup	ricotta cheese	50 ml.

To make the filling, boil the peas and beans in the meat stock for 15 minutes. Reserve the stock. Grind the peas and beans in a mortar and pass them through a sieve. Lightly fry the scallions in a little butter, then mix them into the sieved peas and beans. Add the egg yolks, cinnamon, cloves, nutmeg and sugar. Season with a little pepper, then add the ⅓ cup [75 ml.] of Parmesan cheese plus the ricotta cheese, and mix all together well.

Use this mixture to fill the tortellini. Cook them in the reserved stock for five minutes, and serve them sprinkled with the Parmesan cheese, sugar and cinnamon.

BARTOLOMEO SCAPPI
OPERA DELL'ARTE DEL CUCINARE

Stuffed Wine-Pasta Triangles with Walnut Sauce
Pansoti con la Salsa di Noci alla Ligure

To serve 4

2¾ cups	sifted flour	675 ml.
⅓ cup	dry white wine	75 ml.
	salt	
3 or 4 tbsp.	water	45 or 60 ml.
⅓ cup	freshly grated Parmesan cheese	75 ml.
	Green filling	
¾ lb.	Swiss chard, stems removed	⅓ kg.
¼ lb.	borage, stems removed	125 g.
1	garlic clove, chopped	1
1	egg	1
½ cup	ricotta cheese	125 ml.
⅓ cup	freshly grated Parmesan cheese	75 ml.
	salt and freshly ground pepper	
	Walnut sauce	
1¼ cups	walnuts	300 ml.
2 tbsp.	bread crumbs, soaked in water and squeezed dry	30 ml.
	salt	
¼ cup	olive oil	50 ml.
¼ cup	sour milk (optional)	50 ml.

To make the filling, cook the chard and borage in a very little salted water for about five minutes, then squeeze them dry and put them through a food mill into a bowl. Add the garlic, egg, ricotta and Parmesan cheese. Season with salt and pepper, and mix until well blended.

Make the pasta dough by mixing the flour with the wine, a pinch of salt and some water. Knead until smooth and firm. Roll out the dough and cut it into 3-inch [8-cm.] triangles. To make each of the pansoti, put a little of the filling on a triangle, fold it in half to form another, narrower triangle, and press the edges together well.

Blanch the walnuts for a few minutes, remove the outer skins, then pound the walnuts in a mortar with the bread crumbs and a little salt to produce a smooth, thick sauce. Stir in the olive oil and the sour milk, if using.

Cook the pansoti in plenty of boiling salted water until *al dente*. Drain well, place in a heated serving dish and mix the pansoti with the walnut sauce. Serve hot with the remainder of the grated Parmesan cheese.

ANNA MARTINI (EDITOR)
PASTA AND PIZZA

Tortellini with Cream and Truffles

Tortellini alla Panna con Tartufi

To serve 6 to 8

1½ lb.	pasta dough (recipe, page 164)	¾ kg.
1 cup	heavy cream	¼ liter
3½ oz.	white truffles, sliced	100 g.
6 tbsp.	butter, 5 tbsp. [75 ml.] melted	90 ml.
3	egg yolks, lightly beaten	3
	freshly grated Parmesan cheese	

Veal, pork and prosciutto filling

¼ lb.	boneless lean veal, chopped	125 g.
¼ lb.	boneless lean pork, chopped	125 g.
¼ lb.	prosciutto, fat and lean parts chopped separately	125 g.
¼ cup	olive oil	50 ml.
1	garlic clove	1
1	sprig fresh rosemary	1
	salt and pepper	
½ cup	dry white wine	125 ml.
1	egg	1
⅔ cup	freshly grated Parmesan cheese	150 ml.
	grated nutmeg	

To prepare the filling, first heat the oil in a saucepan and brown the chopped veal, pork and the fatty part of the prosciutto. Season with the garlic, rosemary, and salt and pepper to taste. Add the wine and cook until the liquid in the pan is reduced by half. Cover and cook slowly for 10 minutes or so. Discard the garlic and rosemary, and grind the cooked meat with the lean part of the ham. Bind the mixture with the egg, cheese and a sprinkling of nutmeg.

Roll out the pasta dough paper-thin and cut it into 2-inch [5-cm.] circles. Put a little of the filling in the center of each circle, fold over and press the edges together. With the seam on the outside, curve the filled pasta to form a ring and press the ends together. Cook the tortellini in plenty of boiling salted water with 1 tablespoon [15 ml.] of butter until *al dente*. With a slotted spoon, transfer the tortellini from the water to a saucepan. Add 4 tablespoons [60 ml.] of the melted butter and the cream to the saucepan. Heat, stirring constantly. Remove from the heat, and thicken the mixture with the egg yolks and a few spoons of cheese. Pour the tortellini onto an ovenproof platter, and sprinkle with the truffles. Pour the remaining melted butter over the truffles and sprinkle them with a little additional cheese. Put the dish into a preheated 450° F. [230° C.] oven for a few minutes and serve immediately.

FEAST OF ITALY

Lithuanian Meat Dumplings

Kołduny Litewskie

To serve 4

2 cups	flour	½ liter
2	eggs	2
¼ cup	water	50 ml.
1 quart	boiling meat stock (recipe, page 167)	1 liter

Beef-and-onion stuffing

½ lb.	boneless lean beef, finely chopped	¼ kg.
1	onion, finely chopped	1
½ lb.	suet, chopped	¼ kg.
	salt and pepper	
	marjoram	

Place the flour on a board, add the eggs and a little water, and work the mixture into a dough with your finger tips. Knead the dough, adding the remaining water little by little. Roll the dough thin and cut out 2-inch [5-cm.] rounds.

To prepare the stuffing, put the beef and suet into a bowl and mix thoroughly. Add salt, pepper and marjoram to taste. Scald the onion in a little of the stock, lift out the onion with a skimmer and add it to the meat. Top each dough circle with a little of the meat mixture, moisten the edges, fold the circle over, and pinch the edges together. Bring the stock to a boil again, put in the dumplings and boil them. Then serve them from the pan. There is no need to add butter or sauce.

MARIA DISSLOWA
JAK GOTOWAĆ

Beef and Sauerkraut Pierogi

To serve 10

2 cups	flour	½ liter
½ tsp.	salt	2 ml.
2	eggs	2
½ cup	warm water	125 ml.
2 or 3 oz.	fat back or salt pork with the rind removed, finely cubed	60 or 90 g.

Beef-and-sauerkraut filling

3 cups	coarsely chopped, boneless lean cooked beef (about 1 lb. [½ kg.])	¾ liter
1½ cups	sauerkraut, the juice pressed and reserved	300 ml.
	salt and pepper	

To make the filling, first grind the beef and sauerkraut together through a food grinder. Add enough sauerkraut juice to moisten the mixture, then salt and pepper to taste. Refrigerate for an hour.

On a kneading board, make a hole in the center of the flour. Drop the salt, eggs and water into the hole. Mix to make a dough and knead the dough until firm. Cover with a warm bowl and let set for 10 minutes. Divide the dough into halves and roll each half out thin on a floured board. With a sharp knife, cut strips of dough about 2 inches [5 cm.] wide and 3 inches [8 cm.] long.

Place a small mound of filling on one side of each strip of dough, fold the other side over and seal the pierogi by pressing and rolling the edges together with your thumb and index finger. Place the pierogi, separated, on a floured cloth and cover lightly with wax paper to keep them moist.

Drop the pierogi into boiling salted water, cook gently for three to five minutes and lift out carefully with a perforated spoon. Fry the fat back or salt pork slowly until the cubes are very crisp and golden. Sprinkle the cubes over the pierogi and dribble some of the fat drippings on top.

ELINOR SEIDEL (EDITOR)
CHEFS, SCHOLARS & MOVABLE FEASTS

Persian Ravioli Soup
Gushe Barreh

To serve 5 or 6

1 cup	flour	¼ liter
¼ tsp.	salt	1 ml.
1¼ quarts	water	1¼ liters
¼ tsp.	ground cinnamon	1 ml.
1 tsp.	dried mint	5 ml.
4 or 5 tbsp.	chopped fresh parsley	60 or 75 ml.
about 2 tbsp.	vinegar	about 30 ml.
	plain yogurt (optional)	
Spiced meat filling		
½ lb.	very lean lamb or beef, finely chopped	¼ kg.
1	small onion, grated	1
1 tsp.	salt	5 ml.
¼ tsp.	pepper	1 ml.
¼ tsp.	ground cinnamon	1 ml.

To make the dough, sift the flour and salt into a bowl. Make a hollow in the center of the flour. Gradually add about ⅓ cup [75 ml.] of water and mix well with a fork or your hands. Turn the dough onto a lightly floured board and knead well until the dough is smooth. Put the dough in the bowl, cover with a cloth towel and let the dough rest for 10 minutes.

To make the filling, put the beef or lamb in a bowl, add the grated onion, salt, pepper and cinnamon and mix well.

Divide the dough into three parts. On a floured board, roll out one part of the dough into a rough circle about 12 to 14 inches [30 to 35 cm.] in diameter. Cut the dough into 1½-inch [4-cm.] squares. Put half a teaspoonful [2 ml.] of the meat mixture in the center of each square and place another square on top (like a sandwich). Pinch the four edges of these ravioli squares together well with your fingers or a fork.

Lightly salt the remaining water, bring to a boil and add the ravioli squares. Let them boil for 15 minutes or until done. Add the cinnamon, mint and parsley to the pan just before removing it from the heat. Season the soup with vinegar to taste. Some people like to eat this soup with yogurt.

MAIDEH MAZDA
IN A PERSIAN KITCHEN

Ravioli with Chicken, Butter and Cream Filling
Agnolotti alla Poggio Gherardo

To serve 4

1 lb.	pasta dough (recipe, page 164)	½ kg.
1	egg, mixed with 1 tbsp. [15 ml.] water	1
	melted butter	
	freshly grated Parmesan cheese	
Chicken, butter and cream filling		
1½ lb.	cooked chicken, boned and skinned	¾ kg.
8 tbsp.	butter	120 ml.
½ cup	light cream	125 ml.
⅓ cup	chopped onion	75 ml.
1	white truffle, chopped (optional)	1
¼ cup	dry white vermouth	50 ml.
	tarragon	
	salt and pepper	

To make the filling, grind the cooked chicken fine by putting it twice through a food grinder. Sweat the onion in the butter. Stir the butter and onion into the chicken and add the rest of the ingredients. Season with a pinch of tarragon, and salt and pepper to taste. Work the mixture to a paste.

Divide the pasta in two and roll each half paper-thin. Leave the paste to rest for half an hour and then put teaspoonfuls of the chicken mixture on one piece of pasta at about 2-inch [5-cm.] distances. Brush very lightly in between with the egg-wash mixture and lay the second sheet of pasta lightly on top. Press down around the little heaps of filling, and then cut out the ravioli with a knife or wheel.

Have ready a large saucepan of boiling salted water and put the ravioli in it. Boil slowly for about eight minutes, take the ravioli out with a strainer and season with melted butter and Parmesan cheese. Serve very hot.

JANET ROSS AND MICHAEL WATERFIELD
LEAVES FROM OUR TUSCAN KITCHEN

Lenten Ravioli

Ravioli di Magro

To serve 6

2½ cups	flour	625 ml.
3	eggs	3
7 tbsp.	butter	100 ml.
2 tsp.	dried sage (optional)	10 ml.
6 tbsp.	freshly grated Parmesan cheese	90 ml.
Cheese-and-fish filling		
3½ oz.	mascarpone cheese	100 g.
1	whole white-fleshed fish (1 lb. [½ kg.]) such as mullet, porgy or whiting	1
¾ cup	dry white wine	175 ml.
1	onion, thinly sliced	1
1 tbsp.	strained fresh lemon juice	15 ml.
	salt	
10 oz.	spinach	300 g.
2 tbsp.	butter	30 ml.
	pepper	
1	egg	1
2 tbsp.	freshly grated Parmesan cheese	30 ml.

Into a wide oval pan or fish poacher, put the white wine, half of the onion, the lemon juice, just enough water to cover the fish and a pinch of salt. When the liquid begins to boil, reduce the heat, put in the fish and simmer, uncovered, for 10 minutes. Remove the pan from the heat and allow the fish to cool in the stock.

Meanwhile, cook the spinach in the water remaining on the leaves after washing for about five minutes or until soft. Drain it, squeeze it thoroughly and chop it. Put the rest of the onion into a skillet, add the 2 tablespoons [30 ml.] of butter and fry gently over very low heat, until the onion is transparent but not brown; add a few drops of water if needed.

Drain the fish, bone and skin it, then flake it. Add the fish to the fried onion, stir, then add the spinach. Season to taste, stir and, keeping the heat low, allow the flavors to mingle for about 10 minutes. Then tip the mixture into a bowl before adding the mascarpone or ricotta cheese, the egg and the Parmesan cheese; mix all together well and adjust the seasoning if necessary.

To make the ravioli, tip the flour onto a board and make a well in the center of the flour. Break the eggs into the well and work them into the flour. Roll out the dough with a rolling pin, cut and shape the ravioli, and stuff them with the fish mixture.

Bring a large saucepan of salted water to a boil. Meanwhile, melt the butter in a small skillet. Add the sage, if using, to the butter and set the skillet aside off the heat.

Cook the ravioli quickly in the rapidly boiling water for five minutes, or until they are soft. Remove them from the saucepan, one or two at a time, with a slotted spoon. Drain in a colander. Arrange the ravioli in a deep heatproof dish or bowl, moisten them with a little of the melted butter, and sprinkle with a little grated Parmesan cheese. Arrange a second layer of ravioli on top, and so on, until all of the ingredients have been used.

Stand the dish in the pan of hot water in which the ravioli was boiled, after taking care to pour off enough of the water so that it comes only three quarters of the way up the sides of the dish. Cover the pan and leave the ravioli for five minutes to absorb the flavors of the butter and cheese.

FERNANDA GOSETTI
IN CUCINA CON FERNANDA GOSETTI

Fettucini and Mushroom Timbale

Timballo ai Funghi

To serve 4

1 lb.	fettucini	½ kg.
	freshly grated Parmesan cheese	
3 cups	puréed tomato (recipe, page 167)	¾ liter
Mushroom sauce		
2½ cups	sliced fresh button mushrooms	625 ml.
4 tbsp.	butter	60 ml.
1	garlic clove, chopped	1
¼ cup	flour	50 ml.
2 cups	meat stock (recipe, page 167)	½ liter
1 tbsp.	chopped marjoram	15 ml.
	salt and pepper	

Cook the fettucini in boiling salted water until nearly soft. Drain and allow the fettucini to cool. Butter a timbale mold or pudding basin about 7 inches [18 cm.] in diameter.

Meanwhile prepare the following sauce: Melt the butter in a frying pan. Add the garlic and mushrooms. Cook until the moisture of the mushrooms has evaporated, then stir in the flour. Add and mix in the stock, marjoram, and salt and pepper to taste. Simmer for 10 minutes.

Coil some of the cool fettucini around the inside of the timbale, well packed and slightly overlapping, until the sides and base of the timbale are covered. Mix the sauce with the remainder of the fettucini and pour into the middle of the mold. Put the mold in a baking dish of water, cover the mold with a saucer, and place it in a preheated 350° F. [180° C.] oven for 40 minutes.

Turn out the mold carefully onto a hot dish and serve with grated Parmesan and a fresh purée of tomatoes.

JANET ROSS AND MICHAEL WATERFIELD
LEAVES FROM OUR TUSCAN KITCHEN

Timbale of Sweetbreads and Macaroni

Timbale de Macaroni aux Ris de Veau

The technique for making a macaroni timbale is demonstrated on pages 41-43.

To serve 6 to 8

½ lb.	long macaroni	¼ kg.
2 lb.	veal sweetbreads, soaked in cold water for 1 hour, blanched for 2 minutes in boiling water, drained, plunged into cold water, and trimmed of tubes, fat and superficial membranes	1 kg.
¼ cup	dry white wine	50 ml.
2 cups	gelatinous veal stock(recipe, page 167)	½ liter
3 or 4	large fresh black truffles, thickly sliced	3 or 4
3 tbsp.	butter	45 ml.

Mirepoix

2	medium-sized carrots, finely chopped	2
1	medium-sized onion, finely chopped	1
2 tbsp.	butter	30 ml.
½	bay leaf, crumbled	½
½ tsp.	thyme	2 ml.

Forcemeat mousseline

1	large chicken breast, skin and fat removed, scraped free of tendons and chopped	1
1	egg white	1
	freshly grated nutmeg	
	salt and pepper	
1¼ cups	heavy cream, chilled	300 ml.

Place the sweetbreads side by side on a teatowel in such a way that they form a neat, even-surfaced mass. Place another teatowel over them and a board on top, with about a 2-pound [1-kg.] weight on the board (a medium-sized can of preserves does well). Leave the sweetbreads under this weight until well cooled and firm (a couple of hours).

To make the mirepoix, melt the butter in a heavy saucepan, add all of the ingredients and cook very gently, stirring regularly for 30 minutes. At the end of this time, the mirepoix should be thoroughly cooked but not browned.

Spread the mirepoix over the bottom of a heavy earthenware casserole of just the right size to hold the sweetbreads in one layer. Place them side by side on the bed of mirepoix. Pour in the white wine and, over high heat (using a heat-diffusing pad for protection), reduce the wine almost completely, gently shaking the receptacle from time to time to discourage anything from sticking to the bottom. Add the stock, bring it to a boil, and reduce the heat so that, covered, a near simmer is maintained. Count 40 minutes of braising time from the time the simmer is reached. Remove the sweetbreads from the sauce, slice them in regular ½-inch [1-cm.] slices, and pass the cooking liquid and the mirepoix through a fine sieve. If the sauce remains plentiful and liquid, reduce it over high heat for a few minutes, stirring constantly. Taste for seasoning. Pour the sauce over the sweetbreads, cool and stir in the truffles.

Cook the macaroni in a large pot of boiling salted water and, when nearly cooked but still quite firm, remove the pot from the heat and leave the macaroni to swell for two or three minutes in the hot water. The strands should remain somewhat firm. Drain them without rinsing and spread the strands of macaroni out, without touching one another, on a cloth towel. Generously butter a 2-quart [2-liter] dome mold or dome-shaped metal mixing bowl. Beginning with a strand of macaroni that has first been fashioned into a compact, flatly spiraled circle or disk and pressed into the central point at the bottom of the mold, continue twining the strands of macaroni end to end in a close-fitting spiral until the entire mold is lined in this manner. Refrigerate the mold until the butter is set firmly. Cut the remaining macaroni into short lengths and stir it into the sweetbreads.

To prepare the forcemeat mousseline, pound the chicken breast in a mortar until it is reduced to a purée. Add the salt, pepper and a pinch of grated nutmeg, and continue working the purée with a pestle. Gradually add the egg white. Force the mixture a tablespoonful [15 ml.] at a time through a fine-meshed nylon drum sieve, removing any debris (nerves or membranes) after each passage. Pack the purée into a bowl (it will chill more rapidly in a metal bowl—an hour on cracked ice is sufficient), smooth the surface of the forcemeat, and press a sheet of plastic wrap over it. Refrigerate until needed. Before using, beat in the cream little by little.

Remove the macaroni mold from the refrigerator. Spread three quarters of the forcemeat mousseline evenly over the entire surface of the macaroni lining. Fill the mold with the sweetbread, truffle and macaroni mixture, pressing it gently into place so as to leave no air pockets. Spread the remainder of the mousseline over the surface. Press a circle of buttered wax paper over the surface, and put the mold to poach in a bain-marie in a preheated 325° F. [160° C.] oven for 45 minutes. (A small trivet such as a metal biscuit cutter should be used to support the round-bottomed mold in the larger utensil. The mold should be immersed by about three quarters in nearly boiling water.) If oven space does not permit, the poaching may be done equally well on top of the stove in a large, covered saucepan. The heat should be kept very low to prevent the water from returning to a boil. Remove the mold from the bain-marie, lift off the buttered paper and allow the timbale to settle for seven or eight minutes before unmolding it onto a round, preheated serving dish. The bit of liquid that drains onto the serving dish can be sponged up with a paper towel. Cut the timbale into pielike wedges at the table.

RICHARD OLNEY
THE FRENCH MENU COOKBOOK

Molded Macaroni Pudding

Timbale de Macaroni

The techniques of preparing a mousseline and assembling a timbale are shown on pages 41-43. For 1 pound [½ kg.] of mousseline, you will need one large chicken breast, one egg white and 1 cup [¼ liter] of heavy cream.

To serve 4

½ lb.	long macaroni	¼ kg.
1 lb.	chicken forcemeat mousseline	½ kg.
2 tbsp.	butter	30 ml.
6	chicken livers, trimmed and halved	6
	salt and pepper	
½ cup	dry white wine	125 ml.
1 cup	velouté sauce (recipe, page 166)	¼ liter
2 tbsp.	tomato sauce (recipe, page 166)	30 ml.
2	thick slices cooked, cured tongue, cut into ½-inch [1-cm.] rounds	2
1¼ cups	sliced fresh mushrooms, sautéed in butter for 1 minute	300 ml.
1	truffle, sliced	1

Cook the macaroni in boiling salted water until firm to the bite. Drain it. Spread the macaroni on a towel. When the macaroni is cold, take the longest strands and coil them around the base and against the sides of a buttered domed mold. Cover the macaroni with a layer of mousseline.

Heat the butter in a pan; add the chicken livers. Season with salt and a little pepper, and sauté rapidly. Sprinkle the livers with the white wine. Reduce the liquid by boiling it fast, then moisten the mixture with about ½ cup [125 ml.] of the velouté sauce and all of the tomato sauce. Remove from the heat. Add the pieces of tongue, the mushrooms, the truffle and the rest of the macaroni, cut into sections. Allow to cool, then use the mixture to fill the interior of the mold. Cover the top of the mold with the remaining mousseline. Set a lid on the mold or cover with heavy foil.

Place the mold on a trivet in a deep pan, add hot water almost to the top of the mold, cover the pan and poach the pudding over low heat for 45 minutes. Unmold on a platter and pour the remaining velouté sauce around the pudding.

URBAIN DUBOIS
ÉCOLE DES CUISINIÈRES

Couscous with Lamb

Kousksi bil Ghalmi

Cooking couscous is demonstrated on pages 44-47; the technique for making harissa sauce is shown on page 47. Cardoon is a stalky relative of the artichoke. It is sometimes available in autumn at specialty markets. If not obtainable, substitute ½ pound [¼ kg.] Swiss chard ribs or ½ pound Jerusalem artichokes, peeled and chopped.

To serve 10

1½ lb.	couscous	¾ kg.
1 lb.	boned lean lamb, diced	½ kg.
¼ lb.	lamb fat, diced	125 g.
	salt	
½ tsp.	freshly ground black pepper	2 ml.
1 tbsp.	*harissa*	15 ml.
½ tsp.	cayenne pepper	2 ml.
1	onion, chopped	1
⅔ cup	olive oil	150 ml.
2 quarts	water	2 liters
2 tbsp.	puréed tomato (recipe, page 167)	30 ml.
⅓ cup	dried chick-peas, soaked overnight in water and drained	75 ml.
1	head cardoon, stalks only, scraped and chopped into pieces	1
3 or 4	potatoes, peeled but left whole	3 or 4
2 or 3	carrots, cut into halves	2 or 3
2	small turnips, cut into pieces	2
2 tbsp.	butter	30 ml.
½ tsp.	ground cinnamon	2 ml.
1 tbsp.	crushed dried rose petals (optional)	15 ml.

Put the lamb and lamb fat into the bottom of the *couscoussier*, and season with salt, pepper, *harissa* and cayenne pepper. Add the onion and oil, and sauté for several minutes until the onion browns lightly. Add 1 cup [¼ liter] of the water. Then stir in the puréed tomato and chick-peas, and cook for 15 to 20 minutes. Add the other vegetables, cover with the rest of the water and bring to a boil.

Moisten the couscous with a little cold water, fill the top half of the *couscoussier* without packing the grains too tightly, and put the two halves of the pot together. Time the cooking from the moment the steam begins to rise through the top half. Cook for 30 to 40 minutes, then remove the top half of the pot, empty the couscous onto a dish, sprinkle with a little cold water and mash lightly with a wooden spoon to separate the lumps and aerate the grains. Replace the couscous in the top of the *couscoussier*, put the whole pot back on the heat and bring to a boil a second time.

Empty the couscous onto a serving dish. Skim the fat from the surface of the stew, then add the butter, cinnamon and rose petals. Pour half of the cooking liquid over the couscous and mix well. Pour out the rest of the cooking liquid to serve as a gravy; arrange the meat and vegetables on a separate serving dish. Allow to rest for a moment; serve.

MOHAMED KOUKI
LA CUISINE TUNISIENNE D' "OMMOK SANNAFA"

Couscous with Seven Vegetables

Couscous "Bidaoui" aux Sept Légumes

Oils in hot chilies may make your skin burn and eyes sting; wear rubber gloves when handling them.

To serve 8 to 10

2 lb.	couscous	1 kg.
8	medium-sized onions, thinly sliced	8
1	medium-sized cabbage, halved, cored and cut into pieces	1
4 or 5	tomatoes, quartered	4 or 5
1	small eggplant, cut into pieces	1
6	medium-sized carrots, quartered	6
2 or 3	medium-sized turnips, quartered	2 or 3
1 lb.	pumpkin or butternut squash, quartered, seeded and cut into pieces	½ kg.
2 lb.	veal shank or lamb shoulder, cut up	1 kg.
20 tbsp.	butter	300 ml.
½ tsp.	ground saffron	2 ml.
	salt	
1 tbsp.	pepper	15 ml.
6 quarts	water	6 liters
2	small fresh red chilies, stemmed, seeded and chopped	2
½ cup	chopped fresh coriander	125 ml.

In the bottom half of a *couscoussier*, put the meat, a quarter of the sliced onions, the cabbage and half of the butter. Season with the saffron, salt and pepper, cover with the water and bring to a boil. Put the couscous into the top half of the *couscoussier* and seal the two halves together with a band of cheesecloth soaked in a flour-and-water paste. Steam for 30 minutes from the time the steam begins to escape. Remove the top half of the *couscoussier*, cover the bottom half and let the stew simmer for at least one hour.

Meanwhile, put the couscous in a bowl. Gently lift and stir the grains with a wooden spoon to separate them. Let the couscous cool, sprinkle it with cold water and fluff it again. Continue sprinkling and fluffing until the grains are swollen and saturated. Let the couscous stand for 30 minutes.

About one hour before serving, add the coriander and all of the remaining vegetables, except the pumpkin or squash, to the meat and cabbage. Simmer for about 30 minutes. Cook the pumpkin separately, in a little of the meat cooking liquid, until soft but still intact, about 15 minutes.

Half an hour before the meal, replace the couscous in the top half of the *couscoussier*, reseal the two halves as before and, when the steam begins to rise, remove the couscous and transfer it to a bowl. Add the remaining butter, mix well, and pour over the couscous as much of the meat cooking liquid as it will absorb, fluffing it all the time.

Pile the couscous in a mound on a large, flat round dish. Make a well in the center and fill it with the meat and vegetables. Serve the meat cooking liquid on the side as a gravy.

LATIFA BENNANI SMIRES
LA CUISINE MAROCAINE

Couscous with Chick-peas and Raisins

Couscous "K'dra" aux Raisins Secs et Pois Chiches

The technique of cooking couscous is shown on pages 44-47.

To serve 8 to 10

2 lb.	couscous	1 kg.
1 cup	dried chick-peas, soaked in water overnight and drained	¼ liter
1 lb.	seedless raisins	½ kg.
5 quarts	water	5 liters
12	medium-sized onions, 2 chopped	12
4 lb.	chicken or 2 lb. [1 kg.] lamb shoulder or veal shank, cut into 8 to 10 pieces	2 kg.
	salt	
1 tbsp.	pepper	15 ml.
16 tbsp.	butter (½ lb. [¼ kg.])	¼ liter
¼ tsp.	ground saffron	1 ml.

Pour the water into the bottom of a *couscoussier*. Add the chopped onions, the chick-peas, chicken or meat, a little salt, the pepper, 10 tablespoons [150 ml.] of the butter and the saffron. Bring to a boil over high heat.

Put the couscous in the top half of the pot. Put the top half over the bottom and seal the two parts together with flour-and-water paste. After the steam begins to rise from the top, cook for 30 minutes. Unseal the pot by slitting the hardened paste, then carefully lift off the top half of the pot. Remove the couscous. Put it into a large bowl and toss it gently with a fork to separate the grains. Cool, moisten it with cold water, and toss it again. Repeat until the swollen grains are impregnated with water. Let the couscous rest.

Cook the chicken or meat for 15 to 30 minutes longer or until tender, and remove it from the steamer. Cut the remaining onions into large pieces and add them with the raisins. Bring to a boil. Return the couscous to the top of the steamer, put the two parts together and seal with flour paste as before. When the steam begins to rise again, remove the couscous and pour it back into the bowl. Add the remaining butter in small pieces, stir well, and pour in as much of the stock as the couscous can absorb, stirring continuously.

Arrange the couscous in a mound in the middle of a large round serving dish, make a well in the center, and place the chicken or meat, chick-peas, onions and raisins in the well. Pour the stock into a soup tureen, and serve immediately.

AHMED LAASRI
240 RECETTES DE CUISINE MAROCAINE

Baked Pasta

Sour-Cream Noodles

To serve 4

¼ lb.	thin noodles	125 g.
1 cup	sour cream	¼ liter
1 cup	cottage cheese	¼ liter
⅛ tsp.	pepper	½ ml.
½ tsp.	salt	2 ml.
4 tbsp.	melted butter	60 ml.
1 tsp.	grated horseradish	5 ml.
½ tsp.	dry mustard	2 ml.

Boil the noodles in salted water. Drain. Mix the cottage cheese, sour cream, pepper, salt, melted butter, horseradish and dry mustard together. Add the noodles and put in a buttered baking dish. Bake in a preheated 300° F. [200° C.] oven for one and a half hours.

MARGUERITE GILBERT MC CARTHY
AUNT ELLA'S COOK BOOK

Cavatelli with Cheese

Cavatelli, a long, crinkle-edged shell, holds its shape well.

To serve 4

½ lb.	cavatelli	¼ kg.
1 cup	shredded Cheddar cheese	¼ liter
½ cup	freshly grated Romano or Parmesan cheese	125 ml.
⅓ cup	chopped onion	75 ml.
4 tbsp.	butter	60 ml.
1 cup	hot milk	¼ liter

Bring 6 quarts [6 liters] of salted water to a rolling boil. Add the pasta. Cavatelli normally takes about 20 minutes to cook, but begin testing it after about 10 minutes. Meanwhile, in a saucepan, sauté the onion in the butter until soft. Remove from the heat. When the cavatelli is done, drain and add it to the onion along with the Cheddar and hot milk. Mix lightly and carefully with a rubber spatula. Turn into a buttered ovenproof dish, cover with the grated Romano or Parmesan, and bake in a preheated 350° F. [180° C.] oven for about 10 minutes.

MIRIAM UNGERER
GOOD CHEAP FOOD

Caraway Cheese Noodle Ring

Nudeln mit Kümmelkäse

To serve 6

½ lb.	egg noodles, boiled and drained	¼ kg.
1½ cups	shredded caraway-seed cheese	375 ml.
1 cup	milk, heated to scalding	¼ liter
3	eggs, beaten	3
1 tsp.	salt	5 ml.
	black pepper or cayenne pepper	

Slowly pour the hot milk into the eggs, beating with a whisk until smooth. Add the cheese, salt and a dash of pepper. Combine the milk-cheese mixture with the noodles and spoon evenly into a buttered 1-quart [1-liter] ring mold. Bake at 325° F. [160° C.] until firm, about 45 minutes. Unmold onto a serving platter and fill the center of the ring with buttered mixed vegetables or creamed chicken or curried shrimp and fish.

BETTY WASON
THE ART OF GERMAN COOKING

Czech Farmer Cheese and Noodle Pudding

Topfen-Nudel-Auflauf

To serve 4

½ lb.	wide egg noodles or tagliatelle	¼ kg.
¾ lb.	farmer cheese	⅓ kg.
1 cup	sour cream	¼ liter
	salt	
4	thick slices bacon, diced	4
1	onion, finely chopped	1
1 tbsp.	butter	15 ml.
3	eggs	3

Boil the noodles in salted water until done, drain in a colander, rinse with cold water and drain again. Pass the farmer cheese through a fine sieve, stir in ⅓ cup [75 ml.] of the sour cream and season with salt. Fry the diced bacon with the onion in a skillet until the bacon is crisp.

Grease a deep ovenproof dish with the butter. Place a layer of pasta in the bottom, cover with a layer of the bacon-and-onion mixture, followed by a layer of farmer cheese. Continue in this way until all of the ingredients are used up, finishing with a layer of cheese.

Mix the eggs with the remaining sour cream and pour the mixture over the contents of the dish. Cook in a preheated 350° F. [180° C.] oven for about 45 minutes, or until the top is brown. Serve with a green salad.

GRETE WILLINSKY
KOCHBUCH DER BÜCHERGILDE

Whole-Wheat Macaroni, Russian-Style

To serve 6 to 8

½ lb.	whole-wheat macaroni	¼ kg.
8 tbsp.	butter	120 ml.
1½ cups	sour cream	375 ml.
1 lb.	cottage cheese	½ kg.
1 cup	shredded Cheddar cheese	¼ liter
1	red onion, thinly sliced	1
2	scallions, chopped	2
1	green pepper, seeded, deribbed and chopped	1
2 cups	shredded cabbage	½ liter
½ lb.	fresh mushrooms, sliced	¼ kg.
1	carrot, chopped	1
1 tsp.	caraway seeds	5 ml.
2 tbsp.	*tamari* sauce	30 ml.
	freshly ground black pepper	

Combine the sour cream, cottage cheese, Cheddar cheese, onion, scallions and green pepper. Sauté the prepared cabbage, mushrooms, carrot and the caraway seeds in 4 tablespoons [60 ml.] of the butter.

Boil the macaroni in salted water until barely done. Drain and mix with the remaining butter. Combine everything. Add the *tamari* sauce and lots of freshly ground black pepper.

Place in a buttered casserole, cover, and bake in a preheated 350° F. [180° C.] oven for 40 minutes. Serve with fresh tomato slices sprinkled with basil.

MOLLIE KATZEN
THE MOOSEWOOD COOKBOOK

Léa's Macaroni and Cheese

Macaroni au Gratin de Léa

To serve 6

10 oz.	elbow macaroni	300 g.
2 tbsp.	freshly grated Swiss cheese	30 ml.

Béchamel sauce

2 tbsp.	butter	30 ml.
1 tbsp.	flour	15 ml.
2 cups	milk	½ liter
	salt and white pepper	

Cook the macaroni in plenty of boiling salted water until it is *al dente*—about 15 minutes. As soon as the macaroni is done, refresh it under cold running water. Drain, then put it into a pan over boiling water to keep it warm.

Prepare the béchamel slowly. It has to simmer to acquire its velvety texture. Bring the milk to a boil in a small pan and have it boiling when you add it to the roux. Melt 1 tablespoon [15 ml.] of the butter in a saucepan, sprinkle in the flour, and stir with a wooden spoon until the flour starts to take on color and begins to give off an aroma like baking brioche. Then add half of the boiling milk, stirring constantly with a wire whisk. When the mixture has thickened, let it simmer for a few minutes and decide if you need to add any more milk to obtain a velvety yet light-textured sauce. Add salt and pepper, then simmer for 15 to 20 minutes.

Place the well-drained macaroni in a gratin dish and cover with the béchamel, thinned or stretched with more milk if necessary. The sauce should barely be level with the top of the macaroni.

Sprinkle with the grated cheese and dot with the remaining tablespoon of butter, then run the dish quickly under the broiler to brown the top.

MADELEINE PETER
FAVORITE RECIPES OF THE GREAT WOMEN CHEFS OF FRANCE

Macaroni and Cheese with Wine

To serve 6

½ lb.	macaroni, boiled and drained	¼ kg.
2 cups	cubed sharp Cheddar cheese	½ liter
½ cup	sweet white wine	125 ml.
2 tbsp.	butter, softened	30 ml.
½ tsp.	prepared mustard	2 ml.
2	eggs, beaten	2
1½ cups	half-and-half cream	375 ml.
2 or 3 tbsp.	chopped, peeled, canned green chilies	30 or 45 ml.
½ cup	fine dry bread crumbs, mixed with 2 tbsp. [30 ml.] melted butter	125 ml.

Combine all of the ingredients except the bread crumbs; mix well. Place in a buttered 1½-quart [1½-liter] baking dish. Sprinkle with the buttered bread crumbs, cover and bake in a preheated 350° F. [180° C.] oven for 40 to 50 minutes. To thicken the liquid in the casserole, let it stand for five to 10 minutes before serving.

MICHAEL ROY
MIKE ROY'S AMERICAN KITCHEN

Macaroni with Béchamel au Gratin

The technique of making macaroni and cheese is demonstrated on pages 50-51. The author suggests you may substitute ziti, ziti tagliati, penne or other medium-sized tubular pastas for the macaroni.

	To serve 4	
1 lb.	macaroni	½ kg.
3 cups	béchamel sauce flavored with nutmeg (recipe, page 166)	¾ liter
	freshly grated Parmesan cheese	
½ lb.	mozzarella cheese	¼ kg.
	fresh bread crumbs	

Cook the pasta and mix it with half of the béchamel, some grated Parmesan and freshly ground pepper. Put some of the béchamel in the bottom of a buttered baking dish, cover with a layer of macaroni-and-béchamel mixture, sprinkle with more Parmesan, and top with slices of mozzarella and a few more tablespoons of béchamel. Make another layer of macaroni, Parmesan and béchamel, sprinkle with bread crumbs, dot with butter and brown in a hot (400° F. [200° C.]) oven.

VINCENZO BUONASSISI
PASTA

Mom's Macaroni and Cheese

	To serve 4	
¼ lb.	whole-wheat or buckwheat macaroni	125 g.
½ lb.	Cheddar cheese, shredded	¼ kg.
1¼ cups	hot milk	300 ml.
6 tbsp.	dry bread crumbs or ¾ cup [175 ml.] fresh bread crumbs	90 ml.
1	medium-sized onion, finely chopped	1
1	green pepper, halved, seeded, deribbed and finely chopped	1
	finely chopped fresh parsley or watercress	
3 or 4	scallions, finely chopped (optional)	3 or 4
1 tsp.	sea salt	5 ml.
2	eggs, beaten	2
	paprika	

Cook the macaroni in boiling salted water until it is tender but still firm. Drain it.

Pour the hot milk over the bread crumbs and cheese in a big bowl. Add the onion, green pepper, lots of parsley or watercress, the scallions—if using—and the salt. Stir in the eggs, then mix in the cooked macaroni.

Put the mixture into a buttered casserole dish. Sprinkle it with paprika.

Bake in a preheated 350° F. [180° C.] oven for about 30 minutes, or until the top of the macaroni and cheese is firm and golden brown.

JULIE JORDAN
WINGS OF LIFE

Macaroni Gratin

Le Macaroni au Gratin

	To serve 4 to 6	
1 lb.	long macaroni	½ kg.
1 quart	milk	1 liter
	salt	
¼ tsp.	quatre épices	1 ml.
	freshly ground black pepper	
	nutmeg	
4 tbsp.	butter, softened and cut into small pieces	60 ml.
1 cup	shredded Gruyère cheese	¼ liter
⅔ cup	freshly grated Parmesan cheese	150 ml.
½ cup	dry bread crumbs	125 ml.

Cook the macaroni in boiling salted water until it is *al dente*—about 15 minutes. Drain the macaroni and keep it hot. Heat the milk to boiling, add a pinch of salt, the *quatre épices* and a little pepper, and grate in some nutmeg. Simmer just below the boiling point for five minutes.

Mix the butter and shredded Gruyère cheese with the hot macaroni, stirring well to prevent the cheese from sticking together in lumps. Put the macaroni in an ovenproof dish and cover with all but 1 cup [¼ liter] of the milk. Put the dish in a preheated 425° F. [220° C.] oven and bake for 15 minutes. Remove from the oven. If the macaroni seems dry, add a little of the remaining milk. Sprinkle the baked macaroni with the Parmesan cheese mixed with the bread crumbs. Return it to the oven and bake at 450° to 475° F. [230° to 240° C.] for 10 minutes or until well browned. Or place the dish under a hot broiler for a few minutes to brown the top.

Serve in the baking dish. If the macaroni is not to be served immediately, it can be kept warm in the oven with the heat turned off.

ALBIN MARTY
FOURMIGUETTO: SOUVENIRS, CONTES ET RECETTES DU LANGUEDOC

Marvelous Macaroni and Cheese

To serve 4

½ lb.	elbow macaroni	¼ kg.
2 cups	grated sharp Cheddar cheese	½ liter
3 tbsp.	butter	45 ml.
¼ cup	chopped onion	50 ml.
¼ cup	flour	50 ml.
½ tsp.	salt	2 ml.
⅛ tsp.	pepper	½ ml.
1 cup	heavy cream	¼ liter
½ cup	dry white wine	125 ml.

Cook the macaroni until just tender. Drain. Heat the butter and cook the onion in it until soft, about 10 minutes. Stir in the flour, salt and pepper. Slowly add the cream and wine and cook over low heat, stirring constantly, until this sauce is thickened. Add the cheese and stir until melted. Mix together the macaroni and the cheese sauce. Put into a greased 1½-quart [1½-liter] casserole. Bake in a preheated 350° F. [180° C.] oven for 15 minutes or until thoroughly heated. Serve with buttered fresh leaf spinach.

EDITORS OF HOUSE & GARDEN
HOUSE & GARDEN'S NEW COOKBOOK

Tagliarini with Cheese

Tagliarini al Formaggio

To serve 4

4 cups	flour	1 liter
3	eggs	3
½ cup	milk	125 ml.
	salt	
14 tbsp.	butter	210 ml.
1¼ cups	shredded Gruyère cheese	300 ml.
1⅓ cups	freshly grated Parmesan cheese	325 ml.
1 cup	fresh white bread crumbs	¼ liter

Place the flour in a bowl with a pinch of salt and break the eggs into the center. Mix well, adding the milk gradually to make a smooth paste. Let the dough stand in a cool place for 30 minutes. Roll out the dough very thin and let it dry. Cut it into long, thin strips (tagliarini).

Bring a large pan of salted water to a boil, add the tagliarini and simmer over very low heat until tender. Beat 12 tablespoons [180 ml.] of the butter until soft and stir in the Gruyère and Parmesan cheeses. Drain the tagliarini and place a layer in the bottom of a 2-quart [2-liter] ovenproof dish. Dot the tagliarini with some of the cheese-and-butter mixture. Repeat the layers until the dish is full, finishing with cheese. Sprinkle the top with the bread crumbs and dot with the remaining 2 tablespoons [30 ml.] of butter. Bake in a preheated 400° F. [200° C.] oven for 15 minutes, or until the top is golden. Serve in the baking dish, very hot.

ANDRÉ L. SIMON
CHEESES OF THE WORLD

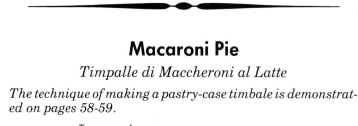

Macaroni Pie

Timpalle di Maccheroni al Latte

The technique of making a pastry-case timbale is demonstrated on pages 58-59.

To serve 6

1 lb.	macaroni	½ kg.
	pastry dough (recipe, page 164, but reduce the quantities by a third)	
1 quart	milk	1 liter
1 cup	freshly grated Parmesan cheese	¼ liter
4 tbsp.	butter	60 ml.
	salt and freshly ground pepper	
5 oz.	mozzarella cheese, thinly sliced	150 g.
3	eggs, hard-boiled and quartered	3

Roll out the pastry dough and use it to line a large casserole or deep pie dish, reserving about one third of the dough for the pastry lid.

Half-cook the macaroni in boiling salted water in one pan and bring the milk slowly to a boil in another pan. Drain the macaroni and finish cooking it in the milk, but take care not to overcook it. Drain away the excess milk, leaving the macaroni very moist, and mix the macaroni with the Parmesan cheese and butter. Place the macaroni in the pastry-lined casserole or pie dish, arranging it in layers seasoned with salt and pepper, and separated by slices of mozzarella cheese and the quartered hard-boiled eggs. Take care that the layers are all packed well together. Put on the pastry lid, folding it over all the way around to effect a good seal between the lid and the pastry lining.

Cook in a preheated 375° F. [190° C.] oven for 40 minutes, or until the pastry is crisp and nicely colored.

IPPOLITO CAVALCANTI
CUCINA TEORICO-PRATICA

Vermicelli Soufflé

To serve 4 to 6

¼ lb.	vermicelli, lightly browned in butter, boiled and drained (about 2 cups [½ liter])	125 g.
3	large eggs, the yolks separated from the whites	3
2 cups	sour cream	½ liter
1 cup	freshly grated Parmesan cheese	¼ liter
1 tbsp.	finely chopped fresh parsley	15 ml.
2 tbsp.	finely chopped onion	30 ml.
	salt and freshly ground pepper	
	butter	

Preheat the oven to 350° F. [180° C.].

Combine the egg yolks and sour cream, and blend well. Add the cheese, parsley, onion, salt and pepper to taste, and the vermicelli. Beat the egg whites until stiff but not dry and gently fold them into the vermicelli mixture. Butter a 6-cup [1½-liter] soufflé dish and fill it with the vermicelli mixture. Set the soufflé dish in a pan of hot water and bake in the preheated oven for 45 minutes, until puffed and browned.

JUNIOR LEAGUE OF THE CITY OF NEW YORK
NEW YORK ENTERTAINS

Baked Hungarian Egg-Barley Noodles

Tarhonya

Tarhonya are small Hungarian egg noodles, shaped like grains of barley. They are made in two sizes: The fine size is used in soup and the coarse size as an accompaniment to an entrée, as here. They are obtainable in stores selling Middle European foods.

To serve 6

¾ lb.	coarse tarhonya (1½ cups [375 ml.])	⅓ kg.
3 tbsp.	butter	45 ml.
1 tsp.	salt	5 ml.
1½ tsp.	paprika	7 ml.
	water	

In a heatproof casserole, brown the noodles in the butter, stirring to brown them on all sides. Add the salt, paprika and enough water to cover the noodles. Cover the casserole, and cook in a preheated 350° F. [180° C.] oven for about one hour, or until all of the liquid has been absorbed and the noodles are flaky, like well-cooked rice.

CHARLOTTE ADAMS
THE FOUR SEASONS COOKBOOK

Maruzze with Blueberries

Maruzze is another name for pasta shells.

To serve 4

½ lb.	maruzze	¼ kg.
1 cup	blueberries	¼ liter
8 tbsp.	butter	120 ml.
about 6 oz.	canned Italian-style tomato paste	about 175 g.
about ½ cup	red wine	about 125 ml.
	crystal salt	
¼ lb.	aged Gruyère cheese, grated	125 g.

Cook the maruzze as if they were macaroni, in a large pot filled with boiling salted water, until they are *al dente* —still chewy. Drain them, rinse under hot running water, then carefully drain again, shaking vigorously to get all of the water out of the shells. While they are cooking, make the sauce in a small copper pan.

Melt the butter, thicken it by blending in 1 or 2 tablespoons [15 or 30 ml.] of the tomato paste, thin it with 1 or 2 tablespoons of the red wine, add salt to taste, and finally adjust it by thickening or thinning it to the consistency of heavy cream. Simmer gently, covered, until needed.

Wash and dry the blueberries. Liberally butter a shallow baking dish. Put in the drained maruzze with the blueberries on top. Alternately shake the dish and gently stir the contents with a wooden spoon. After two or three minutes of this, almost all of the blueberries will have disappeared into the shells. Pour on the sauce and stir so that the sauce, too, runs into the shells. Sprinkle the top with the grated cheese.

Preheat the oven to 350° F. [180° C.]. Put the dish in the oven and leave it until the sauce begins bubbling, usually in about 20 minutes.

ROY ANDRIES DE GROOT
FEASTS FOR ALL SEASONS

Baked Macaroni with Peas

To serve 4 to 6

½ lb.	elbow macaroni, farfalle or other medium-sized pasta	¼ kg.
1 cup	freshly shelled peas	¼ liter
4 tbsp.	butter	60 ml.
1	large onion, finely chopped	1
1 or 2	garlic cloves, finely chopped	1 or 2
2 or 3	sprigs fresh parsley, finely chopped	2 or 3
	salt and pepper	

Parboil the peas in salted water until tender. Drain. Heat the butter, add the onion and garlic, and simmer until the onion is soft. Add the parsley, salt and pepper. Meanwhile, cook the pasta in boiling salted water. Drain, and turn the pasta into a buttered casserole. Add the peas and the onion mixture, stirring gently but well. Bake the casserole in a preheated 350° F. [180° C.] oven for 15 minutes.

ROBIN HOWE
THE PASTA COOKBOOK

Eggplant Stuffed with Sausage, Sage and Macaroni

To serve 8

¼ lb.	elbow macaroni, boiled and drained	125 g.
2	large eggplants	2
1 lb.	hot Italian sausages, removed from their casings	½ kg.
1 tsp.	chopped fresh sage or ½ tsp. [2 ml.] dried sage	5 ml.
1	medium-sized onion, chopped	1
2	garlic cloves, finely chopped	2
¾ cup	freshly grated Parmesan cheese	175 ml.
3 cups	canned Italian-style tomatoes, drained and the liquid reserved	¾ liter
	salt and pepper	

Preheat the oven to 400° F. [200° C.].

Drop the unpeeled whole eggplants into 3 quarts [3 liters] of boiling water. Let them cook for 10 to 15 minutes, depending upon the size of the vegetables. Drain, refresh under gently running cold water and dry on paper towels. Halve each eggplant; remove, chop and reserve the center pulp, leaving ½ inch [1 cm.] of pulp near the skin. If the eggplants lose their shape, which sometimes happens, place them in a preheated 400° F. [200° C.] oven for a few minutes to crisp their skins and help them regain their shape.

Butter a flat ovenproof casserole, large enough to accommodate the four eggplant halves. In a large pan, break up the sausages and sauté them slowly with the onion, garlic and sage. When the sausages are lightly browned, drain the excess fat from the pan and reserve it. Add the chopped eggplant pulp to the sausage mixture and cook until tender, about 10 minutes.

Mix together the macaroni, ¼ cup [50 ml.] of the cheese, half of the sausage mixture, and 1 cup [¼ liter] of the tomatoes. Sprinkle the mixture with salt and pepper to taste, and use it to fill the eggplant shells. Sprinkle the rest of the cheese on top and brush the sides of the eggplants with some of the reserved fat from the pan. Combine the remaining sausage mixture and tomatoes, and put this mixture in the casserole in the empty spaces around the eggplant halves. Bake for 15 minutes.

SHERYL LONDON
EGGPLANT AND SQUASH

Baked Penne and Eggplant Timbale

Timballo di Maccheroni al Forno

This timbale mixture may be baked in a 2-quart [2-liter] soufflé dish or mold, using the techniques shown on pages 56-57.

To serve 4

½ lb.	penne, cooked and drained	¼ kg.
4	small eggplants, trimmed but not peeled, and cut lengthwise into slices ¼ inch thick [6 mm.]	4
	oil	
	flour	
2	eggs, beaten with 3 tbsp. [45 ml.] freshly grated Parmesan cheese, and seasoned with salt and pepper	2
	lard	
about 3½ cups	tomato sauce (recipe, page 166)	about 875 ml.
2	Italian pork sausages, fried until brown, peeled and the meat crumbled	2
1	chicken liver, trimmed, sautéed in butter for 1 minute and chopped	1
1	slice cooked tongue, cut into julienne	1
1	large slice cooked chicken breast	1
½ cup	freshly shelled peas, parboiled for 3 minutes and drained	125 ml.
1	egg, hard-boiled and chopped	1
¼ cup	chopped mozzarella cheese	50 ml.
3 or 4 tbsp.	freshly grated Parmesan cheese	45 or 60 ml.

Fry the eggplant slices in oil, a small batch at a time, until golden on both sides. Drain and dry them well on paper towels. Then flour them and dip them in the seasoned mixture of beaten eggs and grated Parmesan cheese. Fry the slices again until well colored; drain them. Grease four individual 2-cup [½-liter] soufflé dishes with lard and line them with the eggplant slices. Reserve the rest of the slices.

Mix the cooked penne with most of the tomato sauce, reserving a little of the sauce for garnish. Mix in the sausages, chicken liver, tongue, chicken, peas, egg, mozzarella and 2 tablespoons [30 ml.] of the grated Parmesan cheese.

Fill the eggplant-lined dishes with the mixture. Cover them with the remaining eggplant slices. Spread the tops with a little tomato sauce and strew with the remaining grated Parmesan. Cover with foil and bake in a preheated 375° F. [190° C.] oven for 25 minutes. Turn them out and serve as individual portions.

FRANCO LAGATTOLLA
THE RECIPES THAT MADE A MILLION

Noodles with Onions

Nouilles Soubise

	To serve 6	
½ lb.	noodles	¼ kg.
8	medium-sized onions (about 2 lb. [1 kg.]), thinly sliced	8
4 tbsp.	butter	60 ml.
	salt and pepper	
	grated nutmeg	
2 cups	thick white sauce (recipe, page 166)	½ liter
	fine bread crumbs	
	paprika	

Boil the onions for 15 minutes in salted water. Drain well. Heat 3 tablespoons [45 ml.] of the butter in a saucepan and simmer the onions slowly until tender; they should not brown. Season with salt, pepper and a little nutmeg. Stir the onions into the white sauce.

Cook the noodles in a large pan of boiling salted water. Drain well. Put the noodles in a buttered baking dish and cover them with the onion sauce. Sprinkle with bread crumbs and paprika; dot with the remaining butter. Brown in a preheated 400° F. [200° C.] oven for 10 minutes.

MAPIE, THE COUNTESS DE TOULOUSE-LAUTREC
LA CUISINE DE FRANCE

Stuffed Tomatoes

	To serve 6	
¼ lb.	small stars or other small pasta, boiled and drained	125 g.
6	large tomatoes	6
¼ cup	pine nuts	50 ml.
¼ cup	chopped fresh parsley	50 ml.
½ cup	sour cream or plain yogurt	125 ml.
1	garlic clove, crushed to a paste	1
1 tsp.	dried basil	5 ml.
½ tsp.	salt	2 ml.
¼ cup	freshly grated Parmesan cheese	50 ml.
¼ cup	fresh bread crumbs	50 ml.
¼ cup	water, tomato juice or white wine	50 ml.
2 tbsp.	butter	30 ml.

Preheat the oven to 350° F. [180° C.].

Cut a thin slice off the top of each tomato so that you can hollow it out. Discard the slices. Using a grapefruit knife, carefully remove as much pulp as possible without cutting any of the skin. Place the pulp in a large mixing bowl with the pasta, nuts, parsley, sour cream or yogurt, garlic, basil and salt. Combine these ingredients and use the mixture to carefully stuff the tomatoes. Sprinkle the tomatoes with the Parmesan cheese and bread crumbs.

Pour the water, tomato juice or white wine into a baking dish, and place the tomatoes in the dish. Dot with the butter. Bake in the preheated oven for about 20 minutes, basting occasionally with the cooking juices.

KAREN GREEN
THE GREAT INTERNATIONAL NOODLE EXPERIENCE

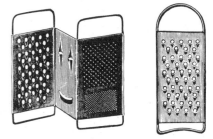

Baked Tomatoes Stuffed with Pasta "Barley"

Pomodoro Ripieni di Orzo

The technique of stuffing tomatoes with pasta is demonstrated on pages 56-57.

	To serve 6	
½ lb.	orzo	¼ kg.
6	large, firm, ripe tomatoes	6
	sugar	
1 tsp.	salt	5 ml.
	freshly ground black pepper	
½ tsp.	dried oregano	2 ml.
½ cup	cubed mozzarella cheese	125 ml.
4 tbsp.	butter	60 ml.
1	onion, finely chopped	1
1 quart	chicken stock (recipe, page 167)	1 liter
4 tbsp.	freshly grated Parmesan cheese	60 ml.

Remove the center pulp and seeds from the tomatoes, hollowing them out well. Lightly sprinkle into each tomato a little sugar, salt, pepper and oregano; place four cubes of mozzarella in each tomato.

Melt the butter in a saucepan and sauté the onion in it until soft; stir in the orzo, stirring well so each grain of pasta is coated. Pour in 2 cups [½ liter] of the stock, stir well, and simmer until it is absorbed, adding more stock gradually until the orzo is about three quarters cooked: firmer than *al dente*. Blend in the Parmesan, stirring it in well.

Spoon the orzo mixture into the hollowed tomatoes, filling them. Place the filled tomatoes in a casserole or baking dish with ½ cup [125 ml.] of hot stock in the bottom of the dish. Bake, covered, in a preheated 400° F. [200° C.] oven for 25 minutes; remove the cover for the last 10 minutes.

JACK DENTON SCOTT
THE COMPLETE BOOK OF PASTA

Beef-Noodle Casserole

To serve 8

½ lb.	broad noodles	¼ kg.
1 lb.	lean ground beef	½ kg.
3 tbsp.	oil	45 ml.
2	medium-sized onions, sliced	2
1	garlic clove, mashed to a paste	1
35 oz.	canned tomatoes	1 kg.
½ cup	tomato paste	125 ml.
1 cup	red wine or water	¼ liter
½ tsp.	paprika	2 ml.
1 tbsp.	salt	15 ml.
1	bay leaf	1
⅛ tsp.	thyme	½ ml.
1 tsp.	marjoram	5 ml.
1 tsp.	Worcestershire sauce	5 ml.
½ tsp.	Tabasco sauce	2 ml.
2 cups	white sauce *(recipe, page 166)*	½ liter
¼ cup	freshly grated Parmesan cheese	50 ml.

Preheat the oven to 375° F. [190° C.]. In a large, heavy skillet, heat the oil until hot; then add the meat, keeping the heat rather high. Stir the meat with a wooden spoon or fork, breaking it into small pieces. Add the onion and garlic to the meat, cover and simmer for two minutes. Add the tomatoes, tomato paste, wine or water, paprika, salt, bay leaf, thyme, marjoram, Worcestershire and Tabasco. Stir the meat and seasonings well, cover and simmer for five minutes.

Select a 2½-quart [2½-liter] baking dish, preferably a deep one. Be precise when selecting the baking dish, since the casserole will shrink somewhat as the noodles soften and the finished dish will look sunken if prepared in anything larger. Spoon half of the meat sauce into the baking dish, then add the uncooked noodles. Cover the noodles with the remaining meat sauce. Spread the white sauce in an even layer over the meat sauce. Bake the casserole in the preheated oven for 40 minutes. Sprinkle with the cheese and bake for 10 minutes more.

Serve directly from the casserole dish.

GREAT COOKS' GUIDE TO PASTA & NOODLE DISHES

Baked Macaroni with Ground Meat

Pasticcio Macaronia

To serve 6 to 8

1 lb.	macaroni	½ kg.
2 lb.	ground lamb, beef or veal	1 kg.
4 tbsp.	butter	60 ml.
1	small onion, finely chopped	1
1	garlic clove, chopped	1
2 tsp.	salt	10 ml.
½ tsp.	pepper	2 ml.
¼ cup	chopped fresh parsley	50 ml.
½ cup	dry white wine	125 ml.
2 or 3	medium-sized tomatoes, peeled and diced	2 or 3
4	eggs, 2 whole, 2 with the yolks separated from the whites	4
1 quart	white sauce *(recipe, page 166)* made with nutmeg	1 liter
2 cups	freshly grated Parmesan cheese	½ liter

Heat 2 tablespoons [30 ml.] of the butter in a large frying pan and sauté the ground meat and onion—stirring frequently—until slightly browned. Add the garlic, salt and pepper, parsley, wine and tomatoes. Cover and cook over medium heat until the meat is cooked and the tomatoes are reduced to a purée, about 15 minutes. Allow the mixture to cool and add the two egg whites.

Make the white sauce. Stir into it 1 cup [¼ liter] of the grated cheese, the two whole eggs and the two egg yolks. Set the sauce aside.

Cook the macaroni in boiling salted water until soft but firm, about 20 minutes. Drain the macaroni and return it to the pan. Add the rest of the butter in small pieces.

Butter a 10-by-14-inch [25-by-35-cm.] baking dish about 2 inches [5 cm.] deep and put half of the macaroni into it. Sprinkle with ½ cup [125 ml.] of grated cheese and cover with the meat filling. Top with the remaining macaroni. Sprinkle with a little cheese and cover with the sauce. Top with the remaining cheese and bake in a preheated 350° F. [180° C.] oven for about 45 minutes or until golden brown. Let sit in a warm place for about 20 minutes, then cut into small squares and serve.

CHRISSA PARADISSIS
THE BEST BOOK OF GREEK COOKERY

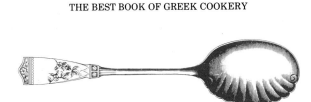

Grated Noodles
with Beef-Heart Filling

Hortobágyi Reszelt Tészta Tüdővel

The original version of this recipe calls for calf's lung, which is not available in the United States. The author recommends using beef heart instead. The techniques of preparing and grating noodle dough are demonstrated on pages 16-17.

This is a most unusual luncheon or supper dish, and it is one of the preparations that tastes quite different from one's expectations.

This 18th Century recipe belongs, to my knowledge, to the very small category that seems to have no close parallel in other nations' recipes.

To serve 8

about 1 cup	flour	about ¼ liter
7	eggs, 2 whole, 2 lightly beaten, 3 with the yolks separated from the whites, and the whites stiffly beaten	7
1 lb.	beef heart, washed and trimmed of fat, arteries and veins	½ kg.
1	small onion, finely chopped	1
2 tbsp.	lard	30 ml.
	salt and pepper	
1 quart	milk	1 liter
1 tbsp.	chopped fresh flat-leafed parsley	15 ml.
½ cup	sour cream	125 ml.

Knead the two whole eggs with enough of the flour to make a very, very hard dough. Grate the dough.

Cook the beef heart in boiling salted water for one hour. Drain, and put it through a food grinder. Sauté the onion in 1 tablespoon [15 ml.] of the lard for about 10 minutes. Mix the onion with the ground beef heart. Add a pinch of pepper and salt to taste. Set aside to cool.

Bring the milk to a boil and simmer the grated noodles in it over low heat, stirring. Cook until the milk is absorbed and the noodles are tender. Add more milk if necessary. Add a little salt and pepper and mix in the chopped parsley. Cool the noodles to lukewarm.

Mix the cooled noodles with the three egg yolks, then fold in the three stiffly beaten egg whites. Grease a heavy 3- to 4-quart [3- to 4-liter] casserole, 3 to 4 inches [8 to 10 cm.] deep, with the remaining lard. Pour the noodle-and-egg mixture into the casserole and pat it down evenly.

Add the two beaten eggs to the beef-heart mixture. Make a hole in the middle of the cooked-noodle mixture in the casserole, and pour in the beef-heart mixture. Spread the top with the sour cream. Bake in a preheated 375° F. [190° C.] oven for 45 minutes.

GEORGE LANG
THE CUISINE OF HUNGARY

Provençal Braised Beef
with Baked Macaroni

Daube à la Provençale

Beef cooked *en daube* is the traditional dish of inland Provence; it is often served with macaronade, or macaroni with cheese. It tastes just as good when reheated, and the leftover meat can be chopped and used in a ravioli filling.

To serve 8

1 lb.	long macaroni	½ kg.
1 tbsp.	butter	15 ml.
⅔ cup	freshly grated Parmesan or aged Gruyère cheese, or a mixture of both	150 ml.
Braised beef		
5 lb.	boneless lean stewing beef, cut into 1½-inch [4-cm.] cubes	2½ kg.
5 oz.	salt pork with the rind removed, blanched in boiling water for 5 minutes, drained and finely diced	150 g.
3 tbsp.	olive oil	45 ml.
5	garlic cloves, crushed	5
2	sprigs thyme	2
3	bay leaves	3
	coarse salt and freshly ground pepper	
2	carrots, quartered lengthwise	2
about 1 quart	red wine	about 1 liter

In an earthenware or cast-iron casserole with a concave lid, briefly sauté the diced pork in the olive oil. Add the beef, garlic cloves, thyme, bay leaves, salt, pepper and the carrots. Pour in the wine, making sure it covers the meat completely. Cover the pot with a piece of buttered wax paper or aluminum foil tied on tightly, then put on the lid. Bring to a boil and simmer for three to four hours. At the end of the cooking time, skim to remove excess fat from the surface.

To make the macaronade, cook the macaroni in plenty of boiling salted water until done, about 20 minutes. Rinse in cold water and drain. Butter a shallow, earthenware baking dish and cover with a layer of macaroni. Sprinkle with some of the cheese, then add a layer of macaroni, and so on until the dish is full, ending with cheese. Moisten well with gravy from the beef. Brown in a preheated 425° F. [220° C.] oven for seven or eight minutes. Serve the macaronade from the baking dish, the braised beef from the casserole.

HENRI PHILIPPON
CUISINE DE PROVENCE

Baked Ditali with Sweet and Hot Italian Sausages

To serve 6

1½ lb.	ditali, boiled until barely chewable and drained	¾ kg.
1 lb.	sweet Italian sausages	½ kg.
1 lb.	hot Italian sausages	½ kg.
1 tbsp.	olive oil	15 ml.
4 cups	tomato sauce *(recipe, page 166)*	1 liter
1½ cups	ricotta cheese	375 ml.
1 cup	freshly grated Parmesan cheese	¼ liter

In a saucepan, heat the oil and brown the sausages evenly. Remove the sausages; cut them into thin slices. Pour the oil out of the pan and discard it, but leave the brown residue. Add the tomato sauce to the same pan; add the sausage slices. Stir, cover and simmer for 20 minutes. Butter a baking dish and spoon a layer of the boiled, drained ditali evenly across the bottom; cover with a layer of sausage slices in tomato sauce. Then spread with a layer of ricotta and sprinkle it with Parmesan cheese. Repeat the layering until all of the pasta, sausages and cheeses are used, ending with a layer of sauce and cheese. Bake, uncovered, in a preheated 350° F. [180° C.] oven for 25 minutes, or until the sauce is bubbling. Serve in warmed individual plates.

MARIA LUISA SCOTT AND JACK DENTON SCOTT
WORLD OF PASTA

Moussaka with Noodles

Musaca cu Tatei

To serve 4 to 6

1 lb.	thin noodles	½ kg.
1 lb.	lean ground pork	½ kg.
1	slice firm-textured white bread, soaked in milk until soft	1
3 tbsp.	finely chopped fresh parsley	45 ml.
3 tbsp.	finely chopped fennel leaves	45 ml.
1	leek, white part only, finely chopped	1
	salt and pepper	
4	eggs	4
2 tbsp.	butter, cut into small bits	30 ml.
	flour	
½ cup	cream	125 ml.
¼ cup	freshly grated cheese	50 ml.

Mix the ground pork with the milk-soaked bread slice. Add 1 tablespoon [15 ml.] of the parsley and fennel, the leek, and

salt and pepper to taste. Boil the noodles, drain, place in a bowl, add two of the eggs and mix well.

Butter the bottom and sides of a casserole and sprinkle with a little flour. Arrange alternately one layer of noodles, then one layer of meat, ending with a layer of noodles on top. Sprinkle each layer with a little chopped parsley and fennel and bits of butter. Place in a preheated 375° F. [190° C.] oven and bake for half an hour.

Meanwhile, prepare a mixture of two eggs well beaten with ½ cup [125 ml.] of cream. Add the grated cheese, mix well and pour over the ingredients in the casserole. Return to the oven and bake slowly until nice and brown, about 20 minutes. Remove from the oven and turn the contents upside down onto a platter. Place another platter on the *musaca* and, holding both platters between your hands, invert them so the crust is on top. Serve very hot on heated plates.

ANISOARA STAN
THE ROMANIAN COOK BOOK

Spaghetti Timbale

Kasseri is a hard, white cheese, made in Greece from sheep's milk, but in the United States from cow's milk.

If the sausages are dry and hard, you can put them through a meat grinder.

To serve 8

2 lb.	thin spaghetti	1 kg.
3 or 4 tbsp.	butter, melted	45 or 60 ml.
2 cups	grated *kasseri* cheese or 6 oz. [175 g.] feta cheese, crumbled	½ liter
7 or 8	thick slices slab bacon or 3 or 4 smoked pork sausage links, cut into small pieces	7 or 8
½ cup	cracker meal	125 ml.
	salt and pepper	
	grated nutmeg	
2 or 3	eggs	2 or 3

Cook the spaghetti in boiling salted water. Drain and return it to the saucepan. Off the heat, pour the melted butter over it. Mix the cheese with the spaghetti. Add the bacon or sausage to the spaghetti and cheese. Add the cracker meal, salt, pepper and nutmeg. Beat the eggs and add them to the mixture. Mix well.

Butter a deep circular cake pan or baking dish and dust it with cracker meal. Carefully fill the mold with the spaghetti mixture and bake in a preheated 375° F. [190° C.] oven for at least 30 minutes. Cool for 15 minutes and unmold the timbale onto a serving platter.

NICHOLAS TSELEMENTES
GREEK COOKERY

Green Pasta Soufflé

Sformato di Tagliatelle Verdi

Making tagliatelle from fresh pasta dough is shown on pages 22-23. For colored-pasta techniques, see page 20.

	To serve 4	
1¾ cups	unbleached flour	425 ml.
1	extra-large egg	1
1 tsp.	olive oil	5 ml.
¼ lb.	spinach, stems removed, washed, boiled in salted water for 2 minutes, drained, squeezed dry and finely chopped	125 g.
	salt	
2½ quarts	cold water	2½ liters
2 tbsp.	vegetable oil	30 ml.
Ham soufflé		
¼ lb.	boiled ham, coarsely chopped	125 g.
3	eggs, the yolks separated from the whites, plus 1 egg white	3
1½ cups	white sauce *(recipe, page 166),* cooled	375 ml.
2 tbsp.	freshly grated Parmesan cheese	30 ml.
	salt and freshly ground white pepper	
	freshly grated nutmeg	
	butter	
	olive oil	

Make the pasta by placing the flour in a mound on a pasta board. Make a well in the center and put in the egg, olive oil, spinach and a pinch of salt. With a fork, first mix together the egg, oil and salt, then begin to incorporate the flour from the inner rim of the well, always incorporating fresh flour from the lower part, pushing it under the dough to keep the dough detached. When half of the flour has been absorbed, start kneading, always using the palms of your hands, not the fingers. Continue kneading in the flour until almost all of it has been incorporated. The small fraction of flour that remains unabsorbed should be passed through a sifter to remove bits of dough and kept to coat the dough during the succeeding steps.

Roll out the dough and cut it into tagliatelle. Set the pasta aside, covered with a cloth kitchen towel.

Place a stockpot containing a large quantity of salted water on the heat. While this water is heating, put the 2½ quarts [2½ liters] of cold water and the vegetable oil together in a large bowl. When the salted water reaches the boiling point, put in the tagliatelle and cook for about 20 seconds or until *al dente.* Drain them, then put them into the cold water for about one minute. Wet a kitchen towel with cold water and spread it out on a pastry board. Lift out the tagliatelle very gently and place them on the damp towel.

To make the soufflé, beat the three egg yolks in a large bowl with a wooden spoon. Add the cooled white sauce and the grated Parmesan. Mix well, then fold in the ham and seasonings very gently. Let the mixture rest for 15 minutes. Meanwhile, beat the four egg whites until stiff.

Add the tagliatelle to the bowl containing the ham mixture, then fold in the egg whites. Toss very gently, taking care not to break up the tagliatelle. Pour carefully into a soufflé dish well greased with butter and a little olive oil, and bake in a preheated 400° F. [200° C.] oven for 40 minutes, or until the soufflé has risen and is golden.

GIULIANO BUGIALLI
THE FINE ART OF ITALIAN COOKING

Noodle and Ham Casserole

Lokshyna and Ham

	To serve 3 or 4	
1 cup	flour	¼ liter
2	eggs, each beaten separately	2
1 tbsp.	water	15 ml.
	salt	
¾ cup	ground or finely chopped ham	175 ml.
1 tbsp.	butter, melted	15 ml.
about ¼ cup	freshly grated cheese	about 50 ml.
¼ cup	light cream	50 ml.
¼ cup	buttered bread crumbs	50 ml.

To prepare the noodles, combine one of the beaten eggs with the flour, water and ¼ teaspoon [1 ml.] of salt to make a stiff dough. Knead on a lightly floured board until the dough is smooth. Cover and let it stand for 30 minutes.

Roll the dough to almost paper-thinness and allow it to dry partially. Turn the dough over in order to dry the other side slightly. It must be neither sticky nor dry and brittle. Cut into strips about 3 inches [8 cm.] wide and stack the strips on top of each other. Cut the strips crosswise into fine shreds. Separate the shreds by tossing them lightly with your fingers. Spread them out to dry.

Drop the noodles into a large quantity of boiling salted water, stir, and cook for about eight minutes. Drain the noodles in a colander or sieve, and then rinse with cold water to prevent them from sticking together. Drain.

Mix the noodles with the melted butter. Mix in the ham and cheese. Combine the remaining egg and the cream and add to the noodle mixture. Taste and add salt if necessary. Spoon the mixture into a buttered baking dish and top with the buttered bread crumbs. Bake in a moderate (350° F. [180° C.]) oven for about 45 minutes or until done.

SAVELLA STECHISHIN
TRADITIONAL UKRAINIAN COOKERY

Sicilian Macaroni and Sardine Pie

Pasta con le Sarde

Bucatini are pierced, hollow pasta similar to macaroni, but thinner than spaghetti.

To serve 6

1 lb.	bucatini or elbow macaroni	½ kg.
1 lb.	fennel bulbs, trimmed	½ kg.
1 lb.	fresh sardines, filleted (about 12 sardines)	½ kg.
½ cup	seedless white raisins, soaked in warm water for 15 minutes and drained	125 ml.
	flour	
1 cup	olive oil	¼ liter
3 or 4	shallots, finely chopped	3 or 4
3	salt anchovies, filleted, soaked in water for 30 minutes, drained and patted dry	3
¼ tsp.	ground saffron, mixed with a little hot water	1 ml.
½ cup	pine nuts	125 ml.
	salt and freshly ground pepper	

Boil the fennel bulbs for 10 minutes in water. Take them out, drain them and cut them into very small pieces. Save the cooking liquid.

Take about four of the sardines and cut them up very small to go into the sauce. Flour the remaining sardines and fry them lightly in about half of the olive oil. Drain them and set them aside.

Heat about ¼ cup [50 ml.] of the olive oil and let the shallots take color in this. Add the chopped-up sardines and crush them in the pan with a spoon. Add the chopped fennel and let the whole cook briefly (about 10 minutes), adding a small amount of the fennel cooking liquid if the mixture begins to dry out.

Heat the remainder of the olive oil separately, then add the anchovies to it. Place the pan on a heat-diffusing pad over very low heat and help the anchovies to melt by stirring them with a fork.

Add to the shallot, sardine and fennel mixture the melted anchovies, the saffron, raisins, pine nuts and a little salt and pepper, and let it all go on cooking for a few minutes.

Meanwhile, cook the pasta: Bring the fennel's cooking liquid to a boil, supplement it if necessary with water, and cook the pasta in this with a little salt. Drain.

Combine the pasta with the sauce. Finally, place a layer of the pasta in an oven dish, with fried sardines on top and more pasta on top of them, and so on, finishing with a layer of pasta. Bake this dish in a preheated 375° F. [190° C.] oven for about 15 minutes.

ALAN DAVIDSON
MEDITERRANEAN SEAFOOD

Stuffed Pasta Shells

To serve 12

1 lb.	large pasta shells, each 2 inches [5 cm.] long, boiled and drained	½ kg.
6 tbsp.	butter	90 ml.
6	garlic cloves, peeled and finely chopped with a little salt	6
6 tbsp.	flour	90 ml.
3 cups	milk with 1 cup [¼ liter] heavy cream	¾ liter
½ cup	finely chopped fresh parsley	125 ml.
6	oil-packed flat anchovy fillets, finely chopped	6
	salt and white pepper	

Cheese-and-prosciutto stuffing

1 lb.	ricotta cheese	½ kg.
½ lb.	small-curd cottage cheese	¼ kg.
¼ cup	freshly grated Parmesan cheese	50 ml.
6	thin slices prosciutto, cut into ⅛-inch [3-mm.] squares	6
3 tbsp.	chopped fresh parsley	45 ml.
3 tbsp.	finely chopped fresh basil or 1 tbsp. [15 ml.] crumbled dried basil	45 ml.
2	egg yolks, beaten	2
	salt and freshly ground white pepper	

Melt the butter in a heavy-bottomed saucepan over low heat. Add the garlic and sauté until it just starts to turn golden brown. Remove from the heat and when the butter has stopped bubbling add the flour. Return to the heat and cook, stirring constantly, for about two minutes. Do not let the flour color. Remove from the heat and add the milk and cream all at once. Immediately beat vigorously with a wire whip until smooth. Put the pan over medium heat and add the parsley and anchovies. Cook, stirring constantly, until the sauce is the consistency of heavy cream. Remove from the heat. Salt and pepper to taste. Reserve uncovered.

In a large bowl, combine the ricotta, cottage cheese, Parmesan, parsley, basil, prosciutto and egg yolks. Add salt and pepper to taste, and mix well. Stuff each shell with some of the cheese mixture, pressing it down lightly to fill out the shape. Using your fingers, press the long sides of each shell lightly together so that the shape of the shell is as it was before boiling. Wipe off any excess filling.

Put about 2 cups [½ liter] of the sauce in the bottom of a baking dish large enough to hold the shells in one layer. Place the stuffed shells in the dish. Pour the remaining sauce over them. Bake in a preheated 375° F. [190° C.] oven for 15 minutes, or until the sauce bubbles. Serve at once.

CHARLOTTE MC NAMARA & LENORE HOWELL
THE BEFORE AND AFTER DINNER COOKBOOK

Hearty Manicotti

To serve 8

½ lb.	manicotti (16 shells), boiled and drained	¼ kg.
	freshly grated Parmesan cheese	

Ricotta-and-mozzarella-cheese filling

2 lb.	ricotta or sieved cottage cheese	1 kg.
½ lb.	mozzarella cheese, diced	¼ kg.
2 tbsp.	chopped fresh parsley	30 ml.
¾ tsp.	basil	4 ml.
½ tsp.	salt	2 ml.

Sausage-and-beef sauce

1 lb.	Italian sausages, each pricked in several places with a fork	½ kg.
1 lb.	lean ground beef	½ kg.
1	medium-sized onion, finely chopped	1
4 cups	puréed tomato (recipe, page 167)	1 liter
6 oz.	canned tomato paste	175 g.
1¼ cups	water	300 ml.
1 tsp.	basil	5 ml.
	salt	
1 tsp.	sugar	5 ml.
½ tsp.	pepper	2 ml.

In a covered Dutch oven over medium heat, cook the sausages in ¼ cup [50 ml.] of the water for five minutes. Uncover; brown the sausages well and drain them on paper towels. Discard the sausage fat, then brown the ground beef with the onion. Stir in the puréed tomato, tomato paste, basil, salt to taste, the sugar, pepper and the remaining water. Cover and simmer for 45 minutes. Cut the sausages into bite-sized pieces and add them to the mixture. Cook for 15 minutes, stirring occasionally.

Meanwhile preheat the oven to 375° F. [190° C.]. In a large bowl, combine the ricotta or cottage cheese, mozzarella, parsley, basil and salt. Stuff this filling into the cooked manicotti shells.

Spoon half of the meat sauce into one 13-by-9-inch [32½-by-23-cm.] or two 9-inch [23-cm.] square baking dishes. Arrange half of the stuffed shells in one layer on top of the sauce. Spoon most of the remaining sauce—reserving about ¾ cup [175 ml.]—over the shells; top with the remaining shells in one layer. Spoon the reserved meat sauce over the top. Sprinkle the manicotti with grated Parmesan cheese. Bake for 30 minutes in the preheated oven.

THE VASHTI EDUCATIONAL CENTER, INC.
PINES AND PLANTATIONS: NATIVE RECIPES OF THOMASVILLE, GEORGIA

Rigatoni Stuffed with Tuna and Ricotta

Rigatoni Ripieni

To serve 6

1 lb.	rigatoni	½ kg.
1 cup	heavy cream	¼ liter
2 cups	freshly grated Parmesan cheese	½ liter
	salt and pepper	
1 tbsp.	butter	15 ml.

Tuna-and-ricotta-cheese filling

7 oz.	canned tuna, drained and flaked	200 g.
1 cup	ricotta cheese, sieved	¼ liter

Cook the rigatoni *al dente* in boiling salted water. Mix the tuna and ricotta to a soft paste. Mix the cream and Parmesan, and salt and pepper to taste. Drain the rigatoni and rinse them with hot water. Load a pastry bag with the tuna-and-ricotta mixture, and squeeze a little of it into each rigatoni. Put the rigatoni side by side in a buttered baking dish. Pour the cream-and-Parmesan mixture over the rigatoni and refrigerate for several hours. When ready to serve, bake in a preheated 400° F. [200° C.] oven for 25 to 30 minutes, or until hot and brown.

WAVERLEY ROOT
THE BEST OF ITALIAN COOKING

Spinach and Cheese Cannelloni

Panzerotti

To serve 4

16	large cannelloni	16
2 cups	white sauce (recipe, page 166)	½ liter

Spinach-and-cheese filling

1 lb.	spinach, stemmed, parboiled for 2 minutes, squeezed dry and chopped	½ kg.
10 oz.	ricotta cheese	300 g.
2⅓ cups	freshly grated Parmesan cheese	575 ml.
5 oz.	*mascarpone* or *crescenza* cheese	150 g.
	salt and freshly ground pepper	
	freshly grated nutmeg	

Put plenty of salted water on to boil for the pasta. When the water boils, put in the cannelloni one at a time, stir and cook over medium heat. When the cannelloni are half-cooked, after five or six minutes for commercial pasta or two minutes for fresh pasta, remove them and plunge them into cold water. Then drain them and spread them out on cloth towels.

While the pasta is cooking, put the chopped spinach into a bowl with the ricotta, about half of the Parmesan, the *mascarpone* or *crescenza,* and a pinch each of salt, pepper and nutmeg. Mix together well.

Thoroughly butter an ovenproof dish large enough to hold the cannelloni in a single layer. Preheat the oven to 350° F. [180° C.]. Fill the cannelloni with the spinach-and-cheese mixture and arrange them in the dish. Sprinkle with the rest of the Parmesan and cover with the white sauce. Place in the oven for about 20 minutes, or until the sauce is bubbling and the surface is lightly colored. Serve.

FERNANDA GOSETTI
IN CUCINA CON FERNANDA GOSETTI

Zucchini and Meat Pie

Crosetti

Caciocavallo is a smooth, white Italian or Sicilian cheese similar to provolone but not smoked as provolone is; it is obtainable at cheese specialty stores.

To serve 6 to 8

1 lb.	mafalde or lasagne	½ kg.
4 or 5	medium-sized zucchini (1½ lb. [¾ kg.], cut into ½-inch [1-cm.] slices	4 or 5
1½ lb.	veal stew meat	¾ kg.
6 tbsp.	olive oil	90 ml.
1	large onion, finely chopped	1
2	garlic cloves, finely chopped	2
2	celery ribs, finely chopped	2
29 oz.	canned Italian-style tomatoes in purée	900 g.
3	sprigs fresh basil or 1 tbsp. [15 ml.] dried basil	3
2	sprigs parsley, chopped	2
1 tsp.	salt	5 ml.
¼ tsp.	black pepper	1 ml.
1 cup	coarsely shredded *caciocavallo* cheese	¼ liter
	freshly grated Parmesan cheese	

In a large skillet, heat 4 tablespoons [60 ml.] of the olive oil and in it brown the zucchini lightly. Set aside.

In the same skillet, sauté the onion, garlic and celery until golden—about five minutes. Transfer to a large saucepan. Add the remaining oil to the skillet and brown the veal lightly on all sides; transfer the veal to the saucepan and stir in the tomatoes, basil, parsley, salt and pepper. Simmer the

sauce slowly until the veal is tender—about one hour. Remove the veal and let it cool. Cut the veal into shreds and return it to the saucepan.

Cook the mafalde in boiling salted water until *al dente.* Drain, rinse with cold water and drain again. Pour a ladle of sauce into a 10-inch [25-cm.] spring-form pan. Add a layer of the mafalde (overlapping the edges of each piece), then layer zucchini, tomato-veal sauce and *caciocavallo* cheese. Continue this layering sequence until all of the pasta and zucchini are used, ending with a layer of mafalde on top. Cut this top layer to fit the circumference of the pan. Cover with the veal sauce and the remaining cheese, and bake in a preheated 350° F. [180° C.] oven for 30 minutes. Let the dish cool for 10 minutes before serving. Cut into wedges and serve with the remaining sauce and grated Parmesan cheese.

ANNA MUFFOLETTO
THE ART OF SICILIAN COOKING

Lasagne with Four Cheeses

Lasagne di Meluzza Comasca

To serve 4

¾ lb.	pasta dough *(recipe, page 164),* cut into lasagne	⅓ kg.
2 oz.	provolone cheese, thinly sliced	50 g.
2 oz.	*caciocavallo* cheese, shredded	50 g.
3½ oz.	mozzarella cheese, thinly sliced	100 g.
⅔ cup	freshly grated Parmesan cheese	150 ml.
5 tbsp.	butter	75 ml.
1 tbsp.	sugar, mixed with 1 tsp. [5 ml.] ground cinnamon	15 ml.

Cook the lasagne in boiling salted water until *al dente,* and spread the pieces out on a towel to dry. Do not let them dry out completely.

Butter a 1½-quart [1½-liter] oven dish, and line the bottom with a layer of lasagne. Cover this with half of the sliced provolone and half of the shredded *caciocavallo.* Add a second layer of lasagne and cover with half of the mozzarella, then half of the Parmesan. Make another layer of lasagne, dot with butter, and sprinkle with half of the cinnamon sugar. Repeat the layers, ending with a layer dotted with butter and sprinkled with cinnamon sugar. Bake in a preheated 350° F. [180° C.] oven for 20 minutes, or until lightly browned. Serve hot.

MASSIMO ALBERINI
CENTO RICETTE STORICHE

Lasagne with Veal and Mozzarella

Lasagne all'Abruzzese

To serve 4

¾ lb.	pasta dough *(recipe, page 164)*	⅓ kg.
1¾ cups	diced mozzarella cheese (about ½ lb. [¼ kg.])	425 ml.
2	eggs, hard-boiled and diced	2
5 tbsp.	butter, melted	75 ml.
	Veal sauce	
½ lb.	lean ground veal	¼ kg.
1 tbsp.	butter	15 ml.
¼ cup	dry white wine	50 ml.
1½ cups	puréed tomato *(recipe, page 167)*	375 ml.
	salt and pepper	
1⅓ cups	freshly grated Parmesan cheese	325 ml.
1	egg	1

Roll out the pasta dough thin and slice it into strips to fit the bottom and sides of your baking dish. Cook the fresh pasta for about one minute in boiling salted water, drain, and put the strips on a cloth kitchen towel to dry.

To make the meat sauce, heat the butter and when it starts to foam, add the ground veal and brown thoroughly. Add the wine and cook rapidly until the smell of the wine disappears. Add the puréed tomatoes and bring the sauce to a boil. Season with salt and pepper. Reduce the heat and simmer. Mix the Parmesan cheese and the egg in a bowl, then stir them gradually into the meat sauce. Simmer the sauce until it thickens.

Butter an ovenproof dish and line the bottom and sides with the pasta strips. Cover with meat sauce, then sprinkle evenly with some of the diced hard-boiled egg and mozzarella cheese. Cover with another layer of pasta and continue in the same way, ending with a layer of pasta. Pour the melted butter over the lasagne and bake the dish in a preheated 350° F. [180° C.] oven for about 15 minutes, or until the top is just beginning to brown. Serve very hot.

ANNA MARTINI (EDITOR)
PASTA AND PIZZA

Lasagne Pie with Sole and Crayfish

Torta di Lasagne di Magro con Gamberi

This is a modern combination of two 16th Century Italian recipes: Fast-Day Pasta and Crayfish Pie. This version was created by Franco Danielli, head chef of the luxury liner Raffaello, in 1973. The technique of making pasta dough is shown on pages 16-19.

To serve 6 to 8

1 lb.	pasta dough *(recipe, page 164)*, rolled out and cut into rectangles 2 by 8 inches [5 by 20 cm.]	½ kg.
12	small sole fillets, skinned	12
15 to 20	live crayfish (about 1 lb. [½ kg.])	15 to 20
10 tbsp.	butter	150 ml.
1 cup	dry white wine	¼ liter
	pepper and salt	
¼ cup	flour	50 ml.
1 cup	freshly grated Parmesan cheese	¼ liter
⅓ cup	brandy	75 ml.
1 tsp.	curry powder	5 ml.
	Wine court bouillon	
1 cup	dry white wine	¼ liter
2 cups	water	½ liter
1	small onion	1
	salt	
5	whole peppercorns	5
2	bay leaves	2

Boil the court-bouillon ingredients together for 15 minutes. Add the crayfish, cover and cook for seven or eight minutes or until the crayfish are red. Shell them and put the heads and shells into a food processor or mortar. Add a little cooking liquid and grind the shells fine. Add the rest of the liquid, strain through a fine sieve and reserve the juices.

In a large skillet, cook the sole fillets over medium heat in 4 tablespoons [60 ml.] of the butter. When they begin to brown, add the white wine, a pinch of ground pepper, and salt to taste. Bring the wine to a boil, simmer for one minute and take the pan off the heat.

In a saucepan, melt 4 tablespoons of the butter and stir in all but 1 teaspoon [5 ml.] of the flour. Cook for one minute, stirring constantly, then whisk in all but ½ cup [125 ml.] of the crayfish cooking juices. Bring to a boil. Remove the sauce from the heat and stir in the grated cheese. Keep the cheese sauce warm, stirring it from time to time to prevent a skin from forming on its surface.

Cook the rectangles of noodle dough in boiling water, two or three at a time, until they are *al dente*, in about three or four minutes. Drain them and lay them side by side on a cloth kitchen towel.

Butter an 8-by-10-inch [20-by-25-cm.] rectangular oven dish and cover the bottom with a layer of lasagne. Pour on a thin coating of the cheese sauce. Add a layer of sole fillets with a little of their cooking juices. Cover with another layer of lasagne, coat with cheese sauce, more sole, and so on until all of the ingredients are used up. The last layer should be of pasta, with cheese sauce poured over. Bake in a preheated 425° F. [220° C.] oven for about 10 minutes, but do not allow the pie to brown.

Meanwhile melt the remaining butter. When it begins to brown, add the crayfish, sauté them for a few minutes, then reduce the heat, add the brandy and carefully ignite it. When the flames die, dissolve the curry powder and the remaining teaspoonful of flour in the remaining crayfish cooking juices and add this mixture to the pan to cook for a few minutes. The sauce should not be too thick.

Serve the pie hot with the crayfish in their sauce.

MASSIMO ALBERINI
CENTO RICETTE STORICHE

Lazanki with Ham

Łazanki z Szynką

The preparation of pasta squares is shown on page 23; the technique of layering pasta is demonstrated on page 53.

To serve 4

2 cups	flour	½ liter
6	eggs, 3 lightly beaten, 3 with the yolks separated from the whites, and the whites stiffly beaten	6
½ lb.	ham, coarsely chopped	¼ kg.
5 tbsp.	butter, softened	75 ml.
½ cup	sour cream	125 ml.

Mix the three beaten eggs with the flour and knead to form a dough. Roll out the dough thin and allow it to dry for about 30 minutes; then cut it into ½-inch [1-cm.] squares. Boil these lazanki in salted water for three to five minutes or until tender. Drain.

Mix the butter with the egg yolks and sour cream, and then stir in the lazanki. Fold in the beaten egg whites. Butter a 1-quart [1-liter] baking dish and put in alternate layers of lazanki and pieces of chopped ham, ending with lazanki. Bake for one hour in a preheated 350° F. [180° C.] oven. The top should be golden brown.

MARIA DISSLOWA
JAK GOTOWAĆ

Spinach Lasagne with Meat Sauce

Lasagne Verdi alla Bolognese

The preparation of spinach-pasta dough appears on page 20. Pancetta is a cut of pork belly similar to bacon but cured with salt and pepper; it is obtainable from Italian delicatessens. If unavailable, substitute lean salt pork or salt-cured ham.

To serve 6

2 lb.	spinach-pasta dough (recipe, page 165)	1 kg.
2 cups	white sauce (recipe, page 166)	½ liter
1 cup	freshly grated Parmesan cheese	¼ liter

Meat sauce

7 oz.	*pancetta*, finely chopped	200 g.
1 lb.	lean ground beef	½ kg.
⅓ cup	finely chopped celery	75 ml.
⅓ cup	finely chopped onion	75 ml.
1	carrot, finely chopped	1
3	chicken gizzards, trimmed and finely chopped	3
1 quart	chicken stock (recipe, page 167)	1 liter
	salt	
8	medium-sized tomatoes, peeled, seeded and chopped	8
14 tbsp.	butter	200 ml.

Roll the spinach pasta out into a thin sheet, and cut it into at least 10 rounds or rectangles, each to fit the shape of the 1½-quart [1½-liter] oven dish that is to be used for the lasagne.

Brown the *pancetta*, salt pork or ham in a saucepan for about five minutes. Add the ground beef, celery, onion, carrot and the gizzards. Cook over fairly brisk heat, stirring frequently, for 20 minutes. Then pour in 1⅓ cups [325 ml.] of the stock and add a pinch of salt. Increase the heat a little and, continuing to stir, cook until the liquid is absorbed, about 20 minutes. Then add the tomatoes and butter and the remainder of the stock. Simmer for at least 90 minutes, or until the mixture is the consistency of a thick sauce.

In fast-boiling salted water, cook the rounds or rectangles of pasta one at a time, until tender but still quite firm, about five minutes. Drain the pasta on cloth kitchen towels.

Moisten the oven dish with a bit of the meat sauce, place a piece of pasta in the bottom and add more meat sauce, a layer of white sauce, then a layer of grated cheese. Cover with a piece of pasta and repeat the process until all of the ingredients are used up, ending with a layer of white sauce. Place in a preheated 400° F. [200° C.] oven and bake for 15 to 20 minutes, or until the top is golden brown. Serve hot.

LUIGI VOLPICELLI AND SECONDINO FREDA
L'ANTIARTUSI: 1000 RICETTE

Fried Pasta

Fried Cheese-stuffed Ravioli
Panzarotti

	To serve 6	
2½ cups	flour	625 ml.
½ cup	olive oil	125 ml.
	salt	
2	egg yolks	2
	tepid water	

Mozzarella-and-Parmesan-cheese stuffing

1 cup	finely diced mozzarella cheese	¼ liter
⅓ cup	freshly grated Parmesan cheese	75 ml.
2	eggs	2
	salt	
¼ lb.	salami or Parma ham, finely diced (optional)	125 g.
	oil for frying	

Sift the flour in a mound on a pastry board or into a bowl. Make a well in the center. Add the oil, a pinch of salt, the egg yolks and about 1 tablespoon [15 ml.] of tepid water. Work the flour into the liquid and knead to a firm dough. Knead the dough until smooth and elastic; gather it into a ball, put it into a lightly floured bowl, cover and leave for about 30 minutes to rest. Roll out into one thin sheet and cut into circles about 2½ inches [6 cm.] in diameter.

To make the stuffing, put the mozzarella into a bowl with the Parmesan cheese, eggs, salt to taste, and the salami or ham, if used. Mix thoroughly and put a teaspoon [5 ml.] of the mixture on each circle of dough. Fold the dough over to cover the filling and seal tightly with the tines of a fork.

Deep fry the panzarotti a few at a time until crisp and golden brown. Drain on paper towels and serve very hot.

ADA BONI
ITALIAN REGIONAL COOKING

Won Tons
Hun Tun

The techniques of filling and shaping won tons are demonstrated on pages 72-73.

	To make about 64 won tons	
2 cups	flour	½ liter
½ tsp.	salt	2 ml.
1	egg	1
about ½ cup	water	about 125 ml.
	oil for deep frying	

Pork-and-vegetable filling

1 lb.	lean ground pork (about 2 cups [½ liter])	½ kg.
½ lb.	spinach, parboiled for 3 minutes, drained, squeezed dry and chopped or ½ cup [125 ml.] chopped celery, cabbage or green beans, parboiled for 5 minutes and drained	¼ kg.
1 tsp.	salt	5 ml.
1 tbsp.	soy sauce	15 ml.
1 tbsp.	cornstarch	15 ml.
1	egg	1
1 tbsp.	peanut or corn oil	15 ml.

Hot-pepper oil

1 tsp.	Szechwan peppercorns	5 ml.
½ cup	corn oil	125 ml.
2 tbsp.	cayenne pepper	30 ml.
1 tsp.	paprika	5 ml.

To make the won-ton wrappers, mix the salt and flour in a mixing bowl. Make a well in the center of the flour and pour in the egg and the water. With your fingers, stir to combine these ingredients (add water if the dough is too dry), then mix and knead until the dough is smooth and soft. Cover the dough with a dry cloth and let it set for 15 minutes.

Divide the dough in half. On a floured surface, roll out one half at a time into a paper-thin sheet about 24 by 12 inches [60 by 30 cm.]. With a sharp knife or pastry wheel, cut 3-inch [8-cm.] squares. Sprinkle a little flour between the pieces and stack them. Cover with a dry towel.

To make the filling, combine the pork, salt, soy sauce, cornstarch, egg and oil. Stir the mixture in one direction until the meat holds together; add the spinach or celery, cabbage or green beans, and mix some more.

While wrapping, cover the stack of won-ton wrappers with a damp cloth to prevent them from drying out.

To fill each won-ton wrapper, place 1 teaspoon [5 ml.] of filling just below one corner. Fold the corner over the filling and roll the wrapper toward the center, leaving 1 inch [2½ cm.] of the opposite corner unrolled. Dip a finger in cold water and moisten one end of the rolled wrapper. Take the two ends of the wrapper in the fingers of both hands and pull the ends toward each other, away from the unrolled corner, until they meet and overlap. Pinch the ends firmly together to seal the won ton. As each won ton is finished, place it on a tray and cover with a dry towel until ready to cook.

To prepare hot-pepper oil, roast the Szechwan peppercorns in a dry frying pan—stirring them often—for about five minutes, or until they are fragrant. Cool, then grind them with a mortar and pestle or in a blender. Heat a wok and add the corn oil. Heat the oil until it just starts to smoke. Turn off the heat, wait for 30 seconds, add the cayenne pepper, roasted Szechwan peppercorns and paprika. Stir well and let the mixture steep until the solids settle. Strain the oil through a strainer lined with a paper towel and discard the solids. Store the oil in a jar without refrigerating it.

When ready to serve, drop a few won tons at a time into oil heated to 335° F. [170° C.] and deep fry for three or four minutes. Drain on paper towels. Serve with wine vinegar and the hot-pepper oil as dips.

FLORENCE LIN
FLORENCE LIN'S CHINESE REGIONAL COOKBOOK

Golden Pasta Croquettes

To make 8 croquettes

2 cups	finely chopped, boiled spaghetti, macaroni or noodles	½ liter
3 tbsp.	finely chopped scallions	45 ml.
1	garlic clove, crushed	1
2 tbsp.	butter or margarine	30 ml.
2 tbsp.	ketchup	30 ml.
½ cup	grated sharp yellow cheese	125 ml.
1 cup	drained cottage cheese	¼ liter
2 tbsp.	chopped fresh parsley, dill or chives	30 ml.
3	eggs	3
about 2 tbsp.	flour	about 30 ml.
	salt and pepper	
	fine dry bread crumbs	
1 tbsp.	water	15 ml.
	fat for deep frying	

Sauté the onions and garlic in the butter or margarine until limp. Mix them in a bowl with the spaghetti, macaroni or noodles, the ketchup, yellow cheese and cottage cheese; add the parsley, dill or chives and two of the eggs. Mix well to combine the ingredients. Add enough of the flour to stiffen the mixture. Season with salt and pepper to taste. Spoon the mixture into a flat dish and spread it evenly. Chill until firm.

Cut the pasta mixture into eight portions and roll each portion with your hands to shape it into an oval croquette. Roll each croquette in bread crumbs; dip it in the remaining egg, beaten with 1 tablespoon [15 ml.] of water; and reroll it in bread crumbs. Chill the croquettes until firm.

Let the croquettes rest at room temperature for one hour before cooking. Deep fry in hot fat (375° F. [190° C.]) until golden brown. Drain on paper toweling.

KAY SHAW NELSON
PASTA: PLAIN AND FANCY

Spaghetti Croquettes

To make 12 croquettes

½ lb.	spaghetti, boiled, drained and chopped	¼ kg.
1 tbsp.	butter	15 ml.
1 tbsp.	flour	15 ml.
¾ cup	milk	175 ml.
¾ cup	grated Cheddar cheese	175 ml.
1 tsp.	salt	5 ml.
¼ tsp.	freshly ground black pepper	1 ml.
¼ tsp.	dry mustard	1 ml.
2	eggs	2
1 tsp.	grated onion	5 ml.
1 tbsp.	chopped fresh parsley	15 ml.
¾ cup	dry bread crumbs	175 ml.
	vegetable oil for deep frying	

Melt the butter in a saucepan. Blend in the flour until smooth. Gradually add the milk, stirring constantly to the boiling point. Mix in the cheese, salt, pepper and mustard; cook over low heat for five minutes. Cool for 15 minutes. Beat one of the eggs and add it to the cheese mixture, mixing thoroughly. Add the spaghetti, onion and parsley. Taste for seasoning. Chill for one hour. Shape into 12 croquettes.

Beat the remaining egg. Dip the croquettes into the egg and then into the bread crumbs. Heat the oil to 375° F. [190° C.]. Fry the croquettes until lightly browned.

MYRA WALDO
THE ART OF SPAGHETTI COOKERY

Fried Won Tons

The technique of making fried won tons is demonstrated on pages 72-73.

	To make 40 to 50 won tons	
2 cups	flour	½ liter
1	egg, lightly beaten	1
¾ cup	cold water	175 ml.
1 tsp.	salt	5 ml.
3 or 4 cups	vegetable oil	¾ or 1 liter

Pork-and-shrimp filling

½ lb.	lean ground pork	¼ kg.
½ lb.	raw shrimp, shelled, deveined and finely chopped	¼ kg.
½	bunch watercress, tough stems removed	½
1	egg, lightly beaten	1
1 tbsp.	dry sherry or Chinese rice wine	15 ml.
2 tbsp.	soy sauce	30 ml.
1 tbsp.	water	15 ml.
1 tbsp.	cornstarch	15 ml.
½ tsp.	salt	2 ml.
	freshly ground black pepper	

Sweet-and-sour sauce

1 cup	sugar	¼ liter
⅔ cup	red wine vinegar	150 ml.
2 cups	water	½ liter
1 tsp.	salt	5 ml.
1 tbsp.	soy sauce	15 ml.
¼ cup	peanut or vegetable oil	50 ml.
2 tbsp.	tree ears, soaked in hot water for 30 minutes and drained	30 ml.
1	sweet red or green pepper, halved, seeded, deribbed and coarsely chopped	1
1	large onion, cut into thin wedges	1
1	carrot, coarsely chopped	1
2	garlic cloves, crushed to a paste	2
1 tbsp.	cornstarch, dissolved in 2 tbsp. [30 ml.] water	15 ml.

To make the sweet-and-sour sauce, combine the sugar, vinegar, water, salt and soy sauce in a saucepan, and place it over medium heat. Stir until the sugar dissolves. Simmer for five to 10 minutes.

Heat the oil in a skillet and add the tree ears, all of the other vegetables and the garlic. Stir fry for five minutes. Add the vegetables to the sweet-and-sour sauce, along with the dissolved cornstarch. Stir well and simmer for 10 minutes. Remove from the heat.

To make the won-ton wrappers, mix together the flour, egg, water and salt. Knead to form a stiff dough and remove to a floured board. Knead for five to 10 minutes until the dough feels smooth and satiny. Roll the dough into a ball, cover it and let it rest for 30 minutes.

Meanwhile, plunge the watercress into a large kettle of boiling water for 30 seconds. Drain, and run under cold water. Squeeze dry and chop fine. Mix together the pork and shrimp in a bowl. Add the watercress and remaining filling ingredients. Mix well.

Knead the dough for a minute or two and roll it out to a thickness of 1/16 inch [2 mm.]; cut it into 3-inch [8-cm.] squares. Cover the squares so that they do not dry out.

Place about a teaspoon [5 ml.] of filling on the center of each square won-ton wrapper. Bring together two opposite corners of the wrapper and pinch the wrapper around the filling, using a little water to make the seal more secure. Pinch the two ends firmly together.

Heat the vegetable oil to 360° F. [180° C.] in a wok or deep-frying pan. Fry the won tons, about 10 at a time, for three minutes or until golden brown. Drain on paper toweling and keep warm in a 250° F. [120° C.] oven while you fry the remaining won tons.

Serve with the sweet-and-sour sauce.

MARIA POLUSHKIN
THE DUMPLING COOKBOOK

Double Noodles Alsace

The technique of preparing sautéed noodles is demonstrated on pages 68-69.

	To serve 4	
½ lb.	fettucini or other narrow egg noodles	¼ kg.
3 tbsp.	butter	45 ml.
¼ cup	shredded Gruyère cheese	50 ml.
½ tsp.	salt	2 ml.
	freshly ground black pepper	
2 tbsp.	light olive oil	30 ml.

Cook the noodles *al dente;* drain them. Melt the butter and stir in half of the noodles. Blend in the cheese, salt and pepper, and simmer for three minutes. Remove from the heat and turn into a heated serving dish. Sauté the remaining noodles in the oil in a frying pan until they are browned, but not too crisp. Ladle these noodles over those in the serving dish; serve in hot bowls.

JACK DENTON SCOTT
THE COMPLETE BOOK OF PASTA

Browned Cabbage Noodles
Kraut Fleckerl

To serve 6 to 8

1 lb.	broad noodles, boiled and drained	½ kg.
4 cups	finely shredded cabbage	1 liter
1 tbsp.	salt	15 ml.
8 tbsp.	butter or rendered chicken fat	120 ml.
½ tsp.	sugar	2 ml.
¼ tsp.	pepper	1 ml.

Sprinkle the salt on the cabbage and let it stand for 20 minutes. Drain thoroughly. Heat the butter or fat in a deep skillet. Mix in the cabbage, sugar and pepper. Cook over very low heat for 45 minutes, stirring frequently. Add the noodles, toss lightly and cook for three minutes.

MYRA WALDO
THE ART OF SPAGHETTI COOKERY

Two-Sides Browned Noodles
Liang Mien Huang

To serve 2 to 4

½ lb.	Chinese egg noodles	¼ kg.
6	large dried mushrooms	6
½ cup	dried flat-tip bamboo shoots	125 ml.
1½ cups	warm water	375 ml.
2 cups	shredded bok choy or Chinese cabbage	½ liter
5 tbsp.	peanut or corn oil	75 ml.
1 tbsp.	soy sauce	15 ml.
½ tsp.	sugar	2 ml.
2 tsp.	cornstarch	10 ml.
1 tsp.	sesame-seed oil	5 ml.

Wash the mushrooms and bamboo shoots and soak them in the warm water for one hour. Squeeze the water out of the vegetables, reserving it for later use. Shred the mushrooms and bamboo shoots fine and set them aside on a plate with the shredded bok choy or Chinese cabbage.

Cook the noodles in boiling water for two or three minutes. Drain and mix in 1 tablespoon [15 ml.] of the peanut or corn oil. Spread the noodles on a plate to cool.

Heat a large skillet until very hot. Add 1 tablespoon of the oil to coat the pan. Spread the cooked noodles in the skillet, smoothing them down. Move the pan, tipping it from side to side, for about five minutes, so that the noodles will shift along the bottom of the pan. The noodles will start to brown. Swirl for another two minutes, then flip the noodle patty over. Add 1 more tablespoon of oil and brown. Transfer to a heatproof platter and keep the patty warm in the oven.

Heat a wok or skillet, and add the remaining 2 tablespoons [30 ml.] of peanut or corn oil. Stir fry the mushrooms, bamboo shoots, and bok choy or Chinese cabbage together for two minutes, or until the vegetables wilt. Add the soy sauce and sugar. Stir to mix.

Strain the reserved mushroom-bamboo-shoot water and slowly pour about ½ cup [125 ml.] of it into the wok. In a cup, combine ¼ cup [50 ml.] of the soaking water with the cornstarch. Discard the remaining soaking water.

When the liquid in the wok begins to boil slowly, stir in the well-blended cornstarch mixture. When the ingredients are coated with a light glaze, add the sesame-seed oil and mix well. Pour the vegetables and sauce on top of the hot noodle patty and serve hot.

FLORENCE LIN
FLORENCE LIN'S CHINESE VEGETARIAN COOKBOOK

Noodle Squares with Cabbage
Káposztás Metélt

The technique of preparing sautéed noodles with cabbage is demonstrated on pages 68-69. If desired, the noodle squares may be made with colored pasta dough (recipe, page 164).

To serve 4

2½ cups	sifted flour	625 ml.
2	eggs	2
	salt	
1 to 3 tbsp.	water	15 to 45 ml.
1	small head cabbage, halved, cored and sliced into thin shreds	1
6 tbsp.	lard	90 ml.
¼ cup	chopped onion	50 ml.
	paprika	
	freshly ground pepper	

Prepare a very firm, dry dough by mixing the flour, eggs, a pinch of salt and enough water to moisten the mixture. Knead the dough until quite firm, divide it into three or four balls and refrigerate for a few hours to dry them.

Then roll each ball of dough out rather thin, cut it into strips ½ inch [1 cm.] wide and then again crosswise, to obtain small, square, flat pieces of pasta. Throw the squares into boiling, salted water and boil for 10 minutes or until cooked through. Drain and hold them under running cold water to prevent sticking.

Meanwhile, fry the cabbage in the lard, together with the chopped onion and a pinch of salt and paprika. Add a little water and simmer until tender.

Mix the cabbage and noodles thoroughly; serve very hot. Season with freshly ground pepper.

LILA DEELEY
FAVORITE HUNGARIAN RECIPES

Spiced Beef Chow Mein

Ngau Yuk Chow Mein

The technique of making a noodle nest is demonstrated on pages 70-71. For this recipe, the beef, scallions, ginger and snow peas should be shredded into strips, or julienne, about ⅛ inch [3 mm.] thick and 2 inches [5 cm.] long.

The beef has to be marinated ahead of time. You may adjust the hotness of the dish by controlling the amount of Tabasco sauce used. The amount listed in the recipe makes a mildly hot gravy. More gravy is needed than usual, since the noodles will absorb quite a bit of it.

To serve 2

1 lb.	Chinese egg noodles, boiled, rinsed in cold water and drained	½ kg.
¾ lb.	boneless lean beef steak, shredded (about 2 cups [½ liter])	⅓ kg.
1 tsp.	sugar	5 ml.
1 tbsp.	cornstarch	15 ml.
3 tbsp.	oyster sauce or 2 tbsp. [30 ml.] light soy sauce	45 ml.
2 cups	meat or chicken stock (recipe, page 167)	½ liter
1½ cups	vegetable oil	375 ml.
⅛ tsp.	salt	½ ml.
2	slices fresh ginger, shredded	2
1	garlic clove, finely chopped	1
2 cups	fresh bean sprouts	½ liter
1 cup	quartered fresh mushrooms	¼ liter
2	scallions, shredded	2
¼ cup	dry sherry	50 ml.
1 cup	shredded snow peas	¼ liter
Soy-sauce marinade		
1 tbsp.	dark soy sauce	15 ml.
1 tbsp.	vegetable oil	15 ml.
¼ tsp.	Tabasco sauce	1 ml.

Mix together the marinade in a bowl and put in the shredded beef to marinate for one hour. Drain before cooking.

Preheat the oven to 200° F. [100° C.].

Mix together the sugar, cornstarch, oyster sauce (or light soy sauce), and meat or chicken stock, and put aside.

Heat a medium-sized frying pan until it becomes hot and dry. Add the vegetable oil. Heat the oil to medium temperature (350° to 365° F. [180° to 185° C.]). Put the noodles into the oil and push them into the middle of the pan with a spatula so they form a round nestlike mass. Fry until a golden brown crust is formed on the bottom (about five to seven minutes); check by slightly lifting this nest to see the bot-

tom. Gently turn the noodles over to fry the other side. When done, remove the nest of noodles to paper towels to drain. Place in the preheated oven to keep warm while draining.

Heat a wok or another frying pan until it is hot and dry. Scoop from the first frying pan about 2 tablespoons [30 ml.] of the oil used to fry the noodles, and place it in the pan that is now being used. Add the salt, then the ginger and garlic, then the drained shredded beef.

Fry while rapidly stirring for half a minute. Turn down the heat, remove the beef to a bowl and put aside.

Turn the heat up again. Put in the bean sprouts, mushrooms and scallions. Stir fry for two minutes. Add the sherry and quickly cover the wok or pan. Cook one minute more. Stir in the sauce mixture made of sugar, cornstarch, oyster sauce, and meat or chicken stock, and cook until this gravy thickens. Put back the beef and add the shredded snow peas. Mix well and turn off the heat.

Take the nest of noodles from the oven and place on a serving platter. Ladle the meat, vegetables and gravy on top of the noodles and serve.

JIM LEE
JIM LEE'S CHINESE COOKBOOK

Special Fried Fresh Egg Noodles with Chicken

Chow San Min

To serve 4

1 lb.	fresh Chinese egg noodles	½ kg.
6 oz.	boneless chicken breast, skinned and thinly sliced	175 g.
3 or 4 tbsp.	peanut oil	45 or 60 ml.
⅓ cup	thinly sliced bamboo shoots	75 ml.
⅔ cup	thinly sliced fresh mushrooms	150 ml.
	salt	
1 tsp.	cornstarch, mixed with a little water	5 ml.
	sesame-seed oil	
2 or 3	scallions, finely chopped	2 or 3

Place the noodles in a saucepan of boiling water for half a minute, then drain them in a strainer and hold them under cold running water for 10 seconds. Drain again, then put the noodles in a hot oiled pan and cook for one minute, turning occasionally. Place the noodles in a warmed serving dish.

Put the chicken into the oiled pan and cook over high heat for half a minute. Add the bamboo shoots and the mushrooms, and cook for another minute. Add salt to taste. Add the cornstarch mixture and a few drops of sesame-seed oil and cook for one minute more.

Place this mixture on top of the noodles and garnish with the finely chopped scallions.

S. K. CHENG (EDITOR)
SHANGHAI RESTAURANT CHINESE COOKERY BOOK

Crisp Fried Vermicelli

Mee Krob

The fish sauce called for is nam pla, a lightly fermented, salty Thai condiment, very similar to Vietnamese nuoc mam. Nam pla and nuoc mam are available at stores specializing in Southeast Asian and Chinese foods. Tree ears, also known as cloud ears, are edible fungi resembling wrinkled, blackish-gray cornflakes. They are sold in Oriental food stores.

To serve 6 to 8

½ lb.	rice vermicelli	¼ kg.
12	dried Chinese mushrooms	12
½ cup	dried tree ears	125 ml.
	oil	
3	garlic cloves, finely chopped	3
1	onion, finely chopped	1
1 lb.	boneless lean pork, finely shredded	½ kg.
1	whole chicken breast, boned, skinned and shredded	1
1 lb.	raw shrimp, peeled and deveined, and cut into pieces	½ kg.
12	scallions, cut into 2-inch [5-cm.] lengths	12
12	green beans, trimmed and cut into thin diagonal slices	12
¼ cup	soy sauce	50 ml.
1 tbsp.	sugar	15 ml.
¼ cup	vinegar	50 ml.
3 tbsp.	fish sauce	45 ml.
1 tsp.	cayenne pepper	5 ml.
¼ cup	chopped fresh coriander leaves	50 ml.

Soak the dried mushrooms and tree ears separately in hot water for 20 minutes. Squeeze the excess water from the mushrooms; remove and discard the mushroom stems and slice the caps. Wash the tree ears well, removing any grit. Cut into bite-sized pieces.

Heat 3 tablespoons [45 ml.] of oil in a wok, fry the garlic and onion for three minutes and, when they begin to color, add the pork and mushrooms and stir fry for eight minutes. Add the chicken and shrimp, and continue to stir fry until they change color and are cooked. Add the scallions, beans and tree ears and fry for one minute. Mix the soy sauce, sugar, vinegar, fish sauce and cayenne pepper together, add to the pan and stir fry for two minutes. Turn off the heat.

In a separate wok, heat a large amount of oil and fry the rice vermicelli a handful at a time. (Do not soak the vermicelli; use it straight from the packet.) The oil should be very hot so the vermicelli will puff and swell immediately. If it does not, it will be tough and difficult to eat, so test the heat of the oil with a little vermicelli first. Turn the vermicelli and fry the other side. Lift it out and drain on paper towels.

Reserve some of the fried vermicelli to garnish the top of the dish and add the rest to the pan containing the other ingredients. Toss everything together and serve immediately, sprinkled with chopped fresh coriander leaves.

CHARMAINE SOLOMON
THE COMPLETE ASIAN COOKBOOK

Noodles in Oyster Sauce, Peking-Style

This dish is only delicately tangy, but it is an example of the true Peking style of cooking. Oyster sauce—a seasoning made from the liquor of oysters, soy sauce and brine—is available in Chinese grocery stores.

To serve 4

½ lb.	narrow, flat Chinese egg noodles	¼ kg.
	oyster sauce	
¼ cup	peanut oil	50 ml.
1	walnut-sized piece of fresh ginger root, slivered or grated	1
3	scallions, white and green parts, sliced into 1-inch [2½-cm.] pieces	3
½ cup	chicken stock *(recipe, page 167)*	125 ml.

Cook the noodles in boiling water until barely done, no more than three minutes. Drain.

Heat the oil over high heat in a wok or deep iron skillet. Add the ginger and scallions and stir fry briskly for two minutes. Keeping the heat high, add the stock a little at a time, stirring constantly until the liquid disappears. When the last of the stock is almost gone, quickly add the noodles and toss until smoking hot. (The noodles will be a bit shiny from the oil left in the pan.)

Serve with small, individual dip dishes of oyster sauce.

STENDAHL
SPICY FOOD

Cellophane Noodles with Dried Shrimp

Fon Sz Ha Mai

For centuries the Chinese have used dehydration as a way of preserving food. In a typical Chinese grocery store you will find hundreds of dried items on sale. The most common seafoods used in this form are dried shrimp, scallops and oysters. For this recipe, choose the medium-large size of shelled dry shrimp. Keep them in a tightly covered jar and they will stay good indefinitely. Fresh shrimp may be used in place of the dried variety; use 1 pound [½ kg.] of fresh shrimp, shelled, split in halves and blanched for one minute.

	To serve 2	
¼ lb.	cellophane noodles	125 g.
1 cup	dried shrimp	¼ liter
2	eggs, lightly beaten	2
3	scallions, white and green parts, cut into 2-inch [5-cm.] lengths and shredded	3
2 cups	shredded lettuce	½ liter
2	slices fresh ginger root, peeled and shredded	2
1	garlic clove, finely chopped	1
1 tsp.	sugar	5 ml.
3 tbsp.	light soy sauce	45 ml.
2 tbsp.	water	30 ml.
¾ cup	vegetable oil	175 ml.
	salt	

Rinse the shrimp and soak them in water for one hour. Drain the shrimp and discard the water. Soak the noodles for 15 to 20 minutes in cold water. Drain them thoroughly and cut into 2-inch [5-cm.] lengths. Mix together the sugar, soy sauce and water, then set aside.

Heat a wok or pan. Add 2 tablespoons [30 ml.] of the oil. Add a pinch of salt. Turn the heat to medium-low, add the lightly beaten eggs and scramble them. Shred the eggs with a spatula; remove from the wok or pan and put aside.

Add 2 more tablespoons of oil to the wok and fry the ginger and garlic until browned. Add the drained shrimp and stir fry for two minutes. Turn the heat to high and add the remainder of the oil, and the noodles and scallions; stir fry for three minutes. Put back the eggs and add the shredded lettuce. Add the soy-sauce mixture prepared earlier. Mix well and turn off the heat at once.

There should be no gravy in this dish. The noodles should be dry, but soft.

JIM LEE
JIM LEE'S CHINESE COOKBOOK

Chinese Crab with Cellophane Noodles

Crabe au Vermicelle de Soja Chinois (Cua Sào Miên)

This dish is served with boiled or fried rice and sprinkled with nuoc mam, a Vietnamese pickled fish sauce, or Chinese fish gravy—both pungent condiments. Black mushrooms are also called dried wood ears; these and dried shiitake mushrooms as well as the condiments can be bought at Oriental food stores. If Oriental mushrooms are not available, substitute other dried mushrooms.

	To serve 4	
14 oz.	cellophane noodles	400 g.
¼ lb.	crab meat, broken up with a fork	125 g.
¼ cup	oil	50 ml.
⅔ cup	pork or chicken stock *(recipe, page 167)*	150 ml.
1	medium-sized onion, chopped	1
2 oz.	black mushrooms, or *shiitake*, soaked in warm water for 2 hours, drained and thinly sliced	60 g.

Soak the noodles in cold water for five minutes, then drain them. Fry them in the oil for about three minutes or until lightly browned, stirring constantly with bamboo chopsticks. Add the stock, then add the onion, mushrooms and crab meat. Cover and simmer for about 15 minutes, or until the mushrooms are tender.

L'ART CULINAIRE CHINOIS ET VIETNAMIEN

Fried Chinese Egg Noodles

Tch'ao Mienn

The technique of frying egg noodles is shown on pages 66-67.

	To serve 4	
½ lb.	Chinese egg noodles	¼ kg.
14 tbsp.	lard	210 ml.
½ lb.	large raw shrimp, peeled and deveined	¼ kg.
6 oz.	pork, finely chopped	175 g.
½ lb.	crab meat, flaked	¼ kg.
	salt	
2 tbsp.	sesame-seed oil	30 ml.
1 tbsp.	vinegar	15 ml.

Cook the noodles in boiling water for three minutes, or until just tender. Drain, rinse in cold water and drain again. Mel

Cream-Puff Dumplings

Gnocchi Parisienne

The authors suggest that the dumplings may be made with Swiss cheese instead of Parmesan. You can also, if you wish, add 1 pound [½ kg.] of spinach that has been blanched, squeezed dry and puréed to the dumpling mixture just before you add the flour. If you do so, reduce the amount of milk by 2 tablespoons [30 ml.].

To serve 6

½ cup	flour	125 ml.
½ cup	milk	125 ml.
6 tbsp.	butter, 2 tbsp. [30 ml.] cut into chunks and 4 tbsp. [60 ml.] melted	90 ml.
½ tsp.	salt	2 ml.
¼ tsp.	freshly ground white pepper	1 ml.
2	large eggs	2
1 cup	freshly grated Parmesan cheese	¼ liter

To make the cream-puff paste, put the milk, butter chunks, salt and pepper into a heavy-bottomed saucepan and bring to a boil slowly. When it has reached a full boil, remove the milk from the heat, add the flour all at once and blend thoroughly. Continue beating until the paste forms a ball.

Return the saucepan to medium heat and continue beating vigorously by flattening the paste against the bottom of the pan, bringing it against the sides, and flipping it over. Repeat this for two or three minutes, or until a grainy film forms on the bottom of the pan. The object is to dry as much of the paste as possible. Be careful not to let it color.

Remove the saucepan from the heat, make a well in the center of the paste, and break in one egg. Smash it a little with your spoon and beat it as fast as possible until the egg is thoroughly absorbed. Repeat with the other egg. Beat until all is smooth and well blended. The paste should be stiff but not heavy. Add ½ cup [125 ml.] of the cheese and mix well.

Butter a shallow baking pan about 8 inches [20 cm.] square or 9 inches [23 cm.] in diameter and set aside. Bring 2 quarts [2 liters] of water to a simmer in a large skillet. With a teaspoon and a small spatula, slip spoonfuls of the paste into the simmering water. Do not let the water boil. Cook the dumplings, uncovered, for about 15 minutes, then test one for doneness—it should be light, fluffy and cooked through. Remove with a slotted spoon and drain on paper towels.

Arrange the dumplings in the baking pan in one layer.

Just before serving, preheat the broiler. Pour the melted butter over the dumplings and sprinkle with the remaining Parmesan cheese. Broil about 2 inches [5 cm.] below the source of heat until brown.

To serve, divide among six warmed plates.

CHARLOTTE MC NAMARA & LENORE HOWELL
THE BEFORE AND AFTER DINNER COOKBOOK

Feathery-light Dumplings

To make 6 dumplings

1 cup	sifted flour	¼ liter
1½ tsp.	baking powder	7 ml.
½ tsp.	salt	2 ml.
2 tbsp.	shortening	30 ml.
⅓ cup	milk	75 ml.
1	egg, beaten	1

Sift together in a bowl the flour, baking powder and salt. Cut in the shortening with a pastry blender until the mixture is crumbly. Pour in the milk; add the egg. Mix only until the flour is dampened—the dough should be lumpy.

To cook, drop by spoonfuls on top of any boiling meat or fruit mixture. Cover tightly and steam for 12 minutes without removing the cover.

NELL B. NICHOLS (EDITOR)
FARM JOURNAL'S COUNTRY COOKBOOK

Napkin Dumpling

Třený Knedlík

To serve 6 to 8

3 cups	flour	¾ liter
10 tbsp.	butter	150 ml.
4	eggs, the yolks separated from the whites, and the whites stiffly beaten	4
¾ cup	milk, mixed with 1 tsp. [5 ml.] salt	175 ml.
4 cups	diced stale white bread, fried in 2 tbsp. [30 ml.] butter	1 liter

Cream the butter. Add the four egg yolks one at a time, mixing well. Add the milk alternately with the flour, by spoonfuls to the butter-egg mixture. Add the bread cubes and mix them in well. Fold in the stiffly beaten egg whites.

Wet a large cloth napkin and wring it out. Place it in a sieve; pour in the dough. Pull the napkin up around the dough and tie it in two places with thread: first right above the mound of dough, then ¾ inch [2 cm.] above the first tie. Tie the napkin corners to the handle of a wooden spoon and place the spoon across a deep pot containing boiling water. The dumpling must be completely submerged, but must not touch the bottom of the pot; it should hang about 2 inches [5 cm.] below the water surface. Cook for 20 minutes, then untie the first thread. Then cook 40 minutes longer. Remove the dumpling from the napkin and slice it with thread. To do this, first slide a piece of thread about 20 inches [50 cm.] long under the dumpling; then switch the ends of the thread from one hand to the other and pull.

JOZA BŘÍZOVÁ
THE CZECHOSLOVAK COOKBOOK

Yeast Dumplings

Hefeklösse

Making yeast dumplings is demonstrated on page 86.

To make 12 dumplings

3¼ cups	flour	800 ml.
1 tbsp.	active dry yeast	15 ml.
¼ cup	tepid water (110° to 115° F. [about 45° C.])	50 ml.
1 tsp.	sugar	5 ml.
1	egg	1
4 tbsp.	butter, melted and cooled	60 ml.
¾ cup	tepid milk (110° to 115° F. [about 45° C.])	175 ml.
1 tsp.	salt	5 ml.
¼ tsp.	grated nutmeg	1 ml.

Pour the tepid water into a small bowl and sprinkle it with the yeast and sugar. Let it stand for two or three minutes, then stir to dissolve the yeast and sugar completely. Set in a warm, draft-free place (such as a turned-off oven) for about five minutes, or until the mixture almost doubles in volume.

In a large mixing bowl, beat the egg with a spoon until it is smooth and well mixed. Beat in the melted butter; add the tepid milk, salt, nutmeg and yeast solution. Then add the flour, ½ cup [125 ml.] at a time, beating well after each addition. Mix with the spoon or your hands until the dough is firm enough to be gathered into a compact ball.

Place the dough on a lightly floured surface and knead it by pushing it down with the heels of your hands, pressing it forward and folding it back on itself. Repeat this procedure for about 10 minutes, lightly flouring the surface from time to time to prevent the dough from sticking.

When the dough is smooth and elastic, place it in a buttered bowl, drape it with a towel and let it rise in a warm, draft-free place for about one hour, or until it doubles in bulk. Then punch the dough down and knead it again for three or four minutes. Flour your hands lightly, pinch off pieces of the dough and shape them into 12 balls about 1½ inches [4 cm.] in diameter.

Spread a damp kitchen towel over a rack set in a large roasting pan and on it arrange the dumplings about 2 inches [5 cm.] apart. Add enough water to the pan to come to within 1 inch [2½ cm.] of the rack. Bring to a boil over high heat, cover tightly and reduce the heat to medium. Steam the dumplings undisturbed for 20 minutes, or until they are firm to the touch. Serve as hot as possible on a large, heated platter. Traditionally, the dumplings are served with meats or stewed fruit compote.

FOODS OF THE WORLD/THE COOKING OF GERMANY

Farina Dumplings

Krupicové Nočky

To make 12 to 15 small dumplings

½ cup	farina	125 ml.
½ cup	milk	125 ml.
2 tbsp.	butter	30 ml.
1	egg, beaten	1
	ground mace	

Bring the milk, salt to taste and farina to a slow boil and stir until thick. Cool. Add the butter, egg and a dash of mace. Drop the mixture in small amounts from a wet spoon into boiling water; simmer for three to five minutes.

JOZA BŘÍZOVÁ
THE CZECHOSLOVAK COOKBOOK

Pumpkin Dumplings

Gnocchi di Zùcca alla Versiliese

To serve 6 to 8

¾ lb.	pumpkin, or substitute winter squash, halved, seeded, cut into cubes about the size of walnuts, and peeled	⅓ kg.
¼ cup	water	50 ml.
	salt	
2	eggs	2
4 cups	flour	1 liter
4 tbsp.	butter	60 ml.
½ cup	freshly grated Parmesan cheese	125 ml.

Put the cubed pumpkin into a deep saucepan, add the water and season with a pinch of salt. Cook slowly, stirring from time to time, for about 20 minutes, or until the pumpkin cubes are reduced to a pulp. Mash the pumpkin or purée it through a sieve or food mill.

Let the purée cool, then add the eggs and enough flour to produce a paste that is thick enough to hold its shape on a spoon. Drop small spoonfuls of the paste into boiling salted water and cook until the dumplings rise to the surface. Remove the dumplings from the water with a skimmer and serve tossed in butter and Parmesan cheese.

MARIÙ SALVATORI DE ZULIANI
LA CUCINA DI VERSILIA E GARFAGNANA

Farina Dumplings with Onion Topping

Halushky

To make 12 to 15 dumplings

¾ cup	farina	175 ml.
¾ cup	flour	175 ml.
2 tsp.	baking powder	10 ml.
1 tsp.	salt	5 ml.
4 tbsp.	butter, cut into small pieces and chilled	60 ml.
2	eggs, lightly beaten	2
¼ cup	milk or buttermilk	50 ml.
	Onion topping	
2	large onions, thinly sliced	2
4 tbsp.	butter	60 ml.

In a large bowl, combine the flour, farina, baking powder and salt. Mix well. Add the butter. Crumble the flour mixture with your finger tips to form a coarse meal. Add the eggs and milk. Stir until the batter is smooth.

Drop the batter by tablespoonfuls into boiling salted water. Cover, and simmer for eight minutes. Cook six to eight dumplings at a time. Remove the cooked dumplings from the water with a slotted spoon and place them in a buttered ovenproof dish. Keep them warm in a 250° F. [120° C.] oven.

To prepare the topping, sauté the onions in the butter until they are light brown and start to crisp. Strew them over the dumplings. Serve with a bowl of sour cream, if you wish.

MARIA POLUSHKIN
THE DUMPLING COOKBOOK

Cabbage Dumplings

To serve 4

1 lb.	cabbage, halved, cored and shredded (about 3½ cups [875 ml.])	½ kg.
4	bread rolls	4
22 tbsp.	butter	330 ml.
2½ cups	milk	625 ml.
2	eggs, plus 4 egg yolks	2
1 cup	flour	¼ liter
1 tsp.	salt	5 ml.
4 tbsp.	lard	60 ml.
1 cup	shredded Gruyère cheese	¼ liter

Dice two of the bread rolls and fry them in 4 tablespoons [60 ml.] of the butter until they are golden brown. Soak the other two rolls in the milk. Cream 14 tablespoons [210 ml.] of the butter and mix it with the whole eggs and the egg yolks, the flour and the salt. Stew the cabbage gently in the lard for about 10 minutes or until it loses its crispness, then combine it with the butter-and-egg mixture. Remove the rolls from the milk, press them through a sieve, then add them to the cabbage mixture with the fried diced bread rolls. Mix well and form the mixture into dumplings about the size of eggs. Cook the dumplings in boiling water for about 15 minutes, or until they are firm and cooked through.

Using a slotted spoon, transfer the dumplings to a serving dish. Melt the remaining butter, pour it over the dumplings, sprinkle shredded cheese on top and serve.

JÓZSEF VENESZ
HUNGARIAN CUISINE

Cheese and Spinach Dumplings

Les Caillettes

The original version of this recipe calls for brousse, a fresh, unsalted sheep's-milk cheese —the Provençal equivalent of ricotta. Because brousse is unavailable in the United States, ricotta is substituted for it. The dumplings may be flattened into patty shapes and browned in oil. Whether boiled or fried, these dumplings may be served with brown butter or tomato sauce poured over them. Or you can put the boiled dumplings into a buttered gratin dish, pour over either heavy cream or tomato sauce, sprinkle with Parmesan cheese, and bake in a preheated 400° F. [200° C.] oven for 10 to 15 minutes.

To serve 6

1 lb.	ricotta cheese	½ kg.
1 lb.	spinach, stems removed, leaves washed, squeezed dry and chopped	½ kg.
1 tbsp.	finely chopped fresh parsley	15 ml.
1	garlic clove, finely chopped	1
2 tbsp.	butter	30 ml.
2 cups	flour	½ liter
	salt	
3	eggs	3

Sauté the spinach, parsley and garlic in the butter until they are soft and the liquid from the spinach has evaporated. Set aside to cool.

Mix together the cheese, half of the flour, the spinach mixture and a pinch of salt. Add the eggs and work the mixture well, adding more flour gradually until you have a firm but malleable dough. Divide the mixture into 12 to 15 pieces; form each piece into a thick, short sausage shape.

Roll the dumplings lightly in the remaining flour and toss them into boiling water. Cover and simmer for 15 minutes, then drain.

C. CHANOT-BULLIER
VIEILLES RECETTES DE CUISINE PROVENÇALE

Leek Dumplings

Nioques aux Poireaux

To serve 4 to 6

1 lb.	leeks, washed, coarse green tops removed, and white parts sliced into rounds ⅛ inch [3 mm.] thick	½ kg.
3 quarts	water	3 liters
	salt	
2	medium-sized potatoes, peeled	2
3	eggs	3
	pepper	
about 1 cup	flour	about ¼ liter
½ lb.	Gruyère cheese, shredded	¼ kg.
4 tbsp.	butter, melted, or heavy cream	60 ml.

Bring the water to a boil in a large saucepan. Salt the water lightly, add the leeks and cook them for 15 minutes. With a slotted spoon, remove the leeks; reserve the cooking liquid. Place the leeks in a cloth and twist it to squeeze out excess liquid, then chop the leeks fine. Place the leeks in a bowl.

Cook the potatoes in the leeks' cooking liquid for 20 to 25 minutes. Drain the potatoes, reserving the cooking liquid again, and purée them through a sieve. Mix the purée with the leeks and stir in the eggs one by one. Taste the mixture and season to taste with salt and pepper. Knead in flour, a spoonful at a time, until the mixture becomes a thick but malleable dough.

On a floured pastry board, shape the mixture into long rolls the thickness of your little finger. Cut the rolls into cylinders 1¼ inches [3 cm.] long. Roll each cylinder between your hands until it is pointed at both ends.

Bring the reserved cooking liquid to a boil and plunge about one fourth of the dumplings into it. Adjust the heat to maintain a light boil. The dumplings will float to the surface when they are done. Remove the dumplings with a slotted spoon and drain them on a cloth. Repeat the process to boil the remaining batches of dumplings.

Arrange the dumplings in a buttered ovenproof dish, sprinkling each layer with a handful of Gruyère. Pour a little melted butter or heavy cream over the top. Bake on the top shelf of a preheated 475° F. [250° C.] oven for 15 minutes, or until golden brown. Serve hot.

PIERRE ANDROUET
LA CUISINE AU FROMAGE

Vegetable Dumplings

Gnocchi à la Niçarde

To serve 6 to 8

½ lb.	spinach, stemmed, finely chopped	¼ kg.
½ lb.	Swiss chard, stemmed, finely chopped	¼ kg.
1	head lettuce (about ½ lb. [¼ kg.]), core removed, finely chopped	1
	salt	
8 cups	flour	2 liters
1 tbsp.	olive oil	15 ml.
2	eggs	2
⅔ cup	freshly grated Parmesan cheese	150 ml.
2 tbsp.	butter, melted	30 ml.

Salt the spinach, chard and lettuce lightly and let the greens stand for 30 minutes. Squeeze out any excess liquid. Mix the flour, olive oil, eggs, greens and about ½ cup [125 ml.] of the Parmesan cheese, adding a little water if necessary to form a malleable dough. Let it stand for 30 minutes. Keeping your hands floured, form the dough into small dumplings, rolling them between your palms. Poach the dumplings for about 20 minutes in a covered pan of boiling salted water.

Drain the dumplings, place them on a hot serving dish, and sprinkle them with the melted butter and the remaining Parmesan cheese. Or serve the dumplings in the juice from a Provençal beef daube and sprinkle the cheese over them.

C. CHANOT-BULLIER
VIEILLES RECETTES DE CUISINE PROVENÇALE

Czech Potato Dumplings

To serve 6 to 8

2 lb.	baking potatoes	1 kg.
½ to 1 cup	flour	125 ml. to ¼ liter
½ cup	cracker meal	125 ml.
½ cup	farina	125 ml.
1½ tsp.	salt	7 ml.
¼ tsp.	grated nutmeg	1 ml.
2	egg yolks, beaten	2

Boil the potatoes until tender but not mushy. Drain thoroughly. Peel, then press the potatoes through a ricer or mash them with a fork. Add ½ cup [125 ml.] of the flour, the cracker meal, farina, salt and nutmeg gradually, blending after each addition. Add the egg yolks and blend well. Mix and knead lightly until you have a smooth dough.

Lightly flour a bread board, turn the mixture out and shape it into a long roll about 2½ inches [6 cm.] in diameter.

Cut the roll into 2-inch [5-cm.] slices and shape the slices into balls. Drop the balls into a large pot of boiling water, cover and boil the dumplings for 12 minutes. Test one dumpling by breaking it open. It should look spongy and fairly dry inside, not soggy or doughy. If you are a dumpling novice, you might cook only one dumpling first. If it falls apart in the water, you may add up to ½ cup more flour.

RUTH VENDLEY NEUMANN
CONVERSATION-PIECE RECIPES

Potato Dumplings with Bacon and Cottage Cheese

Strapachka

	To serve 4	
5	medium-sized potatoes, peeled and grated	5
2½ cups	whole-wheat flour	625 ml.
1	egg	1
	salt	
6 tbsp.	lard	90 ml.
4	slices bacon, diced	4
⅔ cup	cottage cheese	150 ml.

Make a dough of the potatoes, flour, egg, ½ teaspoon [2 ml.] of salt and the lard. Knead well, then form the dough into dumplings the size of eggs. Cook the dumplings in a large pan of boiling salted water for about 20 minutes, or until they are fluffy and cooked through. Drain them in a colander and keep them warm. Meanwhile, fry the bacon until crisp. Remove the bacon cracklings from the pan, add the dumplings to the fat and turn them until they are well coated. Serve with the cracklings and the cheese on top.

JÓZSEF VENESZ
HUNGARIAN CUISINE

Potato Dumplings

The technique of shaping potato dumplings with a fork is shown on page 79.

	To serve 2 to 4	
3	medium-sized potatoes	3
1 tbsp.	butter	15 ml.
¼ cup	flour	50 ml.
	salt and pepper	
1	egg, beaten	1
4 tbsp.	butter, melted	60 ml.

Peel, and cook the potatoes in boiling salted water for 15 to 20 minutes or until tender. Drain them thoroughly and press them through a wire sieve or potato ricer, or crush them with a potato masher. Cool slightly, beat in the butter, flour and seasonings, and gradually add enough egg to bind the mixture without making it sticky.

On a floured board, roll the mixture with your hands into a cylinder about ¾ inch [2 cm.] thick. Cut the cylinder into 1-inch [2½-cm.] pieces, and shape each piece into a ball with the flat part of a fork.

Heat salted water until it just trembles, add the dumplings, and poach for 10 to 12 minutes or until firm. Lift out the dumplings with a slotted spoon, drain on paper towels, and arrange in a warmed serving dish. Spoon the melted butter over the dumplings and serve.

ANNE WILLAN (EDITOR)
GRAND DIPLÔME COOKING COURSE, VOLUME 8

Potato Dumplings with Cheese

Zemiakové Halušky s Bryndzou

Bryndza is a Balkan sheep's-milk cheese, similar in taste to the Greek feta, but creamier. It is obtainable at some cheese specialty stores. You can substitute ½ pound [¼ kg.] of feta, 10 ounces [300 g.] of cream cheese or ¾ cup [175 ml.] of sour cream for the bryndza.

	To serve 6 to 8	
8	medium-sized new potatoes, peeled and grated	8
	salt	
2½ cups	flour	625 ml.
4	thick slices bacon, chopped into small pieces	4
½ lb.	*bryndza* cheese, crumbled	¼ kg.
	finely cut fresh chives or dill	

Put the grated potato into a large mixing bowl, salt to taste, add the flour and mix well. When ready, the dough should be firm enough so that it does not stick to the sides of the bowl. On a wooden board, cut the dough into small pieces. Throw these dumplings into a pan of boiling water and boil them uncovered for about 10 minutes. When the dumplings rise to the surface, take them out with a slotted spoon and place them on a serving dish.

While the dumplings are cooking, fry the bacon. Sprinkle the dumplings with the crumbled cheese and scatter the chives over the top. Pour on the bacon pieces with their fat, and serve immediately.

VOJTECH ŠPANKO (EDITOR)
SLOVENSKÁ KUCHÁRKA

Swabian Noodles with Ham
Spätzle mit Schinken

To serve 4

2½ cups	sifted flour	625 ml.
½ tsp.	salt	2 ml.
2	eggs, beaten	2
about ½ cup	water	about 125 ml.
6 to 8	thin slices Westphalian ham	6 to 8
½ lb.	fresh mushrooms, sliced and sautéed in butter	¼ kg.
1	medium-sized onion, sliced and sautéed in butter	1
4 tbsp.	butter	60 ml.
	bread crumbs moistened with melted butter	

To make the noodles, combine the flour and salt in a mixing bowl, make a well in the center, add the eggs and ¼ cup [50 ml.] of the water. Beat until a stiff dough forms, adding more water a little at a time until the dough is thick and firm and comes easily away from the sides of the bowl. Knead the dough until smooth. Let it stand in the bowl for 30 minutes.

Dampen a pastry board with water, place the dough on it, flour the rolling pin lightly and roll out the dough to a thickness of ⅛ inch [3 mm.] or a little thinner. Heat a kettle of salted water to boiling. With a sharp knife, cut off very thin slivers of the dough, transferring them to a plate as they are cut, then pushing them directly into the rapidly boiling water. Do not crowd the kettle. The spaetzle will rise to the surface when cooked, in about five minutes. Remove them with a slotted spoon and drain the spaetzle in a colander. Add more slivers of dough to the boiling water, continuing until all of the dough is cooked.

In a baking dish, arrange alternate layers of spaetzle with the ham slices and the mushrooms and onion. Spread the buttered bread crumbs over the top; place under the broiler or in a preheated 400° F. [200° C.] oven until the crumbs are nicely browned.

BETTY WASON
THE ART OF GERMAN COOKING

Dumpling with Salt Pork
La Mique

This filling peasant dish is typical of the Sarladais district of Périgord in southwestern France.

To serve 6

1¼ cups	flour	300 ml.
4 cups	stale bread cubes	1 liter
3½ oz.	fresh pork fat, diced	100 g.
about ⅓ cup	warm milk, meat stock (recipe, page 167) or water	about 75 ml.
	salt and pepper	
1 tsp.	baking powder	5 ml.
3	eggs	3
1 tbsp.	rendered pork or goose fat, or oil	15 ml.

Salt pork and vegetables

1½ lb.	salt pork with the rind removed, cut into 6 portions and soaked for 12 hours in several changes of water	¾ kg.
¼ lb.	cabbage, coarsely chopped	125 g.
1	onion, quartered	1
1	turnip, peeled and coarsely chopped	1
1	leek, coarsely chopped	1
¼ lb.	Swiss chard, the leaves coarsely chopped	125 g.
2	celery ribs, trimmed and coarsely chopped	2
1 tsp.	ground cloves	5 ml.

Fill a bowl with the cubes of bread and add the diced pork fat. Moisten with enough of the warm milk, stock or water to dampen the bread without softening it. Season, and mix in the baking powder. Beat the rendered pork or goose fat, or oil, with the eggs, lightly as for an omelet. Stir the egg mixture into the bread and fat. Sprinkle the flour over this. To bind the ingredients into a firm but pliable mass, hold the bowl in both hands and toss the contents slowly and lightly. Do not touch the mixture with hands or spoon. When the mixture comes away from the sides of the dish in a mass, form it into a dumpling the shape of a slightly rounded football. Dust it with flour and cover it with a kitchen towel.

Cook the salt pork, vegetables and cloves for one and a half hours in plenty of water. Halfway through the cooking time, add the dumpling. Turn it over with a skimming ladle after about 20 minutes. When cooked, it should have doubled in volume. To serve, slice the dumpling in half crosswise and put it on a serving dish surrounded by the vegetables and topped with the salt pork.

ZETTE GUINAUDEAU-FRANC
LES SECRETS DES FERMES EN PÉRIGORD NOIR

Swabian Beef Stew with Cut Noodles

Gaisburger Marsch mit Spätzle

	To serve 4	
4 cups	flour	1 liter
5	large eggs	5
1 tsp.	salt	5 ml.
	Beef stew	
14 oz.	boneless lean stewing beef, cubed	400 g.
1½ quarts	meat stock *(recipe, page 167)*	1½ liters
4	medium-sized potatoes, diced	4
	salt	
	freshly grated nutmeg	
4 tbsp.	butter or lard	60 ml.
½ cup	chopped onion	125 ml.
2 tbsp.	finely cut fresh chives	30 ml.

Simmer the beef in the meat stock for one hour.

Meanwhile, boil the potatoes in lightly salted water for 10 minutes. Do not overcook or they will become floury. Drain the potatoes, reserving the cooking liquid.

To make the noodles, beat the flour, eggs and salt together vigorously in a bowl until they form a firm dough that contains air bubbles. If the dough is too stiff to roll out, add 1 or 2 tablespoons [15 or 30 ml.] of cold water. Bring a large pan of water to a boil. Spoon approximately one fourth of the dough onto a board. Roll it out thin, then slide the dough sheet so that a strip ¼ inch [6 mm.] wide hangs over the edge of the board. Cut off this strip and drop it into the boiling water. Repeat this procedure until all of the dough sheet is cut into strips, dipping the knife frequently into cold water to keep it from sticking to the dough. Bring the water gently back to a boil and cook the noodles for about 10 minutes, or until they float on the surface of the water. As they come to the surface, remove the noodles with a skimmer and dip them into cold water. When all of the noodles are ready, empty them into a colander, rinse them under cold running water and drain them again. Roll, cut, cook and drain the remaining dough similarly.

Add the cooked potatoes to the beef with ⅔ cup [150 ml.] of the potato cooking liquid. Season to taste and add a pinch of grated nutmeg. Cook for 10 minutes. Heat the butter in a skillet and gently fry the onions until they turn golden.

Add the noodles to the stew and cook for a further five minutes to heat them thoroughly. Before serving, add the fried onions and sprinkle the stew with the chives. Cubes of fried bread can be used as a garnish.

HANS KARL ADAM
DAS KOCHBUCH AUS SCHWABEN

Lamb Stew with Dumplings, Belle Île-Style

Ragoût de "Cunepouds" Bellilois

This recipe is typical of Belle Île, an island off the coast of Brittany, famous for its turnips. Cunepouds are small, sweet balls of dough, studded with raisins, floured, and then cooked in the stew.

	To serve 6	
5 cups	flour	1¼ liters
4	eggs	4
2 tbsp.	sugar	30 ml.
6 tbsp.	seedless raisins	90 ml.
	Lamb stew	
2 lb.	lamb shoulder or breast, cut into 6 pieces	1 kg.
4 tbsp.	butter	60 ml.
2	onions, chopped	2
5 cups	meat stock *(recipe, page 167)*	1¼ liters
	salt and pepper	
1	whole clove	1
1	garlic clove, chopped	1
2 tbsp.	chopped fresh parsley	30 ml.
1	bay leaf	1
½ tsp.	thyme	2 ml.
6	small turnips, peeled and quartered	6

To prepare the dumplings, place 4 cups [1 liter] of the flour in a large bowl, break in the eggs and stir to a smooth dough. Stir in the sugar. Sprinkle the remaining flour on a work surface. Take a piece of dough the size of a small egg, mix in three or four raisins, and roll the dough in the flour to form a ball. Use up all of the dough in this way. The balls of dough must be quite firm so that they do not come apart while they are cooking.

Melt the butter in a heavy pan, add the lamb and brown it lightly over brisk heat. Sprinkle with half of the onions. When the onions have colored, remove them from the pan with the lamb and set them aside. Add any flour left over from rolling the dumplings to the fat in the pan, blend the two and cook slowly until they form a smooth, nut-brown sauce. Return the lamb and onions to the pan and turn them in the sauce. Cover the meat with the stock and add salt, pepper, the clove, garlic, parsley, the remaining uncooked onions, the bay leaf, thyme and turnips. Cover the pan and simmer for 45 minutes.

Add the dumplings to the stew, cover and cook for 45 minutes. Serve the dumplings in a ring around the stew.

ÉDOUARD NIGNON (EDITOR)
LE LIVRE DE CUISINE DE L'OUEST-ÉCLAIR

Pepper Chicken with Dumplings

To serve 6 to 8

2 cups	sifted flour	½ liter
2½ tsp.	baking powder	12 ml.
1 tsp.	brown sugar	5 ml.
	cayenne pepper	
½ tsp.	freshly ground black pepper	2 ml.
¼ tsp.	salt	1 ml.
2 tbsp.	butter	30 ml.
⅔ cup	milk	150 ml.

Pepper chicken

two 2½ lb.	chickens, cut into serving pieces	two 1¼ kg.
16	peppercorns	16
8 tbsp.	butter	120 ml.
1	onion, grated	1
1 cup	dry white wine or vermouth	¼ liter
2 to 3 cups	chicken stock *(recipe, page 167)*	½ to ¾ liter
2	celery ribs with leaves	2
1 tsp.	salt	5 ml.
1 tbsp.	flour	15 ml.
¼ cup	heavy cream	50 ml.
	chopped fresh parsley	
	freshly ground pepper	

To prepare the chicken, melt the butter in a Dutch oven. Add the chicken and onion, and sauté over medium heat until the chicken is light brown; do not let the butter burn.

Add the wine, and enough stock to cover the chicken. Add the celery, peppercorns and salt. Heat the liquid to boiling; reduce the heat. Cover and simmer until tender—one to one and a half hours.

Meanwhile make the dumplings. Sift the flour with the baking powder, brown sugar, a pinch of cayenne pepper, the black pepper and salt. Cut in the butter; blend well with a pastry blender. Stir in the milk, using a fork. Roll out the dough ½ inch [1 cm.] thick on a lightly floured board; cut out 2-inch [5-cm.] circles.

Heat the oven to 275° F. [140° C.]. Remove the chicken to a shallow baking dish; cover with aluminum foil. Keep the chicken warm in the oven.

Strain the chicken cooking liquid and return it to the Dutch oven. Combine the 1 tablespoon [15 ml.] of flour with 2 tablespoons [30 ml.] of the cream; whisk into the strained liquid. Heat to a simmer; place the dumplings on top, without overlapping them. Cook, covered, for 18 to 20 minutes.

Remove the dumplings, using a slotted spoon. Stir the remaining 2 tablespoons of cream into the cooking liquid.

Heat to boiling and boil for one minute. Spoon half of the sauce over the chicken; top with the dumplings. Spoon the remaining sauce over all. Sprinkle with chopped parsley and freshly ground pepper.

BERT GREENE
BERT GREENE'S KITCHEN BOUQUETS

Corned Beef with Hodgils

Hodgil is an old word for "border," no doubt given to these oatmeal dumplings because they are served as trimmings for the boiled beef.

To serve 6

3 cups	rolled oats, pulverized in a blender or food processor	¾ liter
1 tbsp.	finely cut fresh chives	15 ml.
	salt and pepper	

Corned beef

3 to 4 lb.	corned beef, soaked in water overnight and drained	1½ to 2 kg.
1	bay leaf	1
12 to 15	medium-sized carrots, peeled and quartered	12 to 15
4	medium-sized onions, chopped	4
4	parsnips or 1 large rutabaga, peeled and cut into chunks	4
	salt and pepper	

Place the beef in a large pan with the bay leaf. Cover the beef with cold water and slowly bring it to a boil. Cover the pan, reduce the heat and simmer. Calculate the cooking time at 25 minutes to the pound [½ kg.], plus 25 minutes. Add the vegetables one and a half hours before the beef is ready.

To make the hodgils, mix the oats with the chives and seasoning. Skim fat from the top of the beef cooking liquid to bind the oat mixture together, then roll the mixture into balls, making about 10 in all. Let the hodgils stand for 20 minutes, then cook them with the meat for 15 minutes.

Serve the meat with the vegetables and hodgils. Use the cooking liquid to moisten each serving, adjusting the seasoning if necessary.

JANET WARREN
A FEAST OF SCOTLAND

Joe Booker Stew

The technique of cooking dumplings in stew is demonstrated on pages 84-85.

	To serve 6	
2 cups	flour	½ liter
1 tbsp.	double-acting baking powder	15 ml.
½ tsp.	salt	2 ml.
2 tbsp.	butter, cut into ½-inch [1-cm.] bits and softened	30 ml.
1⅓ cups	milk	325 ml.
¼ cup	finely chopped fresh parsley	50 ml.

Beef stew

2 lb.	lean beef chuck, trimmed of excess fat and cut into 1-inch [2½-cm.] cubes	1 kg.
½ lb.	lean salt pork with the rind removed, cut into ¼-inch [6-mm] dice	¼ kg.
4	medium-sized onions, thickly sliced	4
¼ cup	flour	50 ml.
6 cups	water	1½ liters
4	sprigs fresh parsley and 1 small bay leaf, tied together	4
⅛ tsp.	crumbled dried thyme	½ ml.
2 tsp.	salt	10 ml.
	freshly ground black pepper	
2	medium-sized boiling potatoes, peeled and cut into ½-inch [1-cm.] cubes	2
12	medium-sized carrots, cut into ½-inch [1-cm.] pieces	12
1	medium-sized white rutabaga, peeled and cut into ½-inch [1-cm.] cubes	1

In a heavy 12-inch [30-cm.] skillet at least 3 inches [8 cm.] deep, fry the salt-pork dice over medium heat, turning them about frequently with a slotted spoon until they are crisp and brown and have rendered all their fat. Remove the pork bits and discard them.

Add the onions to the fat in the skillet and, stirring frequently, cook for eight to 10 minutes, or until they are soft and delicately brown. With a slotted spoon, transfer the onions to a bowl and set aside.

Pat the beef cubes completely dry with paper towels, roll them in the flour to coat them on all sides and shake off the excess flour. Brown six or seven cubes at a time in the hot fat remaining in the skillet, turning them with a slotted spoon and regulating the heat so that they color evenly without burning. As they brown, add the beef cubes to the onions.

Pour 1 cup [¼ liter] of the water into the skillet and bring it to a boil over high heat, stirring constantly and scraping in the brown particles that cling to the pan. Return the onions and beef and the liquid that has accumulated around them to the skillet. Add the remaining 5 cups [1¼ liters] of water, the parsley and bay leaf, the thyme, salt and a liberal grinding of pepper. Bring to a boil over high heat, reduce the heat to low, cover tightly and simmer for one hour. Skim the fat from the surface of the stew. Then stir in the potatoes, carrots and rutabaga, cover again and simmer the stew for 30 minutes longer.

Meanwhile, to prepare the parsley dumplings, first combine the flour, baking powder and salt and sift them into a deep bowl. Add the butter bits and, with your fingers, rub the flour and fat together until they look like flakes of coarse meal. Add the milk and chopped parsley and beat vigorously with a spoon until the dumpling mixture is smooth.

Remove the parsley and bay leaf from the simmering stew, and drop the dumpling mixture on top of the stew by the heaping tablespoon. Cover tightly and simmer undisturbed for about 10 minutes longer. The dumplings are done when they are puffed and fluffy, and a cake tester inserted in the center of a dumpling comes out clean.

Remove the dumplings and transfer the stew to a preheated bowl or deep platter. Arrange the dumplings on top and serve at once.

FOODS OF THE WORLD
AMERICAN COOKING: NEW ENGLAND

Sweet Pasta and Dumplings

Lenten Spaghetti with Walnuts and Sugar

Spaghetti di Quaresima

	To serve 4	
1 lb.	spaghetti	½ kg.
½ cup	finely chopped walnuts	125 ml.
2 tbsp.	sugar	30 ml.
1 cup	dry bread crumbs	¼ liter
	freshly grated nutmeg	
	salt and freshly ground black pepper	
4 tbsp.	olive oil	60 ml.

Cook the spaghetti in boiling salted water until tender. Drain and put into a warmed deep serving bowl. Combine the walnuts, bread crumbs and sugar, and nutmeg and salt and pepper to taste. Add the walnut mixture and olive oil to the spaghetti. Toss well and serve promptly.

GERTRUDE HARRIS
PASTA INTERNATIONAL

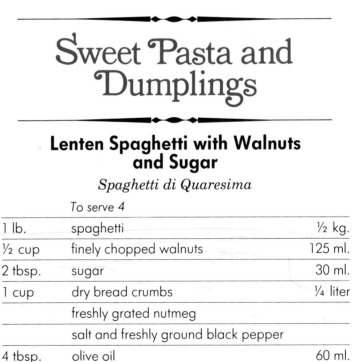

Sweet Buckwheat Vareniki with Cheese Filling

Buckwheat flour is obtainable from health-food stores.

To serve 4 to 6

1 cup	buckwheat flour	¼ liter
1½ cups	all-purpose flour	375 ml.
1 tsp.	salt	5 ml.
2	eggs, the yolks separated from the whites	2
1	egg yolk	1
about ¾ cup	milk	about 175 ml.
	melted butter	
	sour cream	
	fruit syrup	

Cheese filling

1 lb.	dry cottage cheese or farmer cheese	½ kg.
8 tbsp.	butter, softened	120 ml.
1	egg	1
2 tbsp.	sugar	30 ml.

Prepare the filling by pressing the cheese through a sieve into a bowl. With a wooden spoon, beat in the softened butter until well blended. Beat in the egg and sugar. Refrigerate for at least one hour before using.

Into a medium bowl, sift together the two flours and the salt. Add the three egg yolks and enough milk to form a stiff dough. Transfer the dough to a floured board, and knead until the dough feels smooth and satiny—about 10 minutes. Roll the dough into a ball, cover with a cloth towel and let it rest for 30 minutes, or until you are ready to use it.

Divide the dough in half or into thirds. Roll out each portion of dough on a well-floured board until it is as thin as a dime. Use a 3-inch [8-cm.] round cookie cutter to cut out rounds of dough.

Whip the two egg whites until frothy and paint each round of dough with a film of egg white. Place a teaspoon [5 ml.] of the cheese filling on each round. Bring two sides together to form a half moon. Pinch the edges firmly closed.

Bring 7 or 8 quarts [7 or 8 liters] of salted water to a boil and drop in the vareniki, about 10 at a time. Simmer for five to six minutes, or until the vareniki float to the top.

With a slotted spoon, transfer the vareniki to a well-buttered ovenproof dish. Pour a little melted butter over the vareniki and keep them warm in a slow (250° F. [120° C.]) oven until all of them are done and you are ready to serve them. Present with additional melted butter, and with sour cream and fruit syrup.

MARIA POLUSHKIN
THE DUMPLING COOKBOOK

Sweet Dessert Couscous

To blanch almonds and walnuts, drop the nuts in boiling water for a minute or so, drain them and slip off the loosened skins of the nuts with your fingers.

If a handful of raisins or fried almonds is substituted for the nut paste and dates, the dish is called msfouf.

To serve 12

2 lb.	couscous (9 cups [2¼ liters])	1 kg.
11 tbsp.	unsalted butter	165 ml.
1 cup	blanched almonds	¼ liter
1 cup	blanched walnuts	¼ liter
5 tbsp.	granulated sugar	75 ml.
	salt	
½ lb.	dates, pitted and chopped	¼ kg.
	ground cinnamon	
	cold milk	
	confectioners' sugar	

Wash the couscous in a large, shallow pan by pouring water over the grain in a ratio of three parts of water to one part of grain. Stir quickly with your hand and then drain off excess water through a sieve. Return the couscous grains to the pan, smooth them out, and leave them to swell for between 10 and 20 minutes. After roughly 10 minutes, begin—with cupped, wet hands—to work the grains by lifting up handfuls of grain, rubbing them gently and letting them fall back into the pan. Then rake the couscous with your fingers to circulate it and help the grains to swell.

Melt 5 tablespoons [75 ml.] of the butter. Chop the nuts coarse, then pulverize them with the granulated sugar in the blender. Knead the nut mixture with 3 tablespoons [45 ml.] of the melted butter to make a paste.

Fill the bottom of the *couscoussier* with water and bring it to a boil. Then rub the inside of the top part with butter.

Dampen a strip of cheesecloth, dust it with flour, and twist it into a strip the length of the circumference of the rim of the bottom part of the *couscoussier*. Use this to seal the perforated top of the pot to the bottom part. The top and bottom should fit snugly, so that steam rises only through the holes. The perforated top should not touch the broth below. Slowly dribble one quarter of the swollen couscous grains into the steamer, allowing them to form a soft mound. Steam five minutes and gently add the remaining couscous. When all of the grain is in the steamer, reduce the heat to medium and steam for 30 minutes. Do not cover the couscous while it steams.

Remove the top part of the *couscoussier*. Dump the couscous into the large, shallow pan used for washing the grain, and spread the couscous out with a wooden spoon. Sprinkle ½ to 1 cup [125 to 250 ml.] of cold water and 1 teaspoon [5 ml.] of salt over the couscous. Separate and break up any lumps by lifting and stirring the grains gently. Oil your hands lightly and rework the grains—this helps to keep each grain separate. Smooth the couscous out and allow it to dry for at least 10 minutes. If the couscous feels too dry, add another cup of water by handful sprinkles and rake the couscous before each addition.

Toss the drying couscous with the remaining 2 tablespoons [30 ml.] of melted butter. Return the grain to the top container, being sure to reseal the two containers with cheesecloth, and continue steaming 20 more minutes.

Dump the couscous out again and slowly work in about 2 cups [½ liter] of water and 1 tablespoon [15 ml.] of salt. Rub the nut paste between your fingers and toss with the couscous grains.

Steam the dates alone for 15 minutes in the top part of the *couscoussier*. Remove the dates and pile the couscous back for a final steaming of 10 minutes. When the couscous is done, mix it with the dates and remaining 6 tablespoons [90 ml.] of butter. Arrange in an elongated mound and decorate with lines of cinnamon shooting from the top like rays of sunlight. Serve with spoons of ice-cold milk, and with confectioners' sugar separately in a bowl.

PAULA WOLFERT
COUSCOUS AND OTHER GOOD FOOD FROM MOROCCO

Potato Noodles with Poppy Seeds

Zemiakové Rezance s Makom

Ground poppy seeds are obtainable where Central European foods are sold. If unavailable, substitute ground walnuts.

To serve 8

5	medium-sized potatoes, boiled and peeled	5
3 oz.	poppy seeds, ground (about ⅓ cup [75 ml.])	90 g.
1	egg, beaten	1
1½ cups	semolina, or substitute farina	375 ml.
	salt	
4 tbsp.	butter	60 ml.
½ cup	superfine sugar	125 ml.

Press the potatoes through a sieve. Add the egg, semolina and a pinch of salt, and work the mixture into a dough. Roll the dough and cut it into short noodles, slightly thicker than matchsticks. Drop the noodles into boiling salted water, and cook for two or three minutes or until they are soft. Drain the noodles, dot them with the butter and sprinkle them with ground poppy seeds and sugar.

VOJTECH ŠPANKO (EDITOR)
SLOVENSKÁ KUCHÁRKA

Pálffy Noodles

Pálffy Metélt

This Hungarian classic is the *à la financière* of noodle dishes. In the past only financiers could afford it, or aristocrats like Count Pálffy—who introduced the six-year-old prodigy Mozart to the court and the music world of Vienna. As a shortcut you may use ½ pound [¼ kg.] of commercial egg noodles.

To serve 6 to 8

1 cup	flour	¼ liter
5	eggs, 2 whole, 3 with the yolks separated from the whites	5
	salt	
1 quart	milk	1 liter
2-inch	piece vanilla bean	5-cm.
6 tbsp.	unsalted butter	90 ml.
1 cup	raisins, soaked in warm water for 15 minutes and drained	¼ liter
1 tsp.	freshly grated lemon peel	5 ml.
½ cup	sugar	125 ml.
5	sour cooking apples, peeled, cored and halved	5
¼ cup	bread crumbs	50 ml.
¼ cup	ground walnuts	50 ml.
1 tbsp.	fresh lemon juice	15 ml.

Knead the flour, the two whole eggs and a pinch of salt together to make a dough. If the eggs are large you may need a little additional flour. Stretch the dough into a thin sheet and let it rest for 15 minutes. Cut it into strips about ¼ inch [6 mm.] wide. Bring to a boil the milk, vanilla bean, a pinch of salt and 1 tablespoon [15 ml.] of the butter. Reduce the heat and put in the egg noodles. Cook until the noodles absorb all of the liquid, stirring often. This should take 10 to 12 minutes. Mix in the raisins, the remaining butter, the lemon peel, ¼ cup [50 ml.] of the sugar and the three egg yolks.

In a separate pot, cook the apple halves in 1 cup [¼ liter] of water and 2 tablespoons [30 ml.] of the sugar until they are half-cooked. Remove the apples and pat them dry. Sprinkle the bread crumbs in a well-buttered baking-serving casserole of porcelain or heatproof glass. Put three quarters of the noodle mixture in the casserole and pat it down evenly. Place the half-cooked apples, cavities upward, in two even rows on top of the mixture. Fill the apple cavities with walnuts. Cover with the remaining noodle mixture. Bake the noodles in a preheated 375° F. [190° C.] oven for 20 minutes.

Meanwhile, whip the egg whites and beat in the remaining sugar and the lemon juice to make a meringue. Pour the meringue on the partly baked noodle casserole and bake for 15 minutes longer, until the meringue is golden brown.

GEORGE LANG
THE CUISINE OF HUNGARY

Whole-Wheat Noodle Kugel

To serve 6

10 oz.	medium-wide whole-wheat noodles	300 g.
4	eggs, beaten	4
1/3 cup	melted butter	75 ml.
1	apple, peeled, halved, cored and chopped	1
1/2 cup	chopped nuts	125 ml.
2/3 cup	chopped raisins or other dried fruit	150 ml.
1/3 cup	honey	75 ml.
1/2 tsp.	salt	2 ml.
2 tbsp.	strawberry preserves	30 ml.
2 tsp.	grated lemon peel	10 ml.
1/4 cup	fresh lemon juice	50 ml.
1 tsp.	ground cinnamon	5 ml.

Preheat the oven to 325° F. [160° C.]. Cook the noodles in 3 quarts [3 liters] of boiling water to which 1 tablespoon [15 ml.] of oil has been added. Drain, and rinse the noodles with cold water. Drain again. Combine the noodles with the remaining ingredients and turn into a lightly oiled baking dish. Bake in the oven for one hour. Serve warm or cold.

NANCY ALBRIGHT
RODALE'S NATURALLY GREAT FOODS COOKBOOK

Sweet Lasagne au Gratin

Lasagne Zuccherate e Gratinate

To serve 6

1 lb.	lasagne	1/2 kg.
2 cups	milk	1/2 liter
3 tbsp.	sugar	45 ml.
3/4 cup	seedless raisins, soaked in 1 cup [1/4 liter] warm water for 15 minutes and drained	175 ml.
2	eggs, beaten	2
3 tbsp.	dry bread crumbs	45 ml.
1/2 tsp.	ground cinnamon	2 ml.
6 tbsp.	butter	90 ml.

Preheat the oven to 350° F. [180° C.].

Bring the milk to a boil and allow it to cool. Cook the lasagne in boiling salted water for eight minutes. Drain, and put it in a large bowl. Add the sugar, milk, raisins and eggs. Mix well.

Butter a baking dish and dust it with 2 tablespoons [30

ml.] of the bread crumbs. Add the pasta mixture and smooth the top surface. Mix the remaining tablespoon [15 ml.] of bread crumbs with the cinnamon and sprinkle on top. Dot the surface with dabs of butter. Bake in the preheated oven for 20 minutes. Allow the lasagne to cool for five minutes before serving.

JACQUES HARVEY
365 WAYS TO COOK PASTA

Baked Stuffed Noodles

Rakott Metélt

To serve 8

4 cups	flour	1 liter
5	eggs, 2 whole, 3 with the yolks separated from the whites	5
1/4 tsp.	salt	1 ml.
	water	
8 tbsp.	butter, melted	120 ml.
1/2 cup	sugar	125 ml.
3/4 cup	sour cream	175 ml.
1/4	vanilla bean, pounded to a pulp	1/4
1/4 cup	white raisins	50 ml.
2 tbsp.	white bread crumbs	30 ml.
3/4 cup	ground walnuts	175 ml.
1/2 cup	thick apricot jam	125 ml.

Combine the flour, the two whole eggs, the salt and enough water to make a medium-hard dough. Stretch or roll the dough into a thin sheet and cut it into pieces 1 by 4 inches [2½ by 10 cm.].

Bring 4 quarts [4 liters] of water to a boil and boil the noodle pieces for four minutes. Drain, and rinse with cold water. Preheat the oven to 375° F. [190° C.].

Beat together well the three egg yolks, melted butter and half of the sugar. Add the sour cream, vanilla pulp and raisins; stir. Whip the egg whites, add the remaining ¼ cup [50 ml.] of sugar and beat until stiff, then gently stir this meringue into the sour-cream mixture. Combine the noodles and the sour-cream mixture. Butter an 8-by-12-inch [20-by-30-cm.] baking pan and sprinkle it with the bread crumbs.

Spread a third of the noodles on the bottom of the prepared pan. Sprinkle with the ground walnuts. Add another third of the noodles. Spread with apricot jam. Cover with the remaining noodles.

Bake in the preheated oven for 30 minutes. Cut into large squares to serve.

GEORGE LANG
THE CUISINE OF HUNGARY

Noodle Doughnuts

Metélt Fánk

To serve 6 to 8

2 cups	flour	½ liter
3	eggs, 2 lightly beaten	3
2	egg yolks	2
½ tsp.	salt	2 ml.
3 cups	milk	¾ liter
½ cup	crushed blanched almonds	125 ml.
½ cup	granulated sugar	125 ml.
½ tsp.	vanilla extract	2 ml.
1 cup	fresh bread crumbs	¼ liter
½ cup	lard, melted	125 ml.
½ cup	confectioners' sugar	125 ml.

Mix the unbeaten egg, the egg yolks and salt into the flour, making a dry dough. Roll out very thin, and cut into broad noodles. Boil the noodles in the milk until all moisture is absorbed. Stir in the almonds, granulated sugar and vanilla. While still hot, pack the mixture into a large buttered baking pan to form a layer about ½ inch [1 cm.] thick. Cool.

Turn out the cooled noodle mixture onto a board and cut it into rounds with a cookie cutter. Dip each round in the lightly beaten eggs, then in bread crumbs. Fry in the melted lard. Drain, sprinkle with confectioners' sugar and set in a warm oven until all of the rounds are fried. Serve hot.

PAULA POGANY BENNETT AND VELMA R. CLARK
THE ART OF HUNGARIAN COOKING

Farina Dumplings in Milk

Gries Nockerln in Milch

To make about 30 dumplings

¾ cup	farina	175 ml.
6 tbsp.	unsalted butter, softened	90 ml.
2	eggs	2
¼ tsp.	salt	1 ml.
3 cups	milk	¾ liter
2 cups	water	½ liter
2 oz.	semisweet baking chocolate, grated	60 g.
	sugar	

Cream the butter and stir in the eggs. Add the farina and salt, and blend thoroughly. Let the mixture rest in the refrigerator for about 30 minutes to let it swell.

In a deep, wide kettle bring the milk and water to a boil. Reduce the heat. Take about ½ teaspoon [2 ml.] of the mix-

---

ture, pat it quickly into an oblong shape and lower it into the milk mixture. Repeat until all of the mixture is used up. Return the liquid to a boil, reduce the heat and cook the dumplings for two or three minutes.

Without delay, pour the entire contents of the kettle into two 10-inch [25-cm.] ovenproof frying pans, spreading the dumplings so that they lie flat on the bottoms of the pans. Immediately place the pans in a preheated 350° F. [180° C.] oven and bake for 15 to 20 minutes on the lowest rack of the oven until the dumplings turn yellow in color. By then they should be light and fluffy. With a slotted spoon, remove the dumplings to a plate.

Serve at once, sprinkled with grated chocolate and sugar.

LILLY JOSS REICH
THE VIENNESE PASTRY COOKBOOK

Noodle Kugel

To serve 6 to 8

1 lb.	broad egg noodles	½ kg.
	butter	
3	eggs	3
1½ cups	cottage cheese	375 ml.
¾ cup	sour cream or yogurt	175 ml.
½ lb.	cream cheese, softened	¼ kg.
½ tsp.	vanilla extract	2 ml.
2 tsp.	ground cinnamon	10 ml.
¼ cup	honey	50 ml.
	salt	
2	apples, peeled, cored and sliced or 2 peaches, peeled, halved, pitted and sliced	2
Brown-sugar topping		
¼ cup	brown sugar	50 ml.
¼ cup	wheat germ	50 ml.
1 cup	fresh bread crumbs	¼ liter
2 tsp.	ground cinnamon	10 ml.

Cook the noodles in boiling salted water until barely tender. Drain and butter them. Beat together until smooth the eggs, cottage cheese, sour cream or yogurt, cream cheese, vanilla, cinnamon, honey and a few dashes of salt. Add the apples or peaches and the noodles. Put the mixture in a well-buttered casserole. Mix the ingredients for the brown-sugar topping and sprinkle over the noodle casserole. Dot with butter and bake in a preheated 375° F. [190° C.] oven for 35 minutes.

MOLLIE KATZEN
MOOSEWOOD COOKBOOK

Vermicelli Cake

Gâteau de Vermicelles

The technique of preparing vermicelli cake is demonstrated on pages 62-63.

	To serve 6 to 8	
5 oz.	vermicelli	150 g.
4 tbsp.	unsalted butter	60 ml.
1 cup	hot water	¼ liter
1 cup	heavy cream, scalded	¼ liter
½ cup	sugar	125 ml.
⅓ tsp.	salt	1½ ml.
10	whole cloves, the buds separated from the stems, and the buds crushed	10
2 tsp.	grated lemon peel	10 ml.
4	eggs, the yolks separated from the whites	4

Caramel

¼ cup	sugar	50 ml.
2 tbsp.	hot water	30 ml.

Preheat the oven to 325° F. [160° C.].

To make the caramel, mix the ¼ cup [50 ml.] of sugar with the 2 tablespoons [30 ml.] of hot water in a small pan, and cook the mixture to a caramel over medium heat. While the caramel cooks, fill a 6-cup [1½-liter] soufflé dish with hot water from the tap. Empty the dish and wipe it dry. Immediately pour in the caramel, turning the soufflé dish in all directions so the caramel covers the bottom evenly. Let the caramel cool. Butter very heavily the sides of the dish not covered with caramel. Set the dish aside.

Heat the butter in a 9-inch [23-cm.] frying pan. Crush the vermicelli and toss them into the hot butter until half of them have turned brown. Add the 1 cup [¼ liter] of hot water and toss until the vermicelli are almost done. Off the heat, add the scalded cream, the ½ cup [125 ml.] of sugar, the salt, clove buds and grated lemon peel. Mix well. Beat the egg yolks vigorously; mix into the noodle base.

Whip the egg whites until they are stiff enough to carry the weight of a raw egg in its shell without the latter sinking into the egg white bulk by more than ¼ inch [6 mm.]. Fold the egg whites into the noodle base.

Turn into the prepared soufflé dish and bake in the pre-heated oven, without a water bath, for 35 to 40 minutes or until nicely browned. The lack of a water bath will allow the caramel bottom to crisp. The contrast of the crisp caramel with the soft center is one of the pleasures of the cake.

Unmold the cake onto a lightly buttered platter as soon as it is removed from the oven. Serve the vermicelli cake plain or with whipped cream.

MADELEINE KAMMAN
WHEN FRENCH WOMEN COOK

Yeast-Nut Dumpling

Germ Nuss Knödel

	To serve 6 to 8	
about 2 cups	flour	about ½ liter
	milk	
¼ cup	sugar	50 ml.
½ oz.	compressed yeast, finely crumbled, or 1 tbsp. [15 ml.] active dry yeast, dissolved in ¼ cup [50 ml.] tepid water	15 g.
1	egg	1
1	egg yolk	1
¼ tsp.	salt	1 ml.
16 tbsp.	butter (½ lb. [¼ kg.]), cooked until lightly browned	¼ liter

Nut filling

2½ cups	coarsely ground almonds or walnuts	625 ml.
about ¼ cup	sugar	about 50 ml.
2 tbsp.	unsalted butter, melted	30 ml.
½ cup	raisins (optional)	125 ml.

Bread-crumb topping

4 to 6 tbsp.	unsalted butter	60 to 90 ml.
1 cup	bread crumbs	¼ liter
about ⅓ cup	sugar	about 75 ml.

In a small pan, heat milk to lukewarm—using ½ cup [125 ml.] of milk if your yeast is compressed, but only ¼ cup [50 ml.] of milk for dry yeast. Add 1 tablespoon [15 ml.] of the sugar, 5 or 6 tablespoons [75 or 90 ml.] of the flour and the yeast. Combine the ingredients well. Cover the pan with a kitchen towel. Let the yeast mixture rise in a draft-free place until bubbles appear on the surface.

While the yeast is rising, blend together the whole egg, the egg yolk, sugar, salt and several spoons of the flour. Combine this batter with the yeast mixture, gradually adding more flour to form a soft dough.

With a wooden spoon, beat the dough well for about 10 minutes, or until it no longer sticks to either the bowl or the spoon, adding more flour if necessary to get a firm, elastic, satiny dough. Place the dough, covered, in a draft-free warm (but not hot) place. Let the dough rise to at least double its original size. Then punch it down, and let it rise for an additional 15 to 20 minutes.

Prepare the nut filling by mixing the ground nuts with the sugar. Transfer the dough to a well-floured board; roll out to an oblong about 15 by 18 inches [38 by 45 cm.]. Brush the surface with the melted butter. Cover with the nut filling. Scatter raisins on top (optional). Bend up the edges of the two short sides of the dough just enough to keep the filling from escaping, then roll the dough, jelly-roll style, into the shape of a long sausage, stretching it gently to about 18 inches [45 cm.]. Twist the roll into a coil.

Flour a large dinner napkin generously; place the dumpling in its center and tie the opposite corners together loosely, since the dumpling will expand considerably.

While the dumpling is again rising, fill a wide, deep kettle three quarters full with salted water and bring it to a boil. Secured by two wooden spoons, suspend the napkin with the dough in the water. Cover, and boil for about one hour.

Still secured by the wooden spoons, place the napkin bundle in a sieve to let the water escape and the bundle cool down. When you are able to untie the napkin, place the dumpling on a hot platter. Melt the 4 to 6 tablespoons [60 to 90 ml.] of butter for the topping in a small frying pan and add the bread crumbs. Stir until the crumbs are toasted to medium brown. Remove from the heat and combine with the sugar. After pouring some of the topping over the dumpling, cut the dumpling into serving portions. Serve at once, accompanied by the remaining topping and the browned butter.

LILLY JOSS REICH
THE VIENNESE PASTRY COOKBOOK

Burnt-Sugar Dumplings

To serve 6

1½ cups	sifted flour	375 ml.
2½ tsp.	baking powder	12 ml.
3 tbsp.	sugar	45 ml.
¼ tsp.	salt	1 ml.
3 tbsp.	butter	45 ml.
½ cup	chopped walnuts	125 ml.
¾ cup	milk	175 ml.

Burnt-sugar sauce

1½ cups	sugar	375 ml.
2 tbsp.	butter	30 ml.
⅛ tsp.	salt	½ ml.
2 cups	hot water	½ liter

To make the sauce, heat ½ cup [125 ml.] of sugar in a skillet until it melts to a golden brown syrup. Add the butter, salt

and remaining sugar. Add hot water gradually, stirring constantly. Heat to boiling and cook until the sugar is dissolved, about 10 minutes, stirring frequently.

Meanwhile, sift the flour, baking powder, sugar and salt together. Cut in the butter with a pastry blender. Add the walnuts; stir in the milk all at once, mixing only enough to moisten the flour.

Drop the dumpling mixture by tablespoons into the gently boiling caramel sauce. Cover tightly and simmer the dumplings gently for 12 to 15 minutes without removing the lid. Serve the dumplings at once with the sauce.

RUTH BEROLZHEIMER (EDITOR)
CULINARY ARTS INSTITUTE ENCYCLOPEDIA COOKBOOK

Steamed Dumplings
Dampfnudeln

To make 12 dumplings

2½ to 3 cups	flour	625 to 750 ml.
1 tbsp.	active dry yeast	15 ml.
¼ cup	tepid water	50 ml.
¾ cup	milk	175 ml.
8 tbsp.	butter	120 ml.
¼ cup	sugar	50 ml.
1 tsp.	salt	5 ml.

Dissolve the yeast in the water. Combine ¼ cup [50 ml.] of the milk, 4 tablespoons [60 ml.] of the butter, the sugar and salt; bring to a boil, then cool to lukewarm.

Place 2½ cups [625 ml.] of the flour in a mixing bowl, make a well in the center, add the dissolved yeast, then the cooled milk mixture. Mix until blended, then knead until smooth, adding the remaining ½ cup [125 ml.] of flour, if necessary. Cover the dough and let it rise in a warm place for about one and a half hours; when doubled in bulk, punch it down and let it rise again for about half an hour.

Tear off pieces of dough, grease the palms of your hands and roll the pieces of dough to make even balls about 1 inch [2½ cm.] in diameter. Place the remaining ½ cup milk and 4 tablespoons of butter in a large heavy pot or Dutch oven. Put the balls of dough in the pot. Lay a cloth over the top of the pot, then put on the cover. Bring the liquid to a boil on top of the stove, turn the heat as low as possible and cook very slowly until you can hear the butter crackling—which means all of the milk has been absorbed. This takes about 30 minutes. The dumplings will be golden brown and taste much like baked sweet rolls but will be more moist. Serve with meat or stewed fruit.

BETTY WASON
THE ART OF GERMAN COOKING

Sauces and Fillings

Recipes for basic sauces appear in Standard Preparations, pages 166-167.

Veal and Sausage Filling

To make about 2 cups [½ liter] filling

½ lb.	lean ground veal	¼ kg.
½ lb.	sweet Italian sausages, half sweet and half hot Italian sausages, or other well-seasoned pork sausages, peeled and finely crumbled	¼ kg.
2 tbsp.	olive oil	30 ml.
¼ cup	finely chopped onion	50 ml.
⅓ cup	dry bread crumbs	75 ml.
¼ cup	heavy cream	50 ml.
2	eggs	2
2 tbsp.	finely chopped fresh flat-leafed parsley	30 ml.
¼ tsp.	crumbled dried rosemary	1 ml.
½ tsp.	finely chopped lemon peel	2 ml.
¼ tsp.	salt	1 ml.
	freshly ground black pepper	

Heat the oil in a heavy 10- to 12-inch [25- to 30-cm.] frying pan, add the onions and cook them over medium heat for about five minutes, stirring frequently. When they have barely begun to color, add the sausage meat. Increase the heat and, mashing the sausage constantly with a fork to break up lumps, cook until it has rendered most of its fat and turned a light brown. Quickly add the veal and, again mashing it with the fork, cook it for three or four minutes over high heat until it has turned from pink to brown and separated into small granules. Scrape the entire contents of the pan into a strainer and drain the meat of all fat.

In a large bowl, soak the bread crumbs in the cream for three or four minutes, and add the drained meat. Beat together with a spoon until the mixture is fairly smooth, then beat in the eggs one at a time. Stir in the parsley, rosemary, the chopped lemon peel, salt, and a few grindings of pepper, and taste for seasoning.

MICHAEL FIELD
ALL MANNER OF FOOD

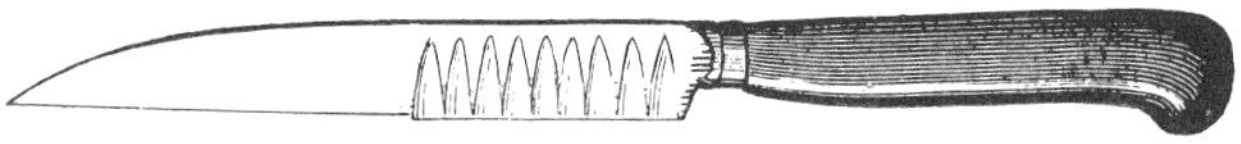

Artichoke Spaghetti Sauce

Salsa di Carciofi

To prepare the artichokes, cut off the stem of each artichoke, remove the outer leaves and cut off about a 1-inch [2½-cm.] slice from the top.

To make about 4 cups [1 liter] sauce

3	medium-sized artichokes, trimmed and thinly sliced	3
3 tbsp.	olive oil	45 ml.
1 tbsp.	butter	15 ml.
1	medium-sized onion, thinly sliced	1
¼ tsp.	finely chopped garlic clove	1 ml.
2 cups	canned Italian-style tomatoes	½ liter
1	bay leaf	1
½ tsp.	dried basil	2 ml.
	salt and pepper	

Heat the oil and butter. Cook the artichokes in the oil and butter, stirring constantly, for three minutes. Add the onion, garlic, tomatoes, bay leaf, basil, and salt and pepper to taste. Simmer, covered, stirring occasionally, until the artichokes are tender.

NIKA STANDEN HAZELTON
THE SWISS COOKBOOK

Chicken Filling for Ravioli

To make 6 to 7 cups [1 ½ to 1 ¾ liters] filling

1 lb.	boneless chicken breasts, skinned, and ground in a food grinder	½ kg.
½ cup	finely chopped onion	125 ml.
1	garlic clove, finely chopped	1
¼ cup	olive oil	50 ml.
½ cup	cracker crumbs, bread crumbs or matzo meal	125 ml.
½ cup	heavy cream	125 ml.
1 lb.	spinach, parboiled for 3 minutes, drained, squeezed dry and chopped	½ kg.
2 tbsp.	chopped fresh parsley	30 ml.
½ tsp.	salt	2 ml.
¼ tsp.	freshly ground black pepper	1 ml.

In a skillet, sauté the onion and garlic in the oil over medium heat for three or four minutes, until the onion is soft but not browned. Add the chicken, turn up the heat, and toss the meat with the onion for a minute or two until the meat is lightly browned. Remove from the heat and transfer to a mixing bowl. Add all of the remaining ingredients to the bowl and blend well. The filling is now ready for use.

PAUL RUBINSTEIN
FEASTS FOR TWELVE (OR MORE)

Veal Stuffing for Ravioli

Farce à Raviolis

For a stuffing with a coarser texture, combine the ingredients with a fork and do not sieve them.

This stuffing can be prepared equally well with leftover cooked veal, chicken or beef. You may need to add a tablespoon [15 ml.] of gravy if the meats are dry; although this stuffing should be firm, it must also be supple.

To make about 2 to 2 ½ cups [500 to 625 ml.] stuffing

5 oz.	boneless lean veal, diced	150 g.
3½ oz.	salt-cured ham or lean salt pork with the rind removed, blanched in boiling water for 5 minutes, drained and diced	100 g.
2 tbsp.	butter	30 ml.
1	onion, thinly sliced	1
1	bay leaf	1
1	sprig thyme	1
¾ cup	white wine, veal or chicken stock (recipe, page 167), or water	175 ml.
½ lb.	spinach, parboiled in salted water for 3 minutes, drained, squeezed dry and finely chopped	¼ kg.
2	egg yolks	2
	salt and pepper	

Brown the veal and salt-cured ham or salt pork in the butter. Add the onion, bay leaf and thyme; moisten with the white wine, stock or water. Cover and simmer over low heat for about one hour. The meat should be well cooked and the liquid almost completely evaporated.

Turn the meat out onto a large plate to cool, discarding the bay leaf and thyme. When cool, pound the meat mixture with the blanched spinach; add the egg yolks, season, and press through a fine sieve.

J. B. REBOUL
LA CUISINIÈRE PROVENÇALE

Tomato Sauce with Tiny Meatballs

Salsa con Polpettine

To make about 3 to 4 quarts [3 to 4 liters] sauce

32 oz.	canned tomatoes, coarsely chopped, with their liquid reserved	1 kg.
¼ cup	finely chopped onion, or 2 garlic cloves, finely chopped	50 ml.
¼ cup	finely chopped fresh parsley	50 ml.
¼ cup	finely chopped fresh basil	50 ml.
3 tbsp.	olive oil	45 ml.
1 tbsp.	finely chopped fresh hot chili (optional)	15 ml.
	salt and pepper	

Tiny meatballs

1 lb.	lean ground beef	½ kg.
1 lb.	lean ground veal or pork	½ kg.
½ cup	finely chopped onion	125 ml.
½ cup	grated Romano cheese	125 ml.
1	garlic clove, finely chopped	1
¼ cup	finely chopped fresh parsley	50 ml.
¼ cup	finely chopped fresh basil	50 ml.
2	eggs	2
2 cups	bread crumbs	½ liter
1½ cups	water or stock (recipe, page 167)	375 ml.

In a large kettle, sauté the ¼ cup [50 ml.] of chopped onion or the two chopped garlic cloves, the parsley and basil in the oil. When the onion or garlic turns delicately brown, add the other ingredients, stir well, and let the sauce cook slowly while preparing the meatballs.

Mix together the beef, the veal or pork, the ½ cup [125 ml.] of chopped onion, the Romano cheese, garlic clove, parsley, basil, eggs, bread crumbs, water or stock, and salt and pepper to taste. Occasionally wetting the palms of your hands, roll the meat mixture into marble-sized balls. Carefully drop the meatballs into the cooking sauce and continue cooking slowly for two hours, stirring occasionally.

WILMA REIVA LA SASSO
REGIONAL ITALIAN COOKING

Mixed Meats Filling for Pasta Cases

Mortadella is a mildly spiced Italian bologna, studded with pieces of fat; it is obtainable from Italian delicatessens.

To make about 2 cups [½ liter] filling

¼ lb.	mortadella	125 g.
2 oz.	prosciutto	60 g.
2 oz.	lean beef	60 g.
2 oz.	pork	60 g.
2 tbsp.	olive oil	30 ml.
	dry, seasoned bread crumbs	
¼ cup	chopped fresh parsley	50 ml.
¼ tsp.	grated nutmeg	1 ml.
	salt and pepper	

Put the mortadella, prosciutto, beef and pork through the fine disk of a food grinder, and combine thoroughly. Sauté the mixture in the olive oil over medium heat. When thoroughly cooked, remove from the heat and mix in enough bread crumbs to make a stiff mixture. Add the parsley and nutmeg, and salt and pepper to taste. Chill for easier handling before filling the pasta of your choice.

IRMA S. ROMBAUER AND MARION ROMBAUER BECKER
JOY OF COOKING

Standard Preparations

Standard Pasta Dough

The techniques of assembling, kneading, rolling and cutting pasta are demonstrated on pages 16-19 and 22-23.

Bread flour or unbleached all-purpose flour is best for handmade pasta dough, although any type of wheat flour can be used. The exact proportion of flour to eggs depends on the type of flour and the size of the eggs used, but about ¾ cup [175 ml.] of flour to one egg is a good mean ratio. If preparing a smaller amount of dough, combine the ingredients in a mixing bowl.

To make about 1 ½ pounds [¾ kg.] fresh pasta, about ¾ pound [⅓ kg.] dried pasta

3 to 4 cups	flour	¾ to 1 liter
4	eggs	4
	salt	
2 tbsp.	olive oil	30 ml.

Mound 3 cups [¾ liter] of the flour on a smooth work surface. Make a well in the center of the flour and break the eggs into

it. Add a generous pinch of salt and the olive oil. With one hand, gradually incorporate the flour from around the edge of the well into the eggs, stirring with your fingers to form a batter. Use the other hand to support the edge of the flour well and prevent the eggs from flowing out. Continue incorporating the flour until the batter becomes a fairly stiff but malleable paste. If the dough is soft or feels moist, work in additional flour, a little at a time.

If the dough is to be rolled out and cut by hand, gather it into a ball and place it on a lightly floured surface. Knead the dough, pressing it flat with the heel of your hand, folding it double and pressing it again. Continue kneading for five to 10 minutes, or until the dough is silky and elastic.

Cover the kneaded dough with plastic wrap or a cloth and let it rest for an hour. Divide it into fist-sized portions. Then roll out each portion of dough on a lightly floured surface until you have a thin circle. The dough can now be cut into the required shapes.

If the dough is to be kneaded and rolled with the aid of a pasta machine, gather it into a ball and briefly knead it by hand. Divide it into fist-sized portions, flatten one with your hand and set the others aside, covered with plastic wrap or a cloth. Open the smooth machine rollers fully, flour the flattened dough and pass it between the rollers. Fold the rolled sheet into thirds, flour the package and turn it 90 degrees before passing it between the rollers again.

Repeat the folding, flouring and rolling four or five times until the dough is smooth. Then decrease the gap between the rollers by several notches and pass the dough through again. Repeat decreasing the gap and rolling the dough until it is thin enough to cut into shape. Hang up the sheet of dough to dry while you repeat the machine-kneading and rolling processes with the remaining portions. Finally, cut the dough into noodles with the aid of the cutting rollers on the machine or cut it into other pasta shapes by hand.

After cutting, the pasta can be used immediately or left to dry at room temperature until brittle, not crumbly — about four hours. You can store the dried pasta — in a tightly covered container or well-sealed plastic bag — in a cool place such as the refrigerator for about a week, or in the freezer for at least a month.

Stiff Pasta Dough

This dough, suitable for grating or shredding, is prepared in the same way as a standard pasta dough *(opposite)*, but during the kneading ¼ cup [50 ml.] of extra flour must be incorporated for every 1 cup [¼ liter] of flour in the standard dough. Continue kneading, constantly working in more flour, until you get a smooth dough that is as stiff as it can possibly be without crumbling. To facilitate grating, cover the dough with plastic wrap and freeze it for about 30 minutes. Remove the dough and grate it coarse onto a sheet of wax paper. If you are not using the shreds immediately, flour them generously to keep them from sticking together.

Colored Pasta Dough

The amount suggested for each ingredient is enough to color the standard pasta dough quantities listed opposite. Should you wish to prepare two or three different pasta colors, divide the quantities of dough and coloring accordingly.

It is simpler to amalgamate the ingredients for colored pasta dough in a mixing bowl than on a flat surface, particularly if you are using small quantities. To compensate for extra moistness when coloring pasta with vegetables (especially spinach), you will need to incorporate extra flour into the dough when kneading it and rolling it out. The technique of kneading and rolling with a pasta machine is demonstrated on pages 18-19.

Green pasta. Parboil ½ pound [¼ kg.] of spinach for about two minutes or chard for five minutes. Drain, rinse in cold water and squeeze the leaves as dry as possible. Purée the spinach or chard through a sieve or food mill, or chop it fine by hand or with a food processor if a pasta machine is to be used. With a fork, combine the spinach or chard with the pasta dough ingredients. Knead and roll out.

Speckled green pasta. Trim, wash, pat dry and chop fine about 6 tablespoons [90 ml.] of mixed fresh herbs: parsley, sorrel, thyme, sage leaves, tarragon, lovage, marjoram, basil, dandelion, rocket, hyssop and tender savory shoots are all suitable. However, the strong herbs—thyme, sage, savory, marjoram and tarragon—do not marry well with some others, so choose your herb mixture carefully. Stir the herbs into the dough ingredients with a fork. Knead and roll out.

Red pasta. Boil two small unpeeled beets in salted water for 40 minutes to one hour or until tender. Peel and chop the beets, then purée them in a food processor. Stir the beet purée into the pasta dough ingredients before kneading the dough and rolling it out.

Orange pasta. Stir about ¼ cup [50 ml.] of well-reduced tomato sauce or puréed tomato into the pasta dough ingredients. Knead and roll out.

Yellow pasta. Add a pinch of ground saffron to the flour and salt for the pasta dough. Mix well. Stir in the eggs and oil. Knead and roll out.

Pastry

For a softer pastry with a distinctive taste *(demonstration, pages 58-59)*, substitute about ½ cup [125 ml.] of olive oil for the butter and one or two eggs for some of the water. Combine all the ingredients in a bowl and blend thoroughly with a fork until the mixture is loosely bound. Knead the dough with your knuckles, sprinkling in more flour if the dough becomes sticky. Gather the dough into a ball, cover with a cloth and refrigerate for about one hour before rolling out.

To make about 1 ½ pounds [¾ kg.] dough		
3½ cups	flour	875 ml.
2 tsp.	salt	10 ml.
24 tbsp.	cold, hard butter (¾ lb. [⅓ kg.]) cut into small pieces	360 ml.
about ½ cup	cold water	about 125 ml.

Sift the flour and salt into a bowl. Add the butter. Rub the butter into the flour with your fingers (or cut the butter into the flour with two knives) until the mixture has a coarse, pebbly texture, with large fragments of butter visible. Stirring lightly with a fork, add just enough water to allow you to gather the dough into a firm ball. Wrap the dough in plastic wrap, wax paper or aluminum foil and chill in the refrigerator for at least 30 minutes before rolling out.

Fritter Batter

Making batter for fritters is demonstrated on pages 74-75.

To make about 2 cups [½ liter] batter		
1 cup	flour	¼ liter
¼ tsp.	salt	1 ml.
2	eggs, the yolks separated from the whites	2
3 tbsp.	olive oil	45 ml.
	cayenne pepper (optional)	
1 cup	beer or water	¼ liter

In a bowl, mix together the flour and salt. Whisk in the egg yolks, oil and, if you wish, cayenne pepper. Gradually add the beer or water, and whisk for only as long as it takes to produce a smooth batter. Let the batter rest for at least one hour at room temperature. Beat the egg whites until soft peaks form, and fold them into the batter just before using it.

Basic White Sauce

This recipe can be used whenever béchamel sauce is called for. If the sauce is to form the basis of a soufflé, use half as much milk, double the quantity of flour and cook for only a few minutes after the milk has come to a boil; also, do not add any heavy cream.

To make about 2 cups [½ liter] sauce		
2 tbsp.	butter	30 ml.
2 tbsp.	flour	30 ml.
2½ cups	milk	625 ml.
	salt	
	white pepper (optional)	
	freshly grated nutmeg (optional)	
	heavy cream (optional)	

Melt the butter in a heavy saucepan over low heat. Stir in the flour to make a roux and cook gently, stirring, for two or three minutes. Pour in all of the milk at once, whisking constantly to blend the mixture smoothly. Increase the heat and continue whisking while the sauce comes to a boil.

Reduce the heat to very low and simmer, uncovered, for about 40 minutes, stirring occasionally to prevent the sauce from developing a top skin or sticking to the bottom of the pan. Season to taste with salt and, if desired, white pepper and a pinch of nutmeg. Whisk again until the sauce is smooth. Add a little heavy cream if you prefer a richer sauce.

Velouté Sauce

To make about 2 cups [½ liter] sauce		
2 tbsp.	butter	30 ml.
2 tbsp.	flour	30 ml.
2½ cups	veal or chicken stock (recipe, page 167)	625 ml.

Melt the butter in a heavy saucepan over low heat and stir in the flour until this roux mixture is smooth. Cook, stirring constantly, for two or three minutes. When the roux stops foaming and is a light golden color, pour in the stock and whisk continuously until the mixture reaches a boil. Move the saucepan half off the heat, so that the liquid on one side of the pan maintains a steady but very light boil. Skim off fat and impurities that form on the surface of the other, calm side of the liquid. From time to time spoon off the skin. Cook for 30 minutes, or until the sauce loses its floury taste and reaches the desired consistency.

Basic Tomato Sauce

When fresh ripe tomatoes are not available, use 3 cups [¾ liter] of drained, canned Italian-style tomatoes.

An alternative method of making the sauce, without using a sieve, is to peel and seed the tomatoes before cooking them: Immerse the tomatoes in boiling water for 30 seconds; remove and peel them. Halve each tomato horizontally and scoop out the seeds. Lightly sauté a finely chopped onion and a chopped garlic clove in a little oil and butter. Add the tomatoes and cook over brisk heat, stirring occasionally, for 10 minutes or until the tomatoes are reduced to a pulp. Season and add herbs to taste. Enrich the sauce, if desired, with 2 tablespoons [30 ml.] of butter at the end of the cooking.

To make about 1¼ cups [300 ml.] sauce		
6	medium-sized very ripe tomatoes, quartered	6
1	bay leaf	1
1	large sprig dried thyme	1
1	onion, sliced	1
1	garlic clove, crushed (optional)	1
about 2 tbsp.	butter (optional)	about 30 ml.
1 tbsp.	finely chopped parsley	15 ml.
1 tbsp.	basil leaves, torn into small pieces	15 ml.
	salt and freshly ground pepper	
1 or 2 tsp.	sugar (optional)	5 or 10 ml.

Place the tomatoes in an enameled, stainless-steel or tinned copper saucepan with the bay leaf and thyme. Add the onion and the garlic, if using. Bring to a boil, crushing the tomatoes lightly with a wooden spoon and cook, uncovered, over fairly brisk heat for 10 minutes or until the tomatoes have become a thick pulp. Remove the bay leaf and thyme.

Tip the tomatoes into a plastic or stainless-steel sieve placed over a bowl and, using a wooden pestle, push them through the sieve. Discard the skins and seeds, and return the sieved tomato pulp to the pan.

Cook, uncovered, over low heat until the sauce is reduced to the required consistency—about 10 to 15 minutes. If you like, whisk in a little butter to enrich the sauce. Taste for seasoning and whisk in the parsley and basil. Sweeten the sauce with the sugar, if using canned tomatoes.

Puréed Tomato

To make about 1 cup [¼ liter] purée

4	medium-sized tomatoes, peeled, seeded and coarsely chopped	4

Place the tomatoes in a heavy enameled, tin-lined copper or stainless-steel saucepan. Stirring frequently, cook the tomatoes over low heat for about 10 minutes, or until most of their juices have evaporated and their flesh has been reduced to a thick pulp. Purée the tomatoes through a food mill or sieve into a bowl. Tightly covered and refrigerated, the purée will keep safely for four or five days.

Meat Sauce

This sauce is sometimes called a Bolognese sauce. It can be made with beef, veal, pork or ham—or any combination of these meats—and may be flavored with such ingredients as garlic, carrots, parsley, lemon peel and meat stock.

To make about 2 ½ cups [625 ml.] sauce

½ lb.	boneless, lean, cooked or raw meat, cut into small pieces or coarsely ground (about 1 cup [¼ liter])	¼ kg.
3 tbsp.	olive oil	45 ml.
1	onion, chopped	1
1	bouquet garni or 1 tbsp. [15 ml.] dried mixed herbs and 1 bay leaf	1
1 cup	wine (optional)	¼ liter
8	medium-sized tomatoes, peeled, seeded and chopped or 4 cups [1 liter] canned Italian-style tomatoes, chopped and drained	8
	salt	

Lightly brown the meat in the oil. Add the onion and cook, stirring occasionally with a wooden spoon, until soft. Then add the herbs. Increase the heat to high, stir in the wine and cook, stirring constantly, until the liquid has almost completely evaporated—in about three or four minutes. Then add the tomatoes.

Cover and simmer gently for one hour or so. Remove the lid toward the end of the cooking time to reduce the liquid and thicken the sauce, until the required consistency is obtained. Season to taste.

Mixed-Meat Stock

This general-purpose strong stock will keep for three or four days if it is refrigerated in a tightly covered container and boiled for a few minutes every day. If frozen, the stock will keep for six months.

To make about 3 quarts [3 liters] stock

2 lb.	beef shank	1 kg.
2 lb.	meaty veal shank, including the shank bone	1 kg.
2 lb.	chicken backs, necks and wing tips plus feet, if obtainable	1 kg.
about 5 quarts	water	about 5 liters
1	bouquet garni, including leek and celery	1
1	garlic bulb	1
2	medium-sized onions, 1 stuck with 2 whole cloves	2
4	large carrots	4

Place a metal rack or trivet in the bottom of a large stockpot to prevent the ingredients from sticking. Fit all of the meat, bones and chicken pieces into the pot and add water to cover by about 2 inches [5 cm.]. Bring slowly to a boil and, with a slotted spoon, skim off the scum that rises. Do not stir, lest you cloud the stock. Keep skimming, occasionally adding a glass of cold water, until no more scum rises—after about 10 to 15 minutes. Add the bouquet garni, garlic, onions and carrots, pushing them down into the liquid so that everything is submerged. Skim again as the liquid returns to a boil. Reduce the heat to very low, cover the pot with the lid ajar and simmer for four to five hours, skimming at intervals. If the meat is to be eaten, remove the veal after one and a half hours, the beef after three hours.

Ladle the stock into a large bowl through a colander lined with a double layer of cheesecloth or muslin. Let the strained stock cool completely, then remove any traces of fat from the surface with a skimmer and a paper towel; if the stock has been refrigerated to cool it, remove the solid fat with a knife.

Veal stock. Replace the beef, beef bones and chicken pieces with about 4 pounds [2 kg.] of meaty veal trimmings—neck, shank or rib tips.

Beef stock. Substitute 4 pounds [2 kg.] of beef short ribs or chuck or oxtail for the veal shank and chicken pieces, and simmer for five hours. The veal shank bone can be omitted if a less gelatinous stock is desired.

Chicken stock. Old hens and roosters yield the richest stock. Use about 5 pounds [2½ kg.] of carcasses, necks, feet, wings, gizzards and hearts, and simmer for two hours.

Lamb stock. Use about 6½ pounds [3 kg.] of lamb shank, bones and neck, and simmer for seven or eight hours.

Recipe Index

All recipes in the index that follows are listed by their English titles except in cases where a food of foreign origin, such as couscous or pesto, is universally recognized by its source name. Entries also are organized by the major ingredients specified in the recipe titles. Foreign recipes are listed by country or region of origin. Recipe credits appear on pages 174-176.

eneral Index/ lossary

uded in this index to the cooking
nonstrations are definitions, in italics,
special culinary terms not explained
where in this volume. The Recipe
ex begins on page 168.

Bean-thread noodles. *See Fen ssu*

Beef: braised for stew, 84; marinated for chow mein, 70; in meat sauce, 12-13

Beef heart: in pasta soufflé, 60-61

Beer: and Chinese pasta, 7; and dumplings, 7; in spaghetti fritters, 74

Beets: frying beet-flavored pasta squares with cabbage and onions, 68-69; in pasta dough, 20, 21

Beurre manié, 40

Blanch: *to plunge food into boiling water for a moment. Facilitates the removal of skins or shells, or softens vegetables or fruits before further cooking;* 33

Boiling pasta, 6, 30-31; for baked macaroni and cheese, 50; dried, 30, 31; filled, 36, 37; fresh, 30, 31; pasta roll, 36-37; ravioli, 36, 37; sauces with boiled pasta, 30, 31, 32-35; in stew, 40; testing doneness, 29, 30, 31

Bok choy: *a sweet-tasting Chinese stalk vegetable.*

Bouquet garni: *mixed herbs — classically parsley, thyme and bay leaf —tied together or wrapped in cheesecloth and used to flavor stocks, sauces and stews.*

Bread crumbs: for baked macaroni and cheese, 50, 51; for croquettes, 75; for dumplings, 78

Bridegrooms. *See Ziti*

Broccoli: blanched, for *primavera,* 33

Buckwheat: flour, 10; noodles, 10, 11. *See also Soba*

Butter: in *beurre manié,* 40; creaming, 82, 83; in roux, 12; in sauce with egg yolks, cheese and cream, 32

Butterflies. *See Farfalle*

Cabbage: combined with pasta squares and onions, 68-69

Cannelloni, 54, 55

Capelli d'angelo (angel's hair), 9

Caramel, 62-63

Carbonara sauce: with dried pasta, 32; with linguini, 28, 35

Cartwheels. *See Ruote*

Celery: in chow mein, 70, 71

Cellophane noodles. *See Fen ssu*

Cepes: in meat sauce, 12, 13

Chard: in pasta dough, 20

Cheese. *See Fontina cheese; Gruyère; Macaroni and cheese; Mozzarella; Parmesan cheese; Pecorino; Ricotta*

Chicken: in eggplant stuffed with penne, meats and cheese, 56-57; forcemeat, 41, 42; poached, in Pennsylvania Dutch stew, 40; in stew with couscous, 44-47

Chick-peas: with couscous, 45

Chou paste: in gnocchi, 80

Chow mein, 70-71

Clams: sauce with linguini, 32, 34

Conchiglie (shells), 9

Conchigliette (small shells), 9

Coriander leaves, 44, 45

Costmary: *a flat-leafed Oriental herb with a slightly bitter, minty flavor. If unavailable, substitute fresh mint.*

Court bouillon: *a flavored cooking liquid, usually made by simmering vegetables and seasonings in water.*

Couscous, 10, 11; cooked with meat-and-vegetable stew, 44-47

Crab: with Chinese noodles and pork, 66-67; frying, 67

Cream: in *carbonara* sauce, 35; in mousseline, 41, 43; in pasta dessert, 62, 63; in pasta pie, 59; sauce made with egg yolks, butter and cheese, 32; in tomato sauce, 12, 43

Croquettes, 74-75; serving, 7

Croutons: in dumpling dough, 82; sautéing bread cubes, 83

Cutting and shaping pasta: butterflies, 22, 23; figure eights, 22; by hand, 22, 23; lazanki and potpie, 22, 23; by machine, 14, 15, 22; mushroom caps, 22

Daisies. *See Margherite*

Dijon mustard: *any mustard produced in Dijon, France. Types range from a smooth, dark, aromatic variety made from brown mustard seeds, to the very strong pale-colored blanc de Dijon, made from white mustard seeds.*

Ditali (thimbles), 8

Dried pasta: in baked macaroni and cheese, 50; boiling, 30, 31; cooked in a stew, 40; deep frying, 65, 72, 74; fritters and croquettes, 74; frying, 65, 66, 72; in lasagne, 52; made with durum wheat, 6; sauces for, 29, 32, 34-35

Dumplings: chou-paste gnocchi, 80-81; cooked in broth, 84-85; dough, 77, 78, 79, 84; flavored with parsley, 76, 84-85; kneading yeast dough, 86; leavened with baking powder, 84-85; leavened with yeast, 86; noodle-shaped, made from batter, 78; potato, with meat sauce, 79; serving, 7; shaping, 78, 79; simmering, 77, 78; soft, steamed on top of a stew, 84-85; steamed, with fruit compote, 86; topping with bread crumbs, 78; wrapping and simmering in cloth napkin, 82-83

Egg flakes, 10, 11

Egg noodles: cooking in milk for croquettes, 74; crisping in olive oil, 68-69; in double noodles, 68-69; flour in, 10; fried, 64; frying in butter, 68; German-style, 10, 11; Oriental, 10; in pasta dessert, 62; spinach, 11; stir-fried, with meat and shellfish, 66-67; whole-wheat, 11. *See also Noodles; Oriental pasta; Tan mien*

Eggplant: as a case for stuffing, 56-57; frying in olive oil, 56

Eggs: in basic pasta dough, 6, 16; in cannelloni, 55; in chou paste, 80; in croquettes and fritters, 74-75; in dumpling dough, 78, 82, 83; in soufflé, 60, 61; whites, in baked lazanki, 53; whites, in dumpling dough, 82; whites, in mousseline, 41, 42; yolks, in *carbonara,* 35; yolks, in dough, 15; yolks, in sauce made with butter, cream and cheese, 32

Farfalle (butterflies), 9; in baked macaroni and cheese, 50; shaping, 22, 23

Fen ssu (bean-thread/cellophane noodles), 10; composition, 38; from mung-bean starch, 10; frying, 66; softening, 29, 38, 66; stir frying with pork, 38-39

Fettucini, 8; baked in a vegetable case, 49; as soufflé filling, 60; spinach-flavored, 8

Filled shapes: boiling, 36, 37; cannelloni, 55; fillings, 24-25; lasagne rolls, 54-55; packages, folded circles and stars, 26-27; pasta roll, 36; poaching, 36, 37; ravioli, 24, 25; sauces for, 29, 36; tortellini in pie, 58-59; tortellini, shaping, 24, 26-27

Fillings: cheese and spinach, 24, 25, 26; eggs and ricotta cheese (cannelloni), 55; for fresh pasta, 24; macaroni and veal sweetbreads (timbale), 41, 42; meat paste made from lamb, 25, 27; meat-and-spinach, 24, 26; mixtures of pasta, in a pie, 48, 58-59; orzo and cheese, 56-57; in pasta packages, 26-27; penne, cheese and meats, 56-57; pork, shrimp and watercress (won ton), 72-73; for ravioli, 24, 26; ricotta cheese, spinach and ham (pasta roll), 36; sausage and veal (lasagne rolls), 54-55; soufflé, 60-61; in tortellini, 26-27; for vegetable containers, 56-57

Fines herbes: *finely chopped fresh herbs —the classic herbs being parsley, chives, tarragon and chervil.*

Flour: in *beurre manié,* 40; buckwheat, 10; in pasta dough, 5, 6, 8, 16; properties of, 16; rice, 5, 10; in roux, 12; soy, 8; wheat, 5, 6, 8, 10, 16

Fontina cheese: in baked macaroni and cheese, 50, 51; on gnocchi, 81

Forcemeat: *finely chopped or ground, seasoned ingredients, mainly meat, fish, poultry or game;* 41, 42

Forcemeat mousseline: made from chicken, 41, 42-43

Fresh pasta: in baked macaroni and cheese, 50; boiling, 30, 31; coloring and flavoring, 20-21; cooked in a stew, 40; cutting and shaping, 22-23; deep-fried, 65, 72-73, 74; fillings for, 24; in fritters and croquettes, 74; frying, 65, 72; in lasagne, 52; making dough, 6, 16-19; sauces for, 29, 32-33; storing, 22

Fried pasta, 65; in butter, 68; cabbage and pasta squares, 68-69; chow mein, 70-71; crisping in oil, 68-69; deep frying, 65, 72, 73, 74-75; double noodles, 68-69; fritters, 74-75; oil for, 74; parboiling pasta, 68; softening pasta, 66; stir-fried Chinese egg noodles, 66-67; won tons, 72-73

Fritters: from spaghetti, 74-75

Fusilli (twists), 8

Garlic: flavoring olive oil, 32, 34; in pesto, 35

Ginger root: in chow mein, 71

Gluten: developing by kneading, 16, 86; in pasta dough, 16; in semolina, 8; in wheat flour, 16

Gnocchi, 80-81

Gratin: *the French term for a crust, usually of cheese or bread crumbs. Formed by spreading the gratin ingredients over the food and placing the dish in a hot oven or under a broiler so that the top crisps. Another meaning is a cooked dish that has such a finish;* 50-51, 81

Green beans: blanched, for *primavera,* 33

Grooved muffs. *See Manicotti rigati*

Gruyère: shredded, for double noodles, 68, 69

Ham: baking with lazanki squares, 53; in croquettes, 74; filling pasta roll, 36; in meat sauce, 12-13; in pasta pie, 59; in pasta soufflé, 61

Harissa sauce: with couscous, 44, 45; making, 47

Harusame/Sai fun (potato-starch noodles), 10

Herb salt: *a mixture of sea salt with ground, dried marine kelp and organically grown herbs. Available at health-food stores.*

Herbs: in cooked tomato sauce, 12-13; in fritters, 74; in pasta dough, 20-21; in uncooked tomato sauce, 32

Hot-pepper oil: in dipping sauce, 72, 73; in marinade, 70

Hot-pepper paste: *a coarse paste made of crushed fresh red chilies and sometimes garlic and other spices. Obtainable at Oriental markets;* 38, 39

Julienne: *a French term for vegetables or other food cut into thin usually matchstick-size —strips.*

Kugeln, 62

Lamb: paste, 25, 27; in stew with couscous, 44-47

Lard: frying Chinese noodles in, 67; frying meat and shellfish in, 67; frying vegetables and pasta squares in, 67; sautéing ground beef heart in, 60

Lasagne, 9; Calabrian, 7; cheeses in, 52; individual rolls, 54-55; in layered casseroles, 8; with meat sauce, white sauce and cheese, 52-53; parboiling, 52; Sicilian, 7; spinach, 9; variations of, 7

Lazanki squares: baking, 53; cutting, 22, 23; parboiling, 53

Linguini, 9; with *carbonara* sauce, 28, 35; with clam sauce, 34; with garlic and olive oil, 34; with pesto, 35

Little stars. *See Stelline*

Lug-lug (thick rice-stick noodles), 10. *See also Rice-stick noodles*

Macaroni, 8; coiled in a mold, 41-43; cut grooved, 8; elbow, 9; vegetable elbow, 8; whole-wheat, 8

fritters, 74-75; testing doneness, 30, 31
Spinach: and cheese filling, 25, 26; egg noodles, 11; fettucini, 8; with ham and ricotta cheese, 36; lasagne, 9; lasagne with meat sauce and cheese, 52-53; and meat filling, 24, 26; parboiling, 21, 24, 25; puréed, in gnocchi dough, 80
Squares: cutting, 22, 23; frying beet-flavored pasta squares with cabbage and onions, 68-69
Steaming: couscous, 10, 29, 45-46; dumplings, 86
Stelline (little stars), 11
Stew: cooking dumplings in, 84-85; couscous, 44-47; meats for stewing, 84; Oriental, with cellophane noodles and pork, 38-39; Pennsylvania Dutch (potpie), 40
Stir fry: *to stir and toss food with a spatula, food shovel or chopsticks for a short time over high heat. A Chinese cooking technique;* 38-39; 66-67, 70
Stock: chicken, 40; in sauce for timbale, 43; straining, 40; veal, 41
Sugar, caramelized, 62
Sweat: *to draw the juices from and soften foods by gently heating them, in*

oil or butter, in a covered saucepan for five to seven minutes.
Sweetbreads, veal: in timbale filling, 41-43
Szechwan peppercorns: *speckled brown peppercorns, mildly hot in flavor with a lemony scent. Obtainable at Chinese markets.*
Tagliatelle: in soufflé filling, 60, 61
Tamari sauce: *a soy sauce made without chemicals or preservatives. Obtainable at health-food stores.*
Tan mien (egg noodles), 10. See Egg noodles; Oriental pasta
Thimbles. See Ditali
Timbale, 41-43
Tomatoes: filling with orzo and baking, 56-57; marinating, 32, 33; in meat sauce, 13; in pasta dough, 20, 21; peeling, 12, 33; puréeing, 13; in stew with couscous, 46-47
Tomato sauce, 12, 13; with herbs, 12, 13; with basil leaves, on pasta roll, 36, 37; in cannelloni, 55; in eggplant stuffed with pasta, 57; enriched with cream, 12, 43; with gnocchi, 80; in lasagne rolls, 54-55; with macaroni timbale, 43; peeling tomatoes, 12; serving, 6-7; simmering

unpeeled tomatoes, 12, 13; uncooked, with herbs, 32, 33
Tongue: in baked eggplant, 56-57
Tortellini: boiling, 37; in a pie, 48, 58-59; shaping, 24, 26-27
Tree ears: *also known as "cloud ears"; small dried fungi, dark brown to black in color. Before use, soak in warm water for 30 minutes.*
Truffle: *an edible wild fungus, sometimes available fresh during the winter at specialty markets in large cities, but usually found canned.*
Twists. See Fusilli
Udon (thick wheat-flour noodles), 10
Veal: braising sweetbreads, 41; filling for timbale, 41, 42; ground, in lasagne rolls, 54-55
Vegetables: with beet-flavored pasta, 68-69; in chow mein, 70-71; containers filled with pasta, 56-57; in pasta pie, 58; in *primavera* sauce, 32, 33; in stew, with beef and dumplings, 84-85; in stew with couscous, 44-47
Vermicelli: baking in pudding with cream and eggs, 62-63
Water bath: *a large pot or vessel of water used to hold a smaller container*

placed on a rack. Used to cook or gently reheat delicate foods; 41, 42
Watercress: blanched, in won-ton filling, 72, 73
Wheat: -flour noodles, 10; in pasta 5, 6, 8, 10, 16; semolina, 6, 8, 10, 1
Wheels. See Rotelle
White sauce, 12; adding to lasagne, 52-53; with gnocchi, 80; lasagne rolls, 54-55; in macaroni c cheese, 50, 51; roux, 12; simmering 12; soufflé base, 60, 61
Whole-wheat: egg noodles, 11; flour, 8; macaroni, 8; shells, 9
Wine: adding to meat sauce, 12; braising sweetbreads in, 41; cooki clams in, 34; serving with pasta or dumplings, 7
Won tons, 72-73
Yam, Chinese: *a large, bland-tasting round-ended root vegetable. Sold at Oriental markets. If unavailable, substitute kohlrabi.*
Yeast: leavening dumplings, 86
Ziti, 8; in baked macaroni and cheese, 50; tagliati, 8
Zucchini: blanched, for *primavera,* 33; in stew with couscous, 46-47

Recipe Credits

The sources for the recipes in this volume are shown below. Page references in parentheses indicate where the recipes appear in the anthology.

Adam, Hans Karl, *Das Kochbuch aus Schwaben.* © Copyright 1976 by Verlagsteam Wolfgang Hölker. Published by Verlag Wolfgang Hölker, Münster. Translated by permission of the publisher(153).
Adams, Charlotte, *The Four Seasons Cookbook.* Copyright 1971 in all countries of the International Copyright Union by The Ridge Press, Inc. Published by Crown Publishers, Inc. By permission of the publisher(126).
Alberini, Massimo, *Cento Ricette Storiche.* Copyright Sansoni Editore, Firenze. Published by Sansoni Editore, Florence, 1974. Translated by permission of G. C. Sansoni Editore Nuova S.p.A.(135, 136).
Albright, Nancy, *Rodale's Naturally Great Foods Cookbook.* © 1977 Rodale Press, Inc. Published by Rodale Press, Inc., Emmaus, Pa. By permission of the publisher(158).
Androuet, Pierre, *La Cuisine au Fromage.* © 1978, Editions Stock. Published by Éditions Stock, Paris. Translated by permission of the publisher(150).
Barry, Naomi and Beppe Bellini, *Food alla Florentine.* Copyright © 1972 by Naomi Barry and Beppe Bellini. Published by Doubleday & Company, Inc. By permission of Brandt & Brandt, Literary Agents, Inc.(98).
Bennett, Paula Pogany and Velma R. Clark, *The Art of Hungarian Cooking.* Copyright 1954 by Doubleday & Company, Inc. Published by Doubleday & Company, Inc. By permission of the publisher(159).
Berolzheimer, Ruth (Editor), *The Culinary Arts Encyclopedic Cookbook.* Copyright © 1971, by Delair Publishing Company, Inc. Published by Delair Publishing Company Inc. By permission of the publisher(161).
Boni, Ada, *Italian Regional Cooking.* English translation © 1969 by Thomas Nelson & Sons and E. P. Dutton & Co. Published by Bonanza Books, a Division of Crown Publishers, Inc. By permission of the publisher(138).

Břízová, Joza, *The Czechoslovak Cookbook.* Translated and adapted by Adrienna Vahala. Copyright © 1965 by Crown Publishers, Inc. By permission of the publisher(147, 148).
Brown, Helen, *Helen Brown's West Coast Cook Book.* Copyright 1952 by Helen Evans Brown. Published by Little, Brown & Co. By permission of the publisher(107).
Bugialli, Giuliano, *The Fine Art of Italian Cooking.* Copyright © 1977 by Giuliano Bugialli. Published by Times Books, a Division of Quadrangle/The New York Times Book Co., Inc. By permission of the publisher(132).
Buonassisi, Vincenzo, *Pasta.* Translated by Elisabeth Evans. U.S./Canadian edition © 1976 by Lyceum Books, Inc., Wilton, Connecticut. Published by Lyceum Books, Inc. By permission of the publisher(93, 98, 124).
Carlton, Jan McBride, *The Old-Fashioned Cookbook.* Copyright © 1975 by Jan McBride Carlton. Published by Holt, Rinehart and Winston, Publishers. By permission of the publisher(146).
Cavalcanti, Ippolito, Duca di Buonvicino, *Cucina Teorico-Pratica.* Sixth Edition. November 1849, Naples(125).
Celli, Elisa and Inez M. Krech, *Naturally Italian.* Copyright © 1978 by Elisa Celli and Inez M. Krech. Published by E. P. Dutton. By permission of the publisher(98).
Chanot-Bullier, C., *Vieilles Recettes de Cuisine Provençale.* Published by Tacussel, Éditeur, Marseilles. Translated by permission of the publisher(149, 150).
Cheng, S. K., (Editor), *Shanghai Restaurant Chinese Cookery Book.* Published in 1936 by the Proprietors of The Shanghai Restaurant, London(142).
Collin, Rima and Richard, *The Pleasures of Seafood.* Copyright © 1976 by Rima and Richard Collin. Published by Holt, Rinehart and Winston, Publishers. By permission of the publisher(110).
Correnti, Pino, *Il Libro d'Oro della Cucina e dei Vini di Sicilia.* © Copyright 1976 Ugo Mursia Editore. Published by Ugo Mursia Editore, Milan. Translated by permission of the publisher(99, 108, 111).
Crossley, Rosemary, *The Dole Cookbook.* Copyright © 1978 by Rosemary Crossley and Prudence Borthwick. Published by Outback Press, Melbourne. By permission of the publisher(95).
Cutler, Carol, *The Six-Minute Soufflé and Other Culinary*

Delights. Copyright © 1976 by Carol Cutler. Published Clarkson N. Potter, Inc. By permission of the publisher
Davidson, Alan, *Mediterranean Seafood.* Copyright © Alan Davidson, 1972. Published by Penguin Books Ltd. London. By permission of the publisher(133).
Deeley, Lilla, *Favorite Hungarian Recipes.* Originally published by Hale, Cushman & Flint, 1938, under the t Hungarian Cookery. Published by Dover Publications, 1972. By permission of the publisher(141).
De Groot, Roy Andries, *Feasts for All Seasons.* Copyright © 1966, 1976 Roy Andries de Groot. Published b McGraw-Hill Book Company. By permission of the publisher(126).
De Zuliani, Mariù Salvatori, *La Cucina di Versilia e Garfagnana.* Copyright © by Franco Angeli Editore, M lano. Published in 1969 by Franco Angeli Editore, Mila Translated by permission of the publisher(100, 148).
Disslowa, Maria, *Jak Gotować.* Published by Instytut Gospodarstwa Domowego, Wydawnictwo Rybitwa. Translated by permission of Agencja Autorska, Warsa for the author(114, 116).
Dubois, Urbain, *Ecole des Cuisinières.* Sixth edition. Published by E. Dentu, Paris, 1887(120).
Engle, Fannie and Gertrude Blair, *The Jewish Festival Cookbook.* Copyright 1954 by Fannie Engle and G trude Blair. Published by the David McKay Company, By permission of the publisher(94).
Famularo, Joe and Louise Imperiale, *The Festive Famularo Kitchen.* Copyright © 1977 by Joe Famularo Louise Imperiale. Published by Atheneum Publishers. B permission of the publisher(98, 109).
Feast of Italy. Copyright © 1973 by Arnoldo Mondad Editore. Originally published in Italy under the title *Cuci all' Italiana,* © 1972 by Arnoldo Mondadori Editore. P lished in the United States by Galahad Books, New Yo By permission of Arnoldo Mondadori Editore(100, 116)
Field, Michael, *All Manner of Food.* Copyright © 1965 1966, 1967, 1968, 1970 by Michael Field. Published by fred A. Knopf. By permission of Jonathan Rude-Field(16
Foods of the World, *American Cooking: Eastern Heartland; American Cooking: New England; The Cooking of Germany.* Copyright © 1971 Time-Life Books Inc.; Copyright © 1970 Time Inc.; Copyright © 1969 Time-Life Bo Inc. Published by Time-Life Books(108; 155; 148).

...cesconi, Jeanne Caròla, *La Cucina Napoletana.* ...yright 1965 by Casa Editrice Fausto Fiorentino, Na- ...Published by Casa Editrice Fausto Fiorentino, Naples, ... Translated by permission of the author(108, 111,

...man, Marion and Felipe P. de Alba, *The Dione* ...s Book of Natural French Cooking.* Copyright © 1977 ...Marion Gorman and Felipe P. de Alba. Published by E. ...utton. By permission of Dominick Abel Literary Agency, ...93).

...etti, Fernanda, *In Cucina con Fernanda Gosetti.* © ...3 Fabbri Editori S.p.A., Milano. Published by Fabbri ...ori S.p.A., Milan. Translated by permission of the pub- ...er(104, 114, 118, 134).

Great Cooks' Guide to Pasta & Noodle ...es.* Copyright © 1977 by Joseph M. Cohen. Pub- ...d by Random House, Inc. By permission of Carol Cut- ...29 — Carol Cutler).

...en, Karen, *The Great International Noodle Experi-* ... Copyright © 1977 by Karen Green. Published by ...eneum Publishers. By permission of the publisher(88, ...100, 128).

...ene, Bert, *Bert Greene's Kitchen Bouquets.* © 1979 by ... Greene. Published by Contemporary Books, Inc. By ...nission of the publisher(154).

...naudeau-Franc, Zette, *Les Secrets des Fermes en* ...gord Noir.* © 1978, Éditions Serg, Paris. Published by ...ons Serg, Paris. Translated by permission of Madame ...naudeau(152).

...ds, Harriet, *More Taste than Money.* Copyright © ...5 by Harriet Hands. Published by Little, Brown & Co. ...ermission of the publisher(101, 104).

...ris, Gertrude, *Pasta International.* Copyright 1978 ...trude Harris. By permission of the publisher, 101 Pro- ...tions, San Francisco(88, 155).

...vey, Jacques, *365 Ways to Cook Pasta.* Copyright ...974 by Jacques Harvey. Published by Doubleday & ...npany, Inc. By permission of the publisher(97, 158).

...wkins, Arthur, *Cook It Quick.* © 1971 by Arthur ...vkins. Published by Prentice-Hall, Englewood Cliffs, ...By permission of the publisher(89).

...elton, Nika, *The Regional Italian Kitchen.* Copyright ...978 by Nika Hazelton. Published by M. Evans and ...pany. By permission of the publisher(91). *The* ...s Cookbook.* Copyright © 1967 by Nika Standen Ha- ...on. Published by Atheneum Publishers. By permission of ...publisher(162).

...er, Edna Eby, *The Art of Pennsylvania Dutch Cook-* ...Copyright © 1968 by Edna Eby Heller. Published by ...bleday & Company, Inc. By permission of the ...lisher(103).

...vitt, Jean, *The New York Times Weekend Cookbook.* ...yright © 1975 by Jean Hewitt. Published by Times ...ks, a Division of Quadrangle/The New York Times ...k Co., Inc. By permission of the publisher(94).

...ker, Alan, *Vegetarian Gourmet Cookery.* Copyright ...970 Alan Hooker. By permission of the publisher, 101 ...ductions, San Francisco(92).

...se & Garden, Editors of, *House & Garden's New* ...kbook.* Copyright © 1967 by The Condé Nast Publica- ...s, Inc. Published by The Condé Nast Publications, Inc. ...ermission of the publisher(125).

...ve, Robin, *The Pasta Cookbook.* © Copyright 1975 ...Robin Howe. Published by Paul S. Eriksson. By permis- ...of the publisher(101, 126).

...att, Enrica and Vernon, *The Complete Book of* ...a.* © 1969 by Enrica and Vernon Jarratt. English trans- ...n © 1975 by Vernon Jarratt. Published by Michael Jo- ...h Ltd., London, 1975. By permission of Erich Linder ...nzia Letteraria Internazionale, Milan, and the au- ...s(90, 96, 105).

...lan, Julie, *Wings of Life: Vegetarian Cookery by Julie* ...an.* © 1976, Julie Jordan. Published by The ...ssing Press, Trumansburg, N.Y. By permission of the ...lisher(124).

Junior League of the City of New York, *New* *Entertains.* Copyright © 1974 by The Junior League of ...v York, Inc. Published by Doubleday & Company, Inc. ...ermission of the publisher(107, 126).

The Junior League of Fayetteville, Inc., *The Caroli-* *na Collection.* Copyright © 1978 by The Junior League, Fayetteville, North Carolina. Published by The Junior League of Fayetteville. By permission of the publisher(94).

Kamman, Madeleine M., *When French Women Cook.* Copyright © 1976 by Madeleine M. Kamman. Published by Atheneum Publishers. By permission of the publisher(92, 160).

Katzen, Mollie, *The Moosewood Cookbook.* © 1977, Mollie Katzen. Published by Ten Speed Press, Berkeley. By permission of the author(123, 159).

Kouki, Mohamed, *La Cuisine Tunisienne d'"Ommok Sannafa."* © by Mohamed Kouki. Published in collaboration with L'Office National des Pêches, Tunis, 1974. Translated by permission of the author(120).

Laasri, Ahmed, *240 Recettes de Cuisine Marocaine.* © 1978, Jacques Grancher, Éditeur. Published by Jacques Grancher, Éditeur, Paris. Translated by permission of the publisher(121).

Lagattolla, Franco, *The Recipes that made a Million.* © Franco Lagattolla 1978. Published by Orbis Publishing Limited, London. By permission of the publisher(113, 127).

Lang, George, *The Cuisine of Hungary.* Copyright © 1971 by George Lang. Published by Atheneum Publishers. By permission of the publisher(130, 157, 158).

L'Art Culinaire Chinois et Vietnamien. Copyright by Établissements Dong-King, Charenton, France, 1958. Published by Établissements Dong-King(144).

La Sasso, Wilma Reiva, *Regional Italian Cooking.* © Wilma Reiva La Sasso 1958. Published by Macmillan Publishing Co., Inc. By permission of the publisher(163).

Lecourt, H., *La Cuisine Chinoise.* © 1968 by Éditions Robert Laffont. Published by Éditions Robert Laffont, Paris. Translated by permission of the publisher(144).

Lee, Jim, *Jim Lee's Chinese Cookbook.* Copyright © 1968 by Jim Lee. Published by Harper & Row, Publishers, Inc. By permission of the publisher(142, 144).

Lin, Florence, *Florence Lin's Chinese Regional Cookbook.* Copyright © 1975 by Florence Lin. Published by Hawthorn Books, a Division of Elsevier-Dutton Publishing Co., Inc. By permission of the publisher(138). *Florence Lin's Chinese Vegetarian Cookbook.* Copyright © 1976 by Florence S. Lin. Published by Hawthorn Books, a Division of Elsevier-Dutton Publishing Co., Inc. By permission of the publisher(141).

London, Sheryl, *Eggplant and Squash.* Copyright © 1976 by Sheryl London. Published by Atheneum Publishers. By permission of the publisher(127).

Lo Pinto, Maria and Milo Miloradovich, *The Art of Italian Cooking.* Copyright 1948 by Doubleday & Company, Inc. Published by Doubleday & Company, Inc. By permission of the publisher(95).

McCarthy, Marguerite Gilbert, *Aunt Ella's Cookbook.* Copyright 1954 by Marguerite Gilbert McCarthy. Published by Little, Brown and Company in association with the Atlantic Monthly Press(122).

McNamara, Charlotte & Lenore Howell, *The Before and After Dinner Cookbook.* Copyright © 1977 by Charlotte NcNamara & Lenore Howell. Published by Atheneum Publishers. By permission of the publisher(133, 147).

Mapie, The Countess de Toulouse-Lautrec, *La Cuisine de France.* Edited by Charlotte Turgeon. Copyright © 1964 by The Orion Press, Inc. Published by Viking Penguin, Inc. By permission of the publisher(128).

Martini, Anna (Editor), *Pasta & Pizza.* English translation copyright © 1977 by Mondadori Milan. Published by St. Martin's Press, New York. By permission of the publisher(106, 115, 136).

Marty, Albin, *Fourmiguetto: Souvenirs Contes et Recettes du Languedoc.* Published by Éditions CREER, F 63340, Nonette, 1978. Translated by permission of the publisher(124).

Mazda, Maideh, *In a Persian Kitchen.* Copyright in Japan, 1960 by Charles E. Tuttle Company, Inc. Published by Charles E. Tuttle Company, Inc., Tokyo, 1960, 1975. By permission of the publisher(117).

Meyers, Perla, *Perla Meyers' from Market to Kitchen Cookbook.* Copyright © 1979 by Perla Meyers. Published by Harper & Row, Publishers, Inc. By permission of the publisher(95, 110).

Miller, Jill Nhu Huong, *Vietnamese Cookery.* Copyright in Japan, 1968, by Charles E. Tuttle Company, Inc. Published by Charles E. Tuttle Company, Inc. By permission of the publisher(102).

Mitchell, Leonard Jan, *Lüchow's German Cookbook.* Copyright 1952 by Leonard Jan Mitchell. Published by Doubleday & Company, Inc. By permission of the publisher(146).

Morton, Marcia Colman, *The Art of Viennese Cooking.* Copyright © 1963 by Marcia Colman Morton. Published by Doubleday & Company, Inc. By permission of The Sterling Lord Agency, Inc.(112).

Muffoletto, Anna, *The Art of Sicilian Cooking.* Copyright © 1971 by Anna Muffoletto. Published by Doubleday & Company, Inc. By permission of the publisher(90, 135, 145).

Nelson, Kay Shaw, *Pasta: Plain and Fancy.* Copyright © 1971 by Kay Shaw Nelson. Published by Hawthorn Books, a Division of Elsevier-Dutton. By permission of Collier Associates, Literary Agents(139).

Neumann, Ruth Vendley, *Conversation-Piece Recipes.* Copyright © 1968 by Ruth V. Neumann. Published by Contemporary Books, Inc. By permission of the author(150).

Nichols, Nell B. (Editor), *Farm Journal's Country Cookbook.* Copyright © 1955 by Farm Journal, Inc. Published by Doubleday & Company, Inc. By permission of Farm Journal, Inc.(147).

Nignon, Édouard (Editor), *Le Livre De Cuisine de L'Ouest-Éclair.* Published in 1941 by l'Ouest-Éclair, Rennes. Translated by permission of Société d'Éditions Ouest-France, Rennes(153).

Olney, Richard, *The French Menu Cookbook.* Copyright © 1970 by Richard Olney. Published by Simon and Schuster. By permission of John Schaffner, Literary Agent, New York(119). *Simple French Food.* Copyright © 1974 by Richard Olney. Published by Atheneum Publishers. By permission of the publisher(145).

Paradissis, Chrissa, *The Best Book of Greek Cookery.* Copyright © 1976 P. Efstathiadis & Sons. Published by Efstathiadis Group, Athens, 1976. By permission of the publisher(129).

Peter, Madeleine, *Favorite Recipes of the Great Women Chefs of France.* Translated and edited by Nancy Simmons. Copyright © 1977 by Éditions Robert Laffont S.A. Copyright © 1979 by Holt, Rinehart and Winston. Published by Holt, Rinehart and Winston, Publishers. By permission of the publisher(123).

Petrov, Dr. L., Dr. N. Djelepov, Dr. E. Iordanov and S. Uzunova, *Bulgarska Nazionalna Kuchniya.* Copyright © by the authors, 1978, c/o Jusautor, Sofia. Published by Zemizdat, Sofia, 1978. Translated by permission of Jusautor Copyright Agency(91).

Pezzini, Wilma, *The Tuscan Cookbook.* Copyright © 1979 by Wilma Pezzini. Published by Atheneum Publishers. Reprinted by permission of Atheneum Publishers(89, 94).

Philpot, Rosl, *Viennese Cookery.* Copyright © 1965 by Rosl Philpot. Published by Hodder & Stoughton Limited, London. By permission of the publisher(146).

Polushkin, Maria, *The Dumpling Cookbook.* Copyright © 1977 by Maria Polushkin Robbins. Published by Workman Publishing Company. By permission of the publisher(140, 149, 156).

Reboul, J. B., *La Cuisinière Provençale.* First published by Tacussel, Éditeur, Marseilles. Translated by permission of the publisher(163).

Reich, Lilly Joss, *The Viennese Pastry Cookbook.* Copyright © 1970 by Lilly Joss Reich. Published by Macmillan Publishing Co., Inc. By permission of the publisher(159, 160).

Rombauer, Irma S. and Marion Rombauer Becker, *Joy of Cooking.* Copyright © 1931, 1936, 1941, 1942, 1943, 1946, 1951, 1952, 1953, 1962, 1963, 1964, 1975 by The Bobbs-Merrill Company, Inc. Published by The Bobbs-Merrill Company, Inc. By permission of the publisher(147).

Root, Waverley, *The Best of Italian Cooking.* Copyright © 1975 by Grosset & Dunlap, Inc. Published by Grosset &

Dunlap, Inc. By permission of the publisher(134).
Ross, Janet and Michael Waterfield, *Leaves from Our Tuscan Kitchen or How to Cook Vegetables.* Copyright © 1973 by Michael Waterfield. Published by Atheneum Publishers. By permission of Atheneum Publishers, New York, and John Murray Ltd., London(106, 107, 118).
Roy, Michael, *Mike Roy's American Kitchen.* Copyright © 1974 by Michael Roy. Published by Harper & Row, Publishers, Inc. By permission of the publisher(123).
Rubinstein, Paul, *Feasts for Twelve or More.* Copyright © 1975 by Paul Rubinstein. Published by Macmillan Publishing Co., Inc. By permission of the publisher(162). *Just Good Food.* Copyright © 1978 by Paul Rubinstein. Published by Charles Scribner's Sons. By permission of the author(109).
Salta, Romeo, *The Pleasures of Italian Cooking.* © Romeo Salta 1962. Published by Macmillan Publishing Co., Inc. By permission of the publisher(101).
Scappi, Bartolomeo, *M. dell'Arte del Cucinare.* Published in Venice, 1610 by Presso Alessandro Vecchi(115).
Schapira, Christiane, *La Cuisine Corse.* © Solar, 1979. Published by Solar, Paris. Translated by permission of the publisher(113).
Schrecker, Ellen, *Mrs. Chiang's Szechwan Cookbook.* Copyright © 1976 by Chiang Jung-Feng, and John E. Schrecker and Ellen Schrecker, Trustees. Published by Harper & Row, Publishers, Inc. By permission of the publisher(103).
Scott, Jack Denton, *The Complete Book of Pasta.* Copyright © 1968 by Jack Denton Scott. Published by Bantam Books by arrangement with William Morrow & Company, Inc. By permission of the author(128, 140).
Scott, Maria Luisa and Jack Denton Scott, *A World of Pasta.* Copyright © 1978 by Jack Denton Scott and Maria Luisa Scott. Published by McGraw-Hill Book Company. By permission of the authors(131).
Seidel, Elinor (Editor), *Chefs, Scholars & Movable Feasts.* © Copyright 1978 University of Maryland University College. Published by University of Maryland University College. By permission of the publisher(116).
Serra, Victoria, *Tia Victoria's Spanish Kitchen.* English text copyright © Elizabeth Gili, 1963. Published by Kaye & Ward Ltd., London, 1963. Translated by Elizabeth Gili from the original Spanish entitled *Sabores: Cocina del Hogar* by

Victoria Serra Suñol. By permission of the publisher(105).
Simon, André L., *Cheeses of the World.* Copyright André L. Simon, 1956. Published by Faber and Faber Ltd., London. By permission of the publisher(125).
Smires, Latifa Bennani, *La Cuisine Marocaine.* © Éditions Alpha G.E.A.M. Published by Éditions Alpha G.E.A.M., Casablanca, 1974(121).
Solomon, Charmaine, *The Complete Asian Cookbook.* Copyright 1976 by Charmaine Solomon. Published by Lansdowne Press, Sydney, and distributed in the United States by McGraw-Hill Book Company. By permission of the author(143).
Špánko, Vojtech, *Slovenská Kuchárka.* © Obzor, Bratislava 1968. Published by Obzor, 1968. Translated by permission of LITA, Slovak Literary Agency, Prague(151, 157).
Stan, Anisoara, *The Romanian Cook Book.* Copyright © 1951 Anisoara Stan. Published by arrangement with Lyle Stuart, The Citadel Press. By permission of The Citadel Press(131).
Stechishin, Savella, *Traditional Ukrainian Cookery.* Copyright 1957, 1959 by Savella Stechishin. Published by Trident Press Limited, Winnipeg. By permission of the publisher(122, 132).
Stendahl, *Spicy Food.* Copyright © 1979 by William Bernal. Published by Holt, Rinehart and Winston, Publishers. By permission of the publisher(97, 143).
Tiano, Myrette, *Pâtes et Riz.* © Solar 1978. Published by Solar, Paris. Translated by permission of Solar(92, 99, 100).
Troisgros, Jean & Pierre, *The Nouvelle Cuisine of Jean & Pierre Troisgros.* Copyright © 1978 in the English translation by William Morrow and Company, Inc. Published by William Morrow and Company, Inc. Originally published under the title *Cuisiniers à Roanne.* Copyright © 1977 by Éditions Robert Laffont S.A. By permission of William Morrow and Company, Inc.(106).
Tselementes, Nicholas, *Greek Cookery.* Copyright 1950, 1952, 1956 by D. C. Divry, Inc., Publishers. Published by D. C. Divry, Inc., Publishers. By permission of the publisher(131).
Ungerer, Miriam, *Good Cheap Food.* Copyright © 1973 by Miriam Ungerer. Published by Viking Penguin, Inc. By permission of the publisher(105, 122).
Uvezian, Sonia, *The Book of Yogurt.* Copyright 1978 by Sonia Uvezian. By permission of the publisher, 101 Produc-

tions, San Francisco(90).
The Vashti Educational Center, Inc., *Pines and Plantations: Native Recipes of Thomasville, Georgia.* Published by The Vashti Auxiliary, Thomasville, Georgia. By permission of The Vashti Educational Center, Inc.(134 — Carol Wight).
Venesz, József, *Hungarian Cuisine.* © by Mrs. József Venesz. Published by Corvina Press, Budapest. By permission of Artisjus Literary Agency, Budapest, for Mrs. József Venesz(146, 149).
Volpicelli, Luigi and Secondino Freda, *L'Antiartusi: 1000 Ricette.* © 1978 Pan Editrice, Milano. Published by Pan Editrice, Milan. Translated by permission of the publisher(137).
Voltz, Jeanne A., *The Flavor of the South.* Copyright © 1977 by Jeanne A. Voltz. Published by Doubleday & Company, Inc. By permission of the publisher(102).
Waldo, Myra, *The Art of Spaghetti Cookery.* Copyright 1964 by Myra Waldo Schwartz. Published by Doubleday Company, Inc. By permission of the author(139, 141).
Warren, Janet, *A Feast of Scotland.* Copyright © 1979 by Janet Warren. Published by Hodder & Stoughton Limited, London. By permission of the publisher(154).
Wason, Betty, *The Art of German Cooking.* Copyright © 1967 by Elizabeth Wason Hall. Published by Doubleday Company, Inc. By permission of the publisher(152, 161).
William, Anne (Editor), *Grand Diplôme Cooking Course, Volume 8.* Published in the U.S.A. by The Danbury Press Division of Grolier, Inc. Copyright © BPC Publishing 19__ and © Phoebus Publishing 1972. By permission of Phoebus Publishing Co., London(151).
Willinsky, Grete, *Kochbuch der Büchergilde.* © Büchergilde Gutenberg, Frankfurt am Main 1958. Published by Büchergilde Gutenberg, 1967. Translated by permission of the publisher(122).
Witty, Helen and Elizabeth Schneider Colchie, *Better Than Store-Bought: a Cookbook.* Copyright © 197__ by Helen Witty and Elizabeth Schneider Colchie. Published by Harper & Row, Publishers, Inc. By permission of the publisher(88).
Wolfert, Paula, *Couscous and Other Good Food from Morocco.* Copyright © 1973 by Paula Wolfert. Published Harper & Row, Publishers, Inc. By permission of the publisher(156).

Acknowledgments

The indexes for this book were prepared by Louise W. Hedberg. The editors are particularly indebted to Maura Bean, U.S. Department of Agriculture, Berkeley, California; Gail Duff, Kent, England; Robert Green, National Macaroni Institute, Palatine, Illinois; and Ann O'Sullivan, Majorca, Spain.

The editors also wish to thank: Caroline Baum, York, England; Eliott Burgess, Majorca, Spain; Paul Canazzaro, L. Della Cella Company, Mineola, New York; Mario Cardullo, Washington, D.C.; Josephine Christian, Bath, England; Emma Codrington, Surrey, England; Clare Coope, London; Nona Coxhead, London; Jennifer Davidson, London; Fiona Duncan, London; Mimi Errington, London; Susan Feller, Alexandria, Virginia; Susan B. Foresman, Arlington, Virginia; Geoffrey Grigson, Swindon, England; Maggie Heinz, London; Marion Hunter, Surrey, England; Brenda Jayes, London; Maria Johnson, Hatfield, England; Alison Kerr, Cambridgeshire, England; Rosemary Klein, London; John Lamb, London; Jim Lee, New York; Dr. Alan Long, The Vegetarian Society, London; Dr. Allen Matthys, National Food Processors Association, Washington, D.C.; Pippa Millard, London; Mrs. Miller, Royal Horticultural Society, Wisley, England; Dilys Naylor, Surrey, England; Edward and Robert New, Cumberland Macaroni Manufacturing Co., Cumberland, Maryland; Jo Oxley, Surrey, England; G. Parmigiani, United Preservers Ltd., London; Reiko M. Ramsey, Japan Trade Center, New York; Craig Sams, Harmony Foods, London; Michael Schwab, London; Cathy Sharpe, Annandale, Virginia; Dr. Virginia Sidwell, National Marine Fisheries Service, Washington, D.C.; Anne Stephenson, London; Lina Stores, London; Germaine Swanson, Germaine's Restaurant, Washington, D.C.; Fiona Tillett, London; Pat Tookey, London.

Picture Credits

The sources for the pictures in this book are listed below. Credits for each of the photographers and illustrators are listed by page number in sequence with successive pages indicated by hyphens; where necessary, the locations of pictures within pages are also indicated — separated from page numbers by dashes.

Photographs by Aldo Tutino: cover, 4, 8-11, 28, 30-35, 37 — top, 38-40, 50-51, 54, 55 — top left, top center and bottom left, 56-57 — top, 62-64, 68-76, 80-86.
Other photographs (alphabetically): Tom Belshaw, 14, 16, 17 — top right and bottom, 18-19, 22 — top and bottom right, 23 — bottom center and bottom right, 24, 25 — top, bottom left and bottom center, 26 — bottom, 53 — top, 55 — top right, center right and bottom right, 79. John Cook, 12 — top, 22 — bottom left, 23 — top and bottom left, 25 — bottom right, 27 — bottom, 78. David Davies, 13 — top. Alan Duns, 17 — top left and top center, 20-21, 26-27 — top, 36-37 — bottom, 48, 58-60, 61 — bottom, 66-67. John Elliott, 12-13 — bottom, 41-43, 52, 53 — bottom, 56-57 — bottom, 61 — top. Edmund Goldspink, 44-47. Louis Klein, 2.
Illustrations: From The Mary Evans Picture Library and private sources and *Food & Drink: A Pictorial Archive from Nineteenth Century Sources* by Jim Harter, published by Dover Publications, Inc., 1979, 6-7, 88-167.
Endpapers: Designed by John Pack.

Library of Congress Cataloguing in Publication Data
Time-Life Books.
  Pasta.
  (The Good cook, techniques and recipes)
  Includes index.
  1. Cookery (Macaroni) 2. Dumplings. I. Title.
II. Series: Good cook, techniques and recipes.
TX809.M17T55   1980   641.8'22   80-18085
ISBN 0-8094-2889-X
ISBN 0-8094-2888-1 (lib. bdg.)
ISBN 0-8094-2891-1 (retail ed.)

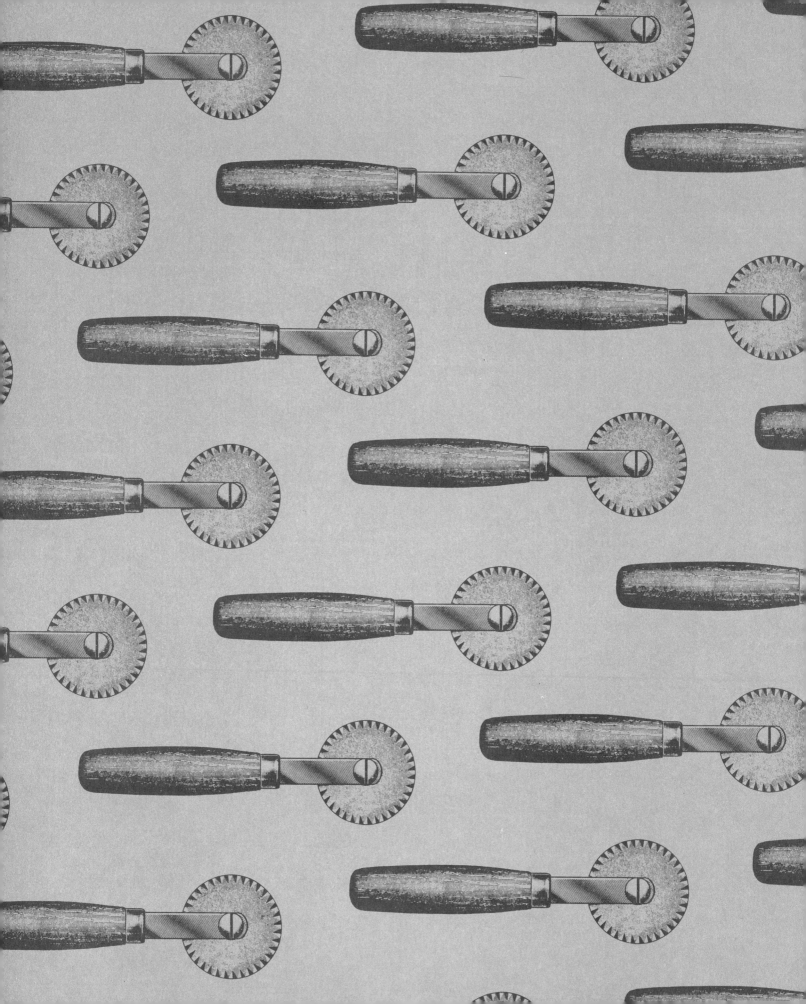